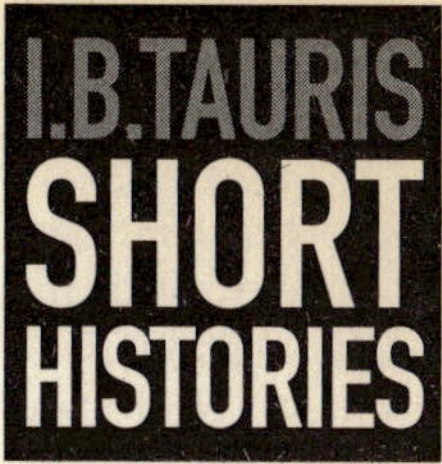

I.B.TAURIS SHORT HISTORIES

I.B.Tauris Short Histories is an authoritative and elegantly written new series which puts a fresh perspective on the way history is taught and understood in the twenty-first century. Designed to have strong appeal to university students and their teachers, as well as to general readers and history enthusiasts, *I.B.Tauris Short Histories* comprises a novel attempt to bring informed interpretation, as well as factual reportage, to historical debate. Addressing key subjects and topics in the fields of history, the history of ideas, religion, classical studies, politics, philosophy and Middle East studies, the series seeks intentionally to move beyond the bland, neutral 'introduction' that so often serves as the primary undergraduate teaching tool. While always providing students and generalists with the core facts that they need to get to grips with the essentials of any particular subject, *I.B.Tauris Short Histories* goes further. It offers new insights into how a topic has been understood in the past, and what different social and cultural factors might have been at work. It brings original perspectives to bear on the manner of its current interpretation. It raises questions and – in its extensive bibliographies – points to further study, even as it suggests answers. Addressing a variety of subjects in a greater degree of depth than is often found in comparable series, yet at the same time in concise and compact handbook form, *I.B.Tauris Short Histories* aims to be 'introductions with an edge'. In combining questioning and searching analysis with informed history writing, it brings history up-to-date for an increasingly complex and globalized digital age.

www.short-histories.com

'While the history of medieval Christianity has been frequently told, this book reorients the traditional narrative in creative ways by making space for all the Abrahamic religions. Offering a global dimension on the one hand, it presents on the other hand an array of materials focused on the British Isles, resulting in a history that is as informative and wide ranging as it is theologically astute. From early medieval wandering monks to late-medieval contentious scholastic disputations, the diverse subjects one might wish for are found here in a compelling account peppered with Evans' customary wit and stylistic flourishes.'

– Willemien Otten, Professor of Theology and the History of Christianity, University of Chicago

'This is an excellent introduction, written with pace and a well-pitched sense of the vast scope of the subject. The reader is briskly conducted from the birth of the Christian faith and its first institutional forms to the establishment of belief and practice under the Roman Empire, to the churches of the Greek East and Latin West in the Early Middle Ages, to the High Middle Ages and finally to the beginnings of the Reformation. Within an epic landscape we are introduced to medieval Christians of all types: monks, nuns, priests, lay men and women, heretics, scholars, popes, kings and peasants. We make the acquaintance, too, of the neighbours of medieval Christendom: the Jewish and Islamic communities, and discover the range of relations that existed between them – from the violence of persecution and holy war to peaceful co-existence. Individual stories give pleasing depth and contour to a study which fully animates the lives of real people as well as providing an engaging survey of a broader, changing culture. The book is very well balanced and structured, its twin themes of dialogue and journey combining to excellent effect and giving the reader the impression of having engaged properly with both. In brief, *A Short History of Medieval Christianity* should be essential reading for all relevant undergraduate courses in the humanities and likewise ought to sell very well to the general public. Written with verve and precision, the book fully conveys the immensity of the topic as well as the sense that it can now be fully grasped and summarised.'

– Giles Gasper, Reader in High Medieval History, Durham University

A Short History of . . .

the American Civil War	Paul Anderson (Clemson University)
the American Revolutionary War	Stephen Conway (University College London)
Ancient China	Edward L Shaughnessy (University of Chicago)
Ancient Greece	P J Rhodes, FBA (Durham University)
Ancient Rome	Andrew Wallace-Hadrill (University of Cambridge)
the Anglo-Saxons	Henrietta Leyser (University of Oxford)
Babylon	Karen Radner (University of Munich)
the Byzantine Empire	Dionysios Stathakopoulos (King's College London)
Christian Spirituality	Edward Howells (Heythrop College, University of London)
the Crimean War	Trudi Tate (University of Cambridge)
English Renaissance Drama	Helen Hackett (University College London)
the English Revolution and the Civil Wars	David J Appleby (University of Nottingham)
the Etruscans	Corinna Riva (University College London)
the Hundred Years War	Michael Prestwich (Durham University)
Irish Independence	J J Lee (New York University)
the Italian Renaissance	Virginia Cox (New York University)
the Korean War	Allan R Millett (University of New Orleans)
Medieval Christianity	G R Evans (University of Cambridge)
Medieval English Mysticism	Vincent Gillespie (University of Oxford)
the Minoans	John Bennet (University of Sheffield)
the Mongols	George Lane (SOAS, University of London)
the Mughal Empire	Michael H Fisher (Oberlin College)
Muslim Spain	Alex J Novikoff (Rhodes College, Memphis)
New Kingdom Egypt	Robert Morkot (University of Exeter)
the New Testament	Halvor Moxnes (University of Oslo)
Nineteenth-Century Philosophy	Joel Rasmussen (University of Oxford)
the Normans	Leonie V Hicks (Canterbury Christ Church University)
the Ottoman Empire	Baki Tezcan (University of California, Davis)

the Phoenicians	Mark Woolmer (Durham University)
the Reformation	Helen Parish (University of Reading)
the Renaissance in Northern Europe	Malcolm Vale (University of Oxford)
Revolutionary Cuba	Antoni Kapcia (University of Nottingham)
the Risorgimento	Nick Carter (Australian Catholic University, Sydney)
the Russian Revolution	Geoffrey Swain (University of Glasgow)
the Spanish Civil War	Julián Casanova (University of Zaragoza)
the Spanish Empire	Felipe Fernández-Armesto (University of Notre Dame) and José Juan López-Portillo (University of Oxford)
Transatlantic Slavery	Kenneth Morgan (Brunel University London)
Venice and the Venetian Empire	Maria Fusaro (University of Exeter)
the Vikings	Clare Downham (University of Liverpool)
the Wars of the Roses	David Grummitt (University of Kent)
the Weimar Republic	Colin Storer (University of Nottingham)

A SHORT HISTORY OF MEDIEVAL CHRISTIANITY

G. R. Evans

Published in 2017 by
I.B.Tauris & Co. Ltd
London • New York
www.ibtauris.com

ISBN: 978 1 78453 282 6 (HB)
ISBN: 9781 7 8453 283 3 (PB)
eISBN: 978 1 78672 223 2
ePDF: 978 1 78673 223 1

A full CIP record for this book is available from the British Library
A full CIP record is available from the Library of Congress

Library of Congress Catalog Card Number: available

Typeset by Free Range Book Design & Production Limited
Printed and bound by T.J. International, Padstow, Cornwall

Contents

List of Maps and Illustrations

MAPS

FIGURES

Preface

There could hardly be a more timely moment to write a book about the way Christianity expanded and entered deeply to the heart of European and Middle Eastern culture during the medieval centuries. Throughout this long Middle Ages, Christianity became the context for almost everyone's life in most of Europe, with few admitting to atheism or even agnosticism.

These were also the centuries when Islam arose and made its own immense geographical impact across many of the same lands. Christianity and Islam had to come to terms, and the Jews in diaspora had to arrive at a working relationship with both. Interfaith encounters between Christians and Jews and in due course Christians and Muslims were always sensitive, socially, economically and politically, as well as in religious terms.

This short book sets the geographical boundaries widely, for the history of medieval Christianity is not just a Western European story. It includes the Orthodox and Monophysite Churches of the Greek-speaking East and the Middle East and parts of North Africa. It is also bold in terms of its time frame. It begins with the end of the ancient world, that period of crucial change when an advanced civilisation died with the collapse of the Roman Empire, and Western Europe in particular found itself faced with an enormous task of reconstruction. These were no 'dark ages' but a time of active recovery of a culture and the framing of much of the doctrine of Church and sacraments which shaped medieval life for ordinary people. The book, but not the story, ends ten centuries later, with the beginning of the modern world in the sixteenth century, when the Christian Church in the West was fragmented by the movements which made up the Reformation.

The religious and cultural accommodations which were painfully worked out in the medieval centuries have recently been adjusting themselves again under the pressures of globalisation, with mass migration into Europe from the Middle East and Africa and the struggle to make multiculturalism 'work' in the twenty-first century. So this is a topical as well as a historical story, for what is happening now is profoundly influenced by the events of the medieval millennium.

Timeline

27 BC	The Roman Republic becomes the Roman Empire, with Augustus the first emperor, ruling until AD 14.
c. AD 0	Jesus born in Bethlehem.
*c.*33	Jesus crucified in Jerusalem.
41	Claudius as second Roman emperor approves an annual spring holiday to celebrate the resurrection of the pagan vegetation god Attis.
*c.*48–50	Christians meet in a 'council' in Jerusalem (Acts 15). Decisions are taken about whether converts to Christianity are bound by the laws of the Old Testament.
49	Jews expelled from Jerusalem by Roman armies.
50–8	Paul's missionary journeys.
*c.*80–90	Acts of the Apostles apparently written by the same author as Luke's Gospel. First-century circulation of the *Didache*, believed to be the *Teaching of the Apostles*.
115–17	Jewish revolts against Roman domination in Egypt, Crete and Libya.
132–5	Bar-Kotchba Jewish revolt against the Romans, destruction of towns in Judaeia, mass enslavement and exile of Jews from Israel.
150–60	*Diatessaron*, written by Tatian in an attempt to reconcile the differences of the Gospel authors in a 'harmony of the Gospels'.
161	Death of Marcus Aurelius, Roman emperor, Stoic philosopher and persecutor of Christians.
165	Death of Justin Martyr, philosopher turned Christian.

c.202	Death of Irenaeus, Bishop of Lyons.
250	Decius, Roman emperor, orders Christians to sacrifice to pagan gods on pain of persecution.
c.250–8	Cyprian, Bishop of Carthage from 248, argues that Christians who had apostatised during the persecution of 250 should be allowed back on certain conditions.
c.299	Arius triggers the Arian heresy which was to divide Christendom for centuries.
306	Constantine becomes Roman emperor.
312	Battle of Milvian Bridge: Constantine has a vision and is converted to Christianity.
313	Edict of Milan. Christianity recognised as the official religion of the empire.
c.320	Athanasius, Bishop of Alexandria, argues against the Arian heresy.
325	Council of Nicaea agrees the Nicene Creed.
337	Emperor Constantine baptised.
347–420	Jerome, translator of the Vulgate Latin Bible.
354–430	Augustine, Bishop of Hippo.
360–435	Cassian, monastic leader in Gaul.
361–3	Emperor Julian the Apostate tries to return the Empire to paganism.
370–410	Alaric, leader of the Goths during invasions of the Roman Empire.
372	Martin of Tours founds the abbey of Marmoutier.
379	Theodosius becomes the last emperor to rule the whole Roman Empire, both East and West (until 395).
381	Council of Constantinople revises the Nicene Creed.
c.385	Priscillian of Avila leads a heretical movement in Spain and is said to be against marriage.
	Fourth-century content of the 'canon' of Scripture is provisionally agreed.
431	Third Council of Ephesus. Nestorius (*c*.386–450), Patriarch of Constantinople, and Eutyches (*c*.378–456) condemned as heretics.
434–53	Attila leads the Huns during invasions of the Roman Empire.
451	Council of Chalcedon triggers lasting schism between Catholic and Monophysite Churches.

c.460–93	Death of Patrick, one of the fifth-century Christian missionaries in Ireland who helped to found Ireland's 'Celtic' Christian tradition.
c.480–524	Boethius, author of the *Consolation of Philosophy* which was written while he was under house arrest awaiting execution.
c.482–565	Justinian, Byzantine emperor and codifier of Roman law.
530	Benedict of Nursia becomes founder of Benedictine monasticism.
c.560–636	Isidore, Bishop of Seville, author of a history of the invasions of Spain in the form of a chronology.
c.563	Columba, Irish abbot and missionary, brings Celtic Christianity to mainland Britain.
589	Third Council of Toledo decrees that Jews may not have Christian wives or concubines, or buy slaves for themselves.
597	Augustine of Canterbury (534–604), sent on a mission to the Anglo-Saxons by Pope Gregory the Great, lands in Kent.
610	Mohammed has a revelation and becomes the Prophet of Islam, a new strictly monotheistic religion.
632	Death in Medina of the Prophet Mohammed.
639	Sixth Council of Toledo enacts Visigothic legislation concerning the Jews.
c.634–87	Cuthbert, Bishop of Lindisfarne.
664	Synod of Whitby, debate over the differences between Celtic and Roman Christians.
c.690	Willibrord becomes a missionary to the Frisians.
711	Muslim army under the Berber Tariq invades southern Spain.
713	Christian–Muslim Treaty of Tudmir (south-eastern Spain).
716	Boniface becomes missionary to the Frisians.
717–867	Iconoclastic controversy.
c.731	Bede, monk of Wearmouth and Jarrow, completes the first *Ecclesiastical History* of the British Isles.
c.735–804	Alcuin, one of the most prominent figures of the Carolingian 'Renaissance'.

750–1258	Abbasid Caliphs rule in Baghdad.
787	Seventh Ecumenical Council called to resolve the iconoclastic controversy.
800	Charlemagne (*c.*742–814) crowned as emperor.
*c.*800–*c*870	Al-Kindi, translator of Greek philosophical writings into Arabic.
858–67	Photios serves as Patriarch of Constantinople (and again from 877 to 886).
863	Methodius (815–85) and Cyril (826–69) begin a Christian mission among the Slavs.
873–4	The Byzantine emperor Basil I has Jews baptised by force.
909–1171	Shia Fatimids rule as Caliphs.
910	Abbey of Cluny founded.
*c.*940–92	Mieszko I, first Christian ruler of Poland.
980–1037	Avicenna, composer of an Arabic encyclopedia of astronomy, cosmology, medicine and mathematics.
1059	Berengar of Tours condemned for heresy for saying that there is no physical change in the bread and wine when they are consecrated at the Eucharist (and again in 1079).
*c.*1005–89	Lanfranc, Abbot of Bec and later Archbishop of Canterbury, campaigner against Berengar.
1054	Schism begins between Greek and Roman Christians.
1085	Toledo reconquered from Muslims by Christian forces.
1090–1153	Bernard, Abbot of Clairvaux and stimulus to the success of the Cistercian order.
*c.*1092–1156	Peter the Venerable, Abbot of Cluny, organises the first translation of the Qur'an into Latin.
1095	Pope Urban II (1088–99) launches the First Crusade at the Council of Clermont.
1098	Anselm (1033–1109), Archbishop of Canterbury, asked by the Pope at the Council of Bari to help mend the schism with the Greek bishops.
1099	Crusader Kingdom of Jerusalem established (lasts until 1291).
1109	Order of Victorine 'canons' founded in Paris.
1118	Military monastic Order of the Templars gains recognition.
1122	Concordat signed at Worms to end the Investiture Contest.

1123	First Lateran Council.
1126–1151	Archbishop Raymond of Toledo makes the cathedral library of Toledo a great translation resource.
1139	Second Lateran Council.
1144	Boy found stabbed to death in Norfolk; Jews of Norwich accused of ritual murder.
1144	Second Crusade called, after Muslims recaptured Edessa.
1151	Death of Suger, Abbot of St Denys near Paris.
1155–1217	Nicetas Choniatas, author of a history of the Byzantine Empire in the twelfth century.
1170	Thomas à Becket, then Archbishop of Canterbury, assassinated in Canterbury Cathedral and becomes a famous martyr with many pilgrims visiting his shrine.
1179	Third Lateran Council.
1187	Saladin (1137/8–93) defeats Christian armies at the Battle of Hattin.
1189–92	Third Crusade led by kings Richard I of England and Philip II of France. Frederick Barbarossa, the German emperor, intends to join them, but dies on the journey.
1202–4	Fourth Crusade.
1204	Crusaders sack Constantinople.
1204–61	Latin Kingdom of Constantinople.
1209–29	Albigensian Crusade against dualist heretics in Spain and south of France.
1210	Newly translated philosophical works of Aristotle condemned at the University of Paris.
1215	Fourth Lateran Council decrees that all Christians must make confession at least once a year.
1216	Pope approves order dedicated to poverty founded by Francis of Assisi (1181/2–1226).
1219	Pope approves order of preachers founded to convert heretics by Dominic Guzman (1170–1221).
*c.*1232	Pope Gregory IX sets up Inquisition.
*c.*1232–*c.*1315	Raymond Lull, born in Mallorca of Catalonian parents, became a missionary to Muslims.
1236	Cordoba reconquered by Christian rulers.
1248	Seville reconquered by Christian rulers.

1256–*c.*1302	Gertrude the Great, woman scholar and mystic at the Abbey of Helfta.
1261–1517	Caliphs of Cairo rule North African and Middle Eastern territories.
1274	Second Council of Lyons.
1321	Death of Dante Alighieri, author of the *Divine Comedy*.
*c.*1324–84	John Wyclif, disseminator of heretical views later taken up by the Lollards in England.
*c.*1342–*c.*1416	Julian of Norwich, hermit and mystic.
*c.*1343–1400	Geoffrey Chaucer, author of the *Canterbury Tales*.
1350–1425	Manuel II Palaiologos, Byzantine emperor, theologian and author of interfaith dialogue.
*c.*1373	Birth of Marjorie Kempe, English mystical writer.
1379–1416	Jerome of Prague, supporter of John Hus.
1382	Archbishop Courtenay expresses concern that preachers were spreading Wyclif's ideas.
1414–18	Council of Constance.
1415	John Hus condemned as a heretic by the Council of Constance for his doctrine of the Church.
1431–49	Council of Florence attempts to mend the Greek–Roman schism of 1054.
1448	Lollard 'heretic' burned at Tower Hill in London. Inquisitions continue against alleged Lollards in England.
1453	Ottomans capture Constantinople and end the Byzantine Empire.
1492	Christopher Columbus (1450/1–1506), an Italian adventurer backed by the Spanish monarchy, discovers America.
1492	Granada captured by Christians.
1492	Jews driven out of Spain by a joint decree of Isabella of Castile and Ferdinand of Aragon.
1498	The Portuguese land at Calicut in a ship captained by Vasco da Gama.

Introduction

THE BEAUTIFUL VISION

Huge pictures of the Last Judgement dominate the west end of many modest medieval churches, such as St Andrew's in Chesterton on the outskirts of Cambridge. Christ is shown judging all souls at the end of the world, with the Virgin Mary sitting beside him on one side and John the 'beloved disciple' on the other. Christ is pointing upwards with his right hand and downwards with his left, to indicate where the blessed and the damned respectively are to spend eternity. Angels blow trumpets to raise the dead ready to be judged in their turn. Above is the shining heavenly city surrounded by its walls. Devils are shown prodding and tormenting the damned through hell's darkly gaping mouth. Members of a congregation regularly gazing at this image when they came to worship would receive the message that they must do all they could to live good lives so as to be among the few who could hope for heaven.

Yet in this life the Christian was offered a foretaste of heaven, a place of beauty, joy and heightened experience. Suger (*c.*1081–1151), abbot of St Denys near Paris, wrote of his delight in the beauty of the church he had restored there as a House of God, and the loveliness of colours that adorned it. To be there called him away from his tedious daily administrative responsibilities and allowed him to glimpse the heights of heaven. The modern visitor to his building, and its much earlier layers beneath the church, can see what he meant. A person could seem to embody some of these beauties in a holy life. In a biography of Thomas More (1478–1535), the author compares the life of More to a lovely garden, a paradise of delights, an epitome of celestial virtues. These virtues include severe self-discipline. The garden walks are paved with the camomile of humility. The borders are set with patience, enamelled with the pinks and violets of poverty. The knots are all of thyme, and here and there is found the hyssop of mortification.[1]

There are many medieval tales of 'journeys' in which the soul makes its way to heaven, 'learning' on the way. The twelfth-century *Vision of Tundal*, the work of a monk, describes an Irish knight who learns the hard way, suffering many torments which are set out in physical detail, until he enters heaven, where his senses are overwhelmed with delights. Dante Alighieri (1265–1321) wrote his *Divine Comedy* in Italian as a travellers' tale, taking his lay readers on a comprehensive tour from hell to heaven, pointing out examples of the kinds of behaviour which have brought various famous people to their eternal destinies.

There was a paradox in all this, because it was also widely believed that the gift of an eternity of bliss lay with God and could not be earned. That had been the insistent teaching of Augustine of Hippo (354–430) and he was probably the most widely read of the early Christian writers who shaped Christian thinking in Western Europe. Nevertheless, the medieval Church encouraged the view that the way one lived now was going to affect the life to be lived in eternity, and that support of that endeavour through the sacraments the Church offered was essential.

It could be a comfort for the poor and underprivileged to believe that having a hard time now improved the chances of heaven later on. The Bible said that for the rich man, getting to heaven would be like threading a camel through the eye of a needle (Matthew 19.24). In this way the laity were presented with a plan for life in which they could try to work their way to heaven by being good and regard social disadvantage as an asset. But that belief also provided support for a secular authority in which good order depended on widespread acceptance of the view that a social hierarchy was part of God's plan.

1

LAUNCHING THE FIRST THOUSAND YEARS OF CHRISTENDOM

WANDERERS IN A RELIGIOUS LANDSCAPE AS A WORLD POWER COLLAPSES

When Christianity began, Rome's influence reached almost to the edges of the known world, which then consisted of Europe, Asia and the coastal strip of North Africa. For centuries before the birth of Jesus of Nazareth, Rome had been building a gigantic power-base, progressively conquering Europe, North Africa and much of the modern Middle East. A vast administrative structure had grown up, in which a well-born citizen might expect to take his turn in office, perhaps even serving as a provincial governor for a period.

Rome had begun as a republic, the 'Senate and People of Rome' (SPQR or *Senatus populusque Romanus*). A generation before Jesus was born, in 27 BC, it became an empire. After a power-struggle commemorated by Shakespeare in *Julius Caesar*, Caesar's adopted son Augustus became the first Roman emperor (27 BC–AD 14). Imperial Rome soon set off down a path towards its ultimate decline and fall as its emperors became corrupt and tyrannical, but it still spread a notable Greco-Roman civilisation across its extensive territories. Infant Christianity, at first a simple religion of the common people, with its emphasis on following the teaching of Jesus, soon began to attract educated followers. They brought

Christianity into contact with classical ideals of the good life and the whole span of ancient philosophy, Greek and Roman. Much absorption, debate and controversy followed as Christianity spelt out its theology in detail.

Rome was a society in which the concept of citizenship reached a high level of sophistication. A person could be proud to say 'I am a Roman citizen (*civis Romanus sum*) not least because citizenship carried privileges. Citizenship could be bought, but Paul of Tarsus was, he insisted, *born* a Roman citizen (Acts 22.28), and Roman officialdom accordingly protected him when he was attacked by a mob and found himself standing trial on charges brought by Jews who were hostile to his Christian mission (Acts 21–6). When he faced an unfair trial, Paul exercised his citizen's right to appeal to Caesar (Acts 25.9–12). The notion of a privileged 'citizenship of heaven' was borrowed and much developed by Augustine of Hippo (354–430) when he wrote his *City of God*, with its theory that God knows who are his own and will enjoy eternity in the 'heavenly city'.

This idea of a 'citizenship' of belonging and privilege had its darker side for the non-citizens. Rome ran on slavery, as did much of the ancient world. Many among the peoples Rome conquered were enslaved, and Christianity seems to have taken root first among the underprivileged and the slaves. There was no early Christian resistance to this social system. Christians who were slaves were told to serve their masters faithfully (Ephesians 6.5–8). Subjection in this world did not matter. In heaven, Christians were to be all one in Christ, in whom there were no Jews or 'Greeks', slaves nor free, males nor females (Galatians 3.28).

The Roman conquerors were generally very broad minded about religion. Roman 'syncretism' simply added the local gods of conquered peoples to the Roman pantheon, equating god with god where possible. For example, the Greek Zeus, king of the gods, could simply be regarded as the Roman Jupiter by another name. In polytheism, one god or goddess more or less presented no special theological challenge. In this system local loyalties could remain strong. The religious devotion of ordinary people concentrated on keeping small spiritual powers, household and other local deities, content with gifts and sacrifices. When the emperor of the day was declared a god, and the people required to worship him, he could be added to the existing deities without disturbing the religious mix. That began early, the deification of the emperor being accepted only gradually in Italy, but serving a useful purpose in ensuring the loyalty of the armies serving in the provinces.

Egypt, Syria, Anatolia and Persia had their own religious systems and they could not all be mapped straightforwardly onto the Greco-Roman pantheon, god for god. Through Roman military conquest and trade, Eastern deities such as Mithras the sun god and Egyptian ones such as Isis and Osiris travelled into the West, remaining still very much themselves in terms of their attributes, rituals and special legends.[1] From Anatolia about the third century BC or possibly through Hannibal's invading Carthaginian armies, arrived the Phrygian cult of the Mother of the gods, the goddess of nature, Cybele. Her cult found a place in Rome on the Palatine Hill and involved exciting rituals including wild dancing and drunken bacchanalia.

Some danger of confusion existed for Christianity from religions with beliefs and practices which could seem to resemble theirs. The goddess Cybele's lover was Attis, the Phrygian vegetation god, who castrated himself, ending his fertility, and died each year only to be resurrected with the spring. The Emperor Claudius (41–54) approved an annual spring holiday for the last two weeks of March each year to celebrate his resurrection, culminating in Hilaria, the feast day when he rose again and banquets were held.[2] Adonis was another god who died and was resurrected in spring, with a cult which seems to have originated in Phoenicia, at Byblos. The Emperor Hadrian (117–38) had the Christian holy place of Jesus' birth used for Adonis worship and a sacred grove put there. The pious Christian Helena, mother of Constantine (272–337), the first Christian emperor, restored it as a sanctuary for Christians and caused a basilica to be built.[3]

The cult of Mithras had its form of 'baptism'. This involved sacrificing a bull over a pit in which the initiates stood and into which the bull's blood flowed. The effect was believed to be that the initiate was made one with the god or somehow deified. Few details of the liturgy and rites have survived. Mithras's devotees were very secretive. They met in caves and underground places for worship and used secret signs to recognise one another.[4] But the early Christians too were considered 'secretive' and links were hinted at.

Peregrinus, the wandering religion-taster, was a creation of the satirist Lucian of Samosata, born about AD 120/125 in Syria,[5] but he was not entirely an invention. Many educated young men of the time

Fig. 1: Aphrodite and Adonis are depicted here on a Greek vase, exemplifying the fleshly amusements the pagan gods of the ancient Mediterranean world were thought to enjoy

spent their youth trying out different philosophies and religions until they found one that suited them. The main questions to which they looked for answers were who, if anyone, was in charge of events and the future of the cosmos and how should one best lead the good life and be happy.

In Lucian's story, Peregrinus came across Christianity in his wanderings when he met Christian 'priests and scribes' in Palestine. He then sought fame by writing and commenting on Christian teaching until he was thrown into prison for it. The local Christians did all they could to rescue him. Widows and orphans could be seen waiting outside the prison from early morning and some Christian leaders bribed their way in to see him, bringing fancy meals and sacred books. That of course only increased his notoriety. People began to arrive from Asia to press for his release, their fares paid by the Christians. Lucian the satirist sneers:

> The poor wretches have convinced themselves [...] that they are going to be immortals and live for all time, in consequence of which they despise death and even willingly give themselves into custody [...] Furthermore [Christ] persuaded them that they are all brothers of one another after they have transgressed once for all by denying the Greek gods and by worshipping that crucified sophist himself and living under his laws. Therefore they despise all things indiscriminately and consider them common property.[6]

Peregrinus the Cynic is just a charlatan, who plans to use his Christian 'membership' for his own profit. Self-appointed Cynics were a common sight in the streets, preaching and begging.

But the experience of 'finding Christianity' on such a philosophical journey could be real enough. In his *Dialogue with Trypho*, Justin Martyr (100–65) explains that after much intellectual wandering he was converted by an old man he met on a seashore who kindled in him a love of Christ and made him understand what the prophets had been foretelling. Justin and Trypho sat down to a discussion before an audience of bystanders. Trypho had heard that Christians ate human flesh and slept promiscuously with one another. But he was a Jew and his real problem with the Christians was that they were not circumcised and did not observe the law. Justin, disposing of the rumours by telling Trypho about the Last Supper, and the nature of the love Christians have for one another, explained that the Old Law had been set aside and superseded. The New Testament contained God-given promises to replace it. There was now a new covenant.[7]

Persecution begins

The monotheistic Jews and Christians would not allow their God to be thrown into this melting pot, and consequently faced centuries of state persecution. Christianity was outlawed in the 80s of the first century by the Emperor Domitian who called it a 'Jewish superstition', but allowed the Jews themselves to keep their civil rights provided they paid the 'Jewish tax' (*fiscus Judaicus*). Domitian's reign ended in his assassination but the political distinction of 'real Jews' from the Christians may have begun to matter. State-driven persecutions specifically of Christians were to run on sporadically for a couple of centuries.

About 161, Melito, Bishop of Sardis in Anatolia (d. 181), sent an *Apologia* to the Roman emperor Marcus Aurelius (121–80). He writes of widespread persecutions of Christians, this activity being treated as a licence to seize people's goods. If this is indeed the emperor's wish, 'well and good'. One would regard a death under such an edict as an honour. Melito merely asks the emperor to look into what is happening and assure himself that those who claim to be acting as his agents are doing so as he would wish. If he finds they are not, Melito hopes he will ensure that the people are not left exposed to this despoiling of their property.

Framing a new institution

It was not long before 'charismatic' preachers claiming to be led by the Holy Spirit began to present a challenge to the very basics of Christian belief. Who was going to be authorised to lead the community and how? What teachings were to be allowed and who would decide? So in these first centuries the Christian 'Church' was not only identifying itself as different from the other religions with which the Roman Empire was awash – it was also busy designing its own institutional arrangements.

There was no Bible to refer to at first, just the Old Testament and a collection of writings, only some of which eventually found their way into the New Testament. Among these was the Acts of the Apostles, written by the same author as Luke's Gospel, probably about AD 80–90. This account describes conflicts between the Christians and the Jews and divisions among the Christians as they tried to decide whether they were a sect of the Jews, keeping to the Old Law, or something quite new.

Acts also describes how the Christians designed a system of organisation for themselves. Leading members such as Paul and Barnabas were despatched from Antioch to Jerusalem seeking help to resolve a controversy as to whether the Law of the Old Testament was to apply to Christians. Should converts who were not Jews be circumcised? Christians met in a 'council' in Jerusalem (Acts 15), about AD 48–50, to discuss this increasingly pressing and divisive question. James, the brother of Jesus, was accepted as the natural leader of the Christians in Jerusalem. He persuaded the meeting (Acts 15.13ff.) that the Christians should reach out to the Gentiles. Paul and Barnabas were entrusted with the task of explaining the decision of the meeting to those at Antioch. They were to be accompanied by Judas and Silas who were also respected as prophets and leaders (Acts 15.32).

This experimental and very personal emergence of leadership was the beginning of what was to evolve into a system of 'ministry' in the Christian Church. The thrust at the beginning was missionary. Jesus had taught his disciples to go out and preach the Gospel and to leave each place promptly and move on if their message was not welcomed, shaking the local dust from their feet (Matthew 10.14). But when they did listen, place by place each new community thus formed became a 'church'. It was to such local 'churches' that Paul and others wrote the letters of guidance and sometimes reproach which can still be read in the New Testament.

The members of a small local church could meet for worship and to celebrate the Last Supper, though they did not at first have church buildings to meet in. But as Christianity spread, a structure had to be devised to serve bigger areas and ensure that the one faith was maintained. A system of dioceses emerged, each presided over by a bishop, with priests looking after local worshipping communities as his 'vicars'. Then dioceses were linked within still larger areas, with the bishop of a major city or metropolis holding the position of 'Metropolitan'. In time an even higher structural level emerged, in which the presiding bishop ('arch'-bishop or patriarch) led a whole province. These patriarchal provinces were 'autocephalous', meaning that they had their own jurisdictions. In the Greek-speaking East there were four such provinces led by the Patriarchs of Alexandria, Antioch, Constantinople and Jerusalem. In the Latin-speaking West there was one patriarchal province, headed by the Bishop of Rome, who made the special claim of being successor to the Apostle Peter, Rome's first bishop. We shall glimpse periods of heated dispute as to which of the five was Primate of all.

This structure was going to help to hold the Church together through synods or councils of bishops, held in provinces and occasionally as 'ecumenical' councils, or councils of the whole Church.[8] These would not be like that first council in Jerusalem. Lay people would not be invited to participate in the voting.

CHRISTIANS, JEWS AND GENTILES: ESTABLISHING PARAMETERS

Distinguishing Christians from Jews

Latin-speaking Christians called non-Christians who kept to the old polytheism 'Gentiles' (*gentiles*), 'natives' (*ethnici*), 'pagans' (*pagani*), even (for some of them were sophisticated intellectuals) 'philosophers' (*philosophi*). Once Islam was founded, Muslims were often called 'Saracens' (*Saraceni*), a term previously used for those who lived as bands of robbers in the deserts of Egypt. The Jews formed a special category because they were bound by race, ritual and custom, not simply by adopted belief.

Jewish resistance to Rome and the diaspora which followed

These were turbulent times for Jews in the lands where Christianity was taking root. The historian Flavius Josephus (37–*c.*100), of high-born Jewish descent, had fought in the first Roman–Jewish War, which was prompted partly by a Jewish aspiration to make such prophecies of the coming of Messiah a reality. Vespasian had found him useful as an educated slave 'interpreter', and when he became emperor in AD 69 he freed him. Josephus took the Imperial family name of Flavius and aligned himself fully with the Roman side.

In AD 70 the Temple in Jerusalem was destroyed when three legions of the Roman army led by the future Roman emperor Titus captured Jerusalem after a siege. The Temple caught fire in the fighting. Many Jews escaped the city through tunnels. The remainder were killed or enslaved.[9] The Emperor Vespasian issued commemorative *Judaea Capta* coins to celebrate the Roman victory. Flavius Josephus wrote a detailed account of what had happened. No one who had known Jerusalem before would have recognised the site if he came upon it now, he says sadly.[10]

Some of those who escaped this catastrophe settled around the Mediterranean and further afield. The Jews everywhere were subjected to an annual tax by the Romans, who continued to class them loosely with the Christians.[11] Christians and Jews, because they refused to worship the gods so comfortably coexisting in the imperial pantheon, were easily bracketed together in the official Roman mind.[12] Yet becoming a Jew was not simply a matter of embracing a faith. It was not an option open to everyone. It was not even an individual choice. Judaism was rooted in a people and the rites of its ancient way of life.

The exiled Jews remained angry. Between 115 and 117 there were Jewish revolts in Egypt, Crete and Libya, killing a large number of Roman citizens and destroying pagan temples. The Jewish rebels, led by the self-styled 'King Lukuas',[13] attacked Alexandria, which had been left largely unprotected by the Roman armies, and set fire to it. The destruction of temples and of the tomb of the great Roman general Pompey of the late republic had the Emperor Trajan's armies quickly on the spot. Nevertheless it took until late 117 for Rome to regain full control of the region. Another Jewish uprising (the Bar Kotchba revolt) in 132–5 led to the destruction of towns in Judaea, mass executions and enslavement, and Jews were forbidden to settle in or near Jerusalem. This time the story was told by Cassius Dio (164–*c*.235), who served his time as a Roman senator. He describes how the Emperor Hadrian had provocatively replaced the destroyed city of Jerusalem by a Roman city to be known as Aelia Capitolina, replacing the Temple of the Jews with a temple to Jupiter. The Jews were outraged.

The Emperor Hadrian (117–38) sent one of his best generals, Julius Severus, to deal with the Jewish resistance. The Jews were starved out, killed or imprisoned piecemeal, villages razed and the territory of Judaea reduced to desolation and decay. The tomb of Solomon collapsed by itself and that was taken to be an ominous sign. It was a war with a high cost to Rome in deaths of its own soldiers but it had its impact on the Jews.[14] Settlements of local pagans moved into former Jewish territories. The area became known as 'Syria Palestina' and Jews were forbidden to settle in or near Jerusalem. The Jews remaining in the area suffered discrimination and social exclusion and special taxes. No Jewish self-government or legal system was allowed to operate. The Jews became an exiled people without a *patria* or 'homeland', and consequently Christians encountered them everywhere as Christianity spread through Europe. This sort of organised Jewish resistance had no parallels among the Christians, but the authorities often confused the two, so it added to the unpopularity of Christians.

Christians and Jews: agreeing to differ

The 'Hellenistic' Jews were Greek speakers who had returned from exile – perhaps with a wider view of the world. Philo Judaeus (*c*.25 BC–*c*.AD 50) was one of the Jewish community in Alexandria. So

'Hellenised' was he that he may not even have known Hebrew.[15] He actively endeavoured to synthesise Greek thought with Judaism.[16] The Aramaic-speaking Jewish Christians did not always welcome these exiles back. In Acts 6.1 the Hellenistic Jewish Christians were complaining that their widows were being left out when food was distributed each day. Stephen, himself a Hellenistic Jewish Christian, was appointed with the community's consent to supervise and ensure that the distribution was fair. Acts 6–7 records the mounting resentment which brought him before the Sanhedrin, the local Jewish Council, accused of blasphemy. The Sanhedrin condemned him and he was stoned to death.

Those Christians who were scattered by the internal persecution that broke out when Stephen was killed travelled as far as Phoenicia, Cyprus and Antioch, spreading the Word among Jews. Acts 11.19–26 describes their wider missionary activities. Some Jews 'from Cyprus and Cyrene' living at Antioch converted some of the Greeks there. When the Christians in Jerusalem heard about this they sent Barnabas to Antioch to find out what was happening. He was pleased with what he saw and encouraged them. He then went to Tarsus to find Paul and brought him back to Antioch, where the two of them worked hard in the mission there for a year. It was here, according to Acts 11.25, that the name of 'Christian' was first applied to the converts. It also seems to have been Paul's initiation into a ministry of mission, and also his first encounter with rivalries and resentments in the young Christian community as it worked out its stance in relation to Judaism.

The persistent question was whether non-Jews who became Christians would be bound by Jewish law. Jesus had taught that the Old Law had been fulfilled not superseded (Matthew 5.17). At the Last Supper he spoke of a 'new covenant' (Luke 22.20).[17] Second Corinthians 3.14 says that the Old Law is still there but Christians serve God in a new way in the Holy Spirit. Romans 7.6 similarly suggests that Christians are released from the obligations of the law to serve in a new way 'in the Spirit'.

When the 'council' held at Jerusalem (Acts 15) decided that that it should not be made unnecessarily difficult for Gentiles to turn to God and become Christians, it was agreed that a letter should be written setting out a digest of points taken from the Old Law which were still appropriate. These were listed as abstaining from eating any food which had been offered in sacrifices to idols; from eating blood and the meat of strangled animals; and from sexual misconduct (Acts 15.19–20). It was agreed to send out the letter to the Gentile believers in Antioch, Syria and Cilicia.

Who were the Christian 'Gentiles'?

Paul came to see himself as the 'apostle to the gentiles' (Romans 11.13). But who were to be regarded as 'Gentiles'? Timothy, Paul's disciple and co-worker as a missionary, had a Christian mother, a Greek father and grandmother of Jewish extraction (2 Timothy 1.5). He had not been circumcised and Paul thought it would be politic to have him circumcised so that he would not cause offence to the Jews when he went among them as a missionary (Acts 16.1–3).

A series of letters was written during the next few years to the communities of Christians Paul now visited, sometimes jointly with others – and especially Timothy, who appears as a co-author in several of his letters. Communities of Christians named after the cities where they lived received letters from Paul: Corinthians, Galatians, Philippians, Thessalonians, Ephesians, Colossians, Romans.[18] Corinth had some recent Jewish immigrants, expelled from Jerusalem in AD 49. There were also Jewish refugees from Rome itself, including fellow tent-makers Prisca and Aquila (Acts 18.1–12 and 1 Corinthians 16.19). Paul apparently visited Rome twice, and was twice imprisoned there. During his first incarceration (Acts 28) he wrote some of the letters which are now in the New Testament. On his release, he set off on another missionary journey (Acts 29). 1 Timothy, Titus and Philemon seem to have been written while he was at Corinth on this journey. But he was arrested again after he had left Corinth (*c.*AD 66) and taken back to Rome, where he wrote his second letter to Timothy (Acts 31–2). This comprehensive mission to the Gentiles also involved encounters with Jews in diaspora. Among the Galatians, the question of what to do about the Old Law was evidently still heated. Local Judaisers were trying to insist that the Old Law must still be obeyed. Writing to the Galatians (Galatians 2.16–17), Paul says, 'If righteousness could be gained through the law, Christ died for nothing!' Paul is also conscious of Jewish criticism when writing to the Thessalonians (1 Thessalonians 2.14–16).

So the separation of the Jewish and the Christian religion was painful and difficult.

CHRISTIANITY STRUGGLES TO LEAVE POLYTHEISM BEHIND

The difficulty of giving up the little gods

This first struggle for Christian identity and separation from Judaism took place in a Roman world where most people had other ideas about religion. Deep in European consciousness, in every tribe and people at the beginning of Christianity, was a nervous sense of being surrounded by a supernatural universe full of living beings. They tended to be perceived as small and personal rather than cosmic. These petty gods had to be placated. They had to be prevented from acting destructively from sheer malice and had to be bribed to persuade them to offer assistance when people needed it. So, pleasing such gods might involve making sacrificial gifts, costly to the person who offered them and involving shedding blood and even death. It was not a matter of *thinking* or *believing* correctly but of *doing* the right thing.

A Roman household god had a shrine in the house.[19] Each day the head of the household would make an offering of food and wine. The Roman poet Horace describes how little crowns of herbs were sometimes placed on the heads of the small statues.[20] They seem to have been treated with the affection of a family pet, but with the same nervous awareness of housing a potentially dangerous animal that even the fondest owners of a Rottweiler might feel.

As Christianity soaked into the social fabric of the late Roman Empire, it brought with it a multitude of 'saints', dead Christians acknowledged as outstanding in their courage in the face of persecution, or for their virtuous lives. Some were martyrs. It remained natural to want to show them respect and to turn to them for help. Augustine of Hippo, born in what is now Algeria in the mid-fourth century, was brought up by a Christian mother and a pagan father. In Africa his mother visited the shrines of the saints in much the spirit in which her neighbours might visit the shrines of the gods. She poured out libations of wine. When Augustine moved to Italy in search of progress in his career as a professor of rhetoric, his mother accompanied him. He comments that at first she kept up this habit of making small propitiatory sacrifices when she came to Milan with him. However, when she learned that Ambrose, the Bishop of Milan, had forbidden it, she humbly stopped at once.[21]

Yet it was natural enough for Christians to adopt the statues of favoured saints to sit in a niche or shrine at home, to be prayed to for help and intercession. In a procession before the Roman Games or for a Christian festival alike, images were carried on floats and the crowds who lined the streets to watch would call out the name of a god or a saint as the image went past, invoking his or her help.[22] In Spain and southern Italy a list of saints and their particular interests was available for consultation. There was, for example, a saint for stomach-ache, one for toothache and several for headaches, others for indigestion or cholera or scrofula.[23]

Apuleius tells a good story

Apuleius (*c.*125–80) was the author of the gossipy *Metamorphoses* (*The Golden Ass*). He was a North African Berber who studied rhetoric at Carthage where Augustine was to teach a later generation of students. He travelled widely and became a great taster of contemporary religions and 'mysteries'. He gives us an insight into the world of thought in which the first Christians found themselves living.

Apuleius describes how the hero of his story 'saw' a woman transform herself into an owl. She took off her clothes and then scooped some ointment out of an alabaster box, rubbed it in her fingers to warm it and then smeared it thoroughly all over herself. Then her body began to vibrate and she became covered in feathers and grew wings. Her nose turned into a beak and her toenails became talons. She let out a tentative hoot, hopped and tried her wings and then took off in swooping flight.[24] The hero of Apuleius' story, whose name is Lucius, thinks he would like to try this himself and he gets a maidservant to bring him a box of ointment from the chest where such things are stored.[25] He too takes off his clothes and smears himself all over with the ointment, but he does not grow feathers. Instead he turns into a donkey. The maid has brought him the wrong ointment. Evidently the magic powers of the different unguents are quite specific and also, it turns out, their antidotes. This provides Apuleius with the thread of his narrative, as Lucius goes on a journey to find some roses, for he is told that only if he eats roses can he be turned back into a human being.

Lucius finds that even as a donkey he retains his human powers of reasoning. Here Apuleius is playing with a theory of the Hermetic tradition his readers would have recognised, that human beings stand in the cosmic 'hierarchy of being' between the purely spiritual (gods, angels, demons) and the simply bestial. We are both spirit and body, and we share with the higher spiritual beings the power of conscious thought. If we behave like beasts, we turn into beasts and lose our reason. It we behave like gods, we actually become more spiritual.[26] Lucius the donkey is, however, not quite reduced to a beast by his behaviour. His first consideration when he finds how he is changed is whether to kick the maidservant. He decides against it.[27]

Little portents are described in the tale. A hen ran about her yard ready to lay her daily egg and when her master praised her she laid at his feet not just the egg but a chick already clad in its feathers. This outcome was regarded as an 'ominous portent'. On the same occasion a crack opened up under the dinner table and a great gush of blood came up from underground. Wine in the cellars began to bubble. A weasel was seen dragging a snake. A dog opened its mouth and a green frog leapt out, then an old sheep turned on the dog, took its throat in its teeth and killed it. It seemed obvious that supernatural powers were sending a message or warning.[28]

A Christian apology

How was a Christian apologist to counter this sort of thing? Augustine of Hippo's *City of God* was written partly to address the challenge of highly educated pagans who had fled to North Africa from the barbarian invasions that were threatening Rome. A professional persuader as a professor of rhetoric, Augustine meets them halfway.[29] He accepts that there are powerful beings which are malign: these 'gods' are real enough, the gods who enjoy the ribald theatrical performances in their honour which he had once found such a temptation himself.[30] But they are in truth fallen angels, God's good creatures who rebelled against him and became 'evil' spirits with malevolent intentions towards humanity. These sinner-demons are just like sinful people.[31] They get upset. They get annoyed. They can be bribed and placated by presents. They are pleased to be honoured and respected. But these capricious and small-minded beings have to be relied on to assist in augury and soothsaying and making magic work and the interpretation of dreams, for they have authentic communication with the supernatural. So he did not expect the Christian to deny the possibility of ill-intentioned supernatural interference.

LET INTO THE SECRET

What did a Christian believe?

Galatians 6.6 may be the first mention of giving instruction in the Christian faith. The *Didache*, which may date from the late first century, was apparently written as a practical manual of instruction for converts, based on the teaching of Jesus as the apostles had relayed it. It concentrates on the way a Christian should behave. He should love God first and then his 'neighbours' as himself (Mark 12.30–31; *Didache*, 1.2). He should do nothing to anyone that he would not want done to him (*Didache*, I.2), bless those who curse him and pray for his enemies (Luke 6.28; *Didache*, 1.3). If bad things happen to him, the Christian should accept them as good, for nothing happens without God's permission (*Didache*, 3.10). The Christian should bear the Lord's yoke as far as he is able (*Didache*, 6.2). He should regard possessions as common (*Didache*, 4.8) and share what he has with the poor. He should have nothing to do with such pagan practices as engaging with omens or astrology or magic, for they all lead to idolatry (*Didache*, 3.4). He is not to indulge in gossip (*Didache*, 3.6) because it can lead him into heresy, or into the sort of talk that leads to division among Christians (*Didache*, 4.3), but instead he should work to make peace where there is any dispute.

This instruction was meant to prepare a convert for baptism. In Acts 8.38, Philip is described as baptising the converted eunuch straight away when he confessed his Christian faith, but the *Didache* expects proper preparation (*Didache*, 7.4–8.1). The purpose of baptism was to cleanse the baptised person of sin and it could be done only once. Tertullian (*c.*160–225) said that to be baptised again would be like trying to wash in the 'dirty bath water' of one's subsequent sinning.[32] So adults prepared carefully as catechumens for baptism, often saving it until as late in life as they dared.

In church they stood in a separate group and left before the consummation of the Eucharist, along with any members of the public who had come to watch the worship, the 'unbelievers' and those whose opinions were not orthodox, the heretics.[33] The holy secret of what followed was protected. Doorkeepers (ostiaries) might keep watch to make sure no outsider was able to see. In their lengthy period of instruction, the catechumens first received 'baby food' teaching and only later food for adults (1 Corinthians 3.1–2 and

Hebrews 5.12–14). For example, a firm grasp of the principle that Christians worship only one God was needed before introducing the doctrine of the Trinity.

About 400, at the request of a deacon in Carthage called Deogratias ('Thanks-be-to-God'), Augustine wrote a Latin guide to 'instructing the uneducated' (*De catechizandis rudibus*). Many catechumens were brought to Deogratias to teach and he found it a heavy responsibility. Augustine tells him to keep it simple. He should explain that the reason why Christ came to earth was to show people how much God loves them. However, such simplicity will not do for educated catechumens who have been reading the Bible and will come with informed questions, ready to out-argue their catechist. Conversely, the catechist should be alert to signs that his pupils are bored and he will have to be cheerful and resilient in the face of feelings of failure.

Augustine had encountered catechumens who came to classes while continuing to enjoy the theatre and gladiatorial combats and lead sinful lives. They argued that they need not amend their lives until they had learned the theology and were ready for baptism.[34] They are quite wrong about that, says Augustine. What if the catechumen arrives with even more false and unchristian aims, believing that becoming a Christian will win him approval and temporal advantages? A man like that[35] needs to be kept on the right road by reminders that the only right reason to become a Christian is the desire to grow fit for heaven.[36]

Only with these questions of right conduct disposed of does Augustine come to the narrative 'theology' of what the faithful Christian should believe.[37] God is all-powerful, good, just and merciful. He made all things: angels and man, and woman to be man's helpmeet. He gave men and women free will as he had given it to the angels. Some of the angels fell, as an omniscient God foresaw they would, and their leader became the Devil. The catechist is then to tell the story of Adam and Eve and how they disobeyed by eating the apple, and emphasise again that God foreknew that this would happen. All men and women now deserve to go to hell but God in his mercy destines some for heaven. This was an important point for Augustine, who held a strong belief in predestination but also insisted that no one could know whether heaven or hell was to be his or her destiny. The catechist should explain that the present visible

Church has both the good and the wicked in it. Only God knows who are his own.[38]

Cyril of Jerusalem (*c.*313–86) offers an almost contemporary glimpse of the method of preparing candidates for Christian baptism in the Greek-speaking East of the Christian world in the fourth century. He evokes the atmosphere vividly and makes it clear that by the fourth century, ritual and order had become far more developed and established than in the period of the *Didache*. His lectures for catechumens begin encouragingly with a Prologue assuring them that they are already beginning to gather blossoms for their heavenly crowns, and it is only a matter of time before the blossoms bear fruit. Their names have been inscribed on a list. They have glimpsed the torches of the bridal procession. They have heard the call and felt the longing for citizenship in heaven. They have been allowed to come and see something of what happens in church. They have observed the order and discipline, the priests, the reading of Scripture and the teaching. Now is the time for them to examine their motives and their present mode of life. If they have come for personal profit or to court a woman or to please a friend, this will not do. They should leave now and come back when they can come with the right motives. Like Augustine, he is concerned to stress that would-be Christians must not put off amending their lives until baptism, but do it now.

Cyril trusts that the Holy Spirit will help his spiritual pupils understand and gain enlightenment if they attend classes regularly (23 lectures survive), but only if they cleanse their conduct and their hearts, forgive their enemies and confess their sins to God. Like the Latin catechumens, they must not tell outsiders what they are learning (CL, Prologue, 12). The Christian mysteries are to be respected.

The fourth lecture covers the ten key points of Christian doctrine. Cyril begins with the warning in Colossians (CL 2.8) about the dangers posed to the Christian by the deceitful contortions of human philosophy. This needs to be balanced by practical Christian living. To be a good Christian, a person must hold the right views and also live rightly. Neither is enough without the other.

The first thing to get right is the doctrine of God. God is one, eternal, unchanging, omnipotent and omnipresent. He is not one god among many as the polytheist pagans say. He is not a Principle of Good set against a Principle of Evil as the dualists claim. God is a

Trinity. He is not a hierarchical Trinity like the one the Platonists describe, but a Trinity of co-eternal equals. Before all ages he was Father, Son and Holy Spirit.

Then comes the right belief about Christ, who is eternally the only-begotten Son of God but historically born of the Virgin Mary as fully human. Humanity was no mere garment he wore. He felt like us and shared all our experiences. He was crucified for our sins, died, was buried and was resurrected. He ascended into heaven and will come again to judge the living and the dead.

As he goes through these key pillars of the Nicene Creed, Cyril touches on the various ways in which philosophers and heretics and adherents of other religions have confused these issues to warn his listeners not to be led astray.

Then he moves to the subject of the soul and its relationship with the body, another matter of great contemporary interest and widespread debate. Some – especially the dualists, who equated spirit with the Good and matter with Evil – claimed that human souls were sparks of the divine trapped in material bodies as a punishment. (We shall hear much more of the dualists.)[39] No, insists Cyril, a human being is divinely created afresh as a person with body and soul.

Nevertheless he accepts the underlying assumption almost universal in the ancient world that the body and its appetites can lead the soul astray. It follows that the good Christian will live with a self-discipline that will subdue the body and its appetites. Much is made of the importance of chastity. Second marriages are permissible, though continence is better for the widowed. In the matter of food, the purpose of fasting is to discipline the body. The Christian should eat moderately and tidily. He should avoid eating meat which has been offered to the pagan gods. He should dress plainly, to cover himself and keep warm.

Of the Scriptures, the catechumen should read or hear read the books of the Old Testament to be found in the Greek version known as the Septuagint. The rest of the content of the Bible was still under discussion. He should not read the apocrypha, whose place in the Scriptures was disputed. He should read the New Testament, but the four Gospels only. Other books pretending to be gospels should be avoided, especially that of the Manicheans. Also to be accepted are the Acts of the Apostles, the letters of James, Peter, John and

Jude and Paul's 14 letters to the young churches. Everything else is to be considered as of secondary rank and dubious authenticity as the Word of God.

The actual baptism

In his Catechetical lectures (CL 19) for those who had just been baptised, Cyril of Jerusalem gives us a vivid picture of a baptism of adults as he reminds the baptised exactly what had now happened to them. The candidates entered the vestibule of the baptistery and there they faced towards the West, the region of darkness where the sun sets, and pointing their hands as though they could see him before them, they renounced Satan 'and all his works', which means all sin (including sins of thought), for sin is Satan's work. Then they renounced all pomp and vanity, such as theatres and horse-racing and the other decadent entertainments of the time. Then they renounced the service of Satan, which would include all sorts of necromancy, idolatry, astrology, magic and so on.

Now they turned to the East and made their professions of faith, saying 'I believe in the Father, and in the Son and in the Holy Spirit and in one baptism of repentance.' Then they entered from this outer chamber into the church for their baptism. This would normally be baptism by immersion or by standing in water, with water poured over their heads.

Teaching after baptism: the secrets revealed

Chrysostom (*c.*349–407) says the Creed was taught only immediately before baptism and Ambrose of Milan mentions in a letter to his sister that he had been teaching it to the advanced students after the ordinary catechumens had been dismissed for the day.[40] The Apostles' Creed as we have it now derives from the statement of faith used in early Roman worship. It got its name because of the legend that each of the apostles had contributed a clause. The Nicene Creed was a formulation of the Council of Nicaea of 325 in an attempt to define a faith untainted by heresy, but it did not come into general use at once. It is not clear that Augustine was familiar with it.

The effect of this secrecy on those preparing for baptism must have been heightened curiosity and the desire to learn these final secrets. What were they? First, the newly baptised were at last allowed to use the Lord's Prayer. Cyril's surviving lectures for learners come to the

Lord's Prayer only towards the end (CL 23). Augustine too indicates that restraint was the practice.

As to the Eucharist itself, Tertullian (*c.*200) wrote of the importance of the protective silence about the 'mysteries'.[41] There must be no risk that catechumens to whom Jesus' words at the Last Supper were revealed should think they were 'eating' a god, as enemies of the Christians accused.[42] The mystery was also a protection of the sacredness of the celebration of the Last Supper. Unsavoury episodes did happen. Chrysostom wrote to Pope Innocent I (Letter I, 3), while he was Patriarch of Constantinople, to describe an occasion when a crowd of soldiers broke into the church on an Easter Sunday and women who had taken off their clothes ready for baptism were forced to flee immodestly dressed. The soldiers forced their way into the place where sacred vessels were kept and the consecrated wine was spilt, so that the 'blood of Christ' fell on their garments.

Into the Middle Ages: the baptism of babies and repenting the sins of a lifetime

This exacting preparation of adults for baptism had to change when at the end of the fourth century in the West baptism as an infant became the norm. That happened partly because of a strengthening conviction that an unbaptised baby would be denied entry to heaven. Infant mortality was high.

Pelagius (*fl.*390–418), a fashionable society preacher in Rome of possible British origins, assured his listeners that they could win God's approval simply by living good Christian lives. Augustine responded by explaining about 'original sin'. This he said was inherited from Adam and Eve after they sinned, and was born in every child. For this alone, God could justly send a new-born infant to hell. He pointed to the selfish greed visible even in suckling babies. Even Pelagian families were known to get their infants baptised just in case.

This change had implications that were going to shape Christian life throughout the Middle Ages, especially in Western Europe. A baptised infant would need to be taught about the faith when he or she was old enough. Cyril of Jerusalem reminded the baptised that baptism offers complete cleansing for the soul in preparation for heaven, but once and for all. Once the sinner was cleansed of all sin, it behoved him or her to sin no more. There must be no turning back after one had put one's hand to the plough (Luke 9.62). The early Christian world had a system of penance for the serious sins of murder, adultery and apostasy. The early Middle Ages had to develop penitential arrangements for the innumerable more minor sins everyone commits. The effects upon the daily experience of medieval Christians were going to be enormous.

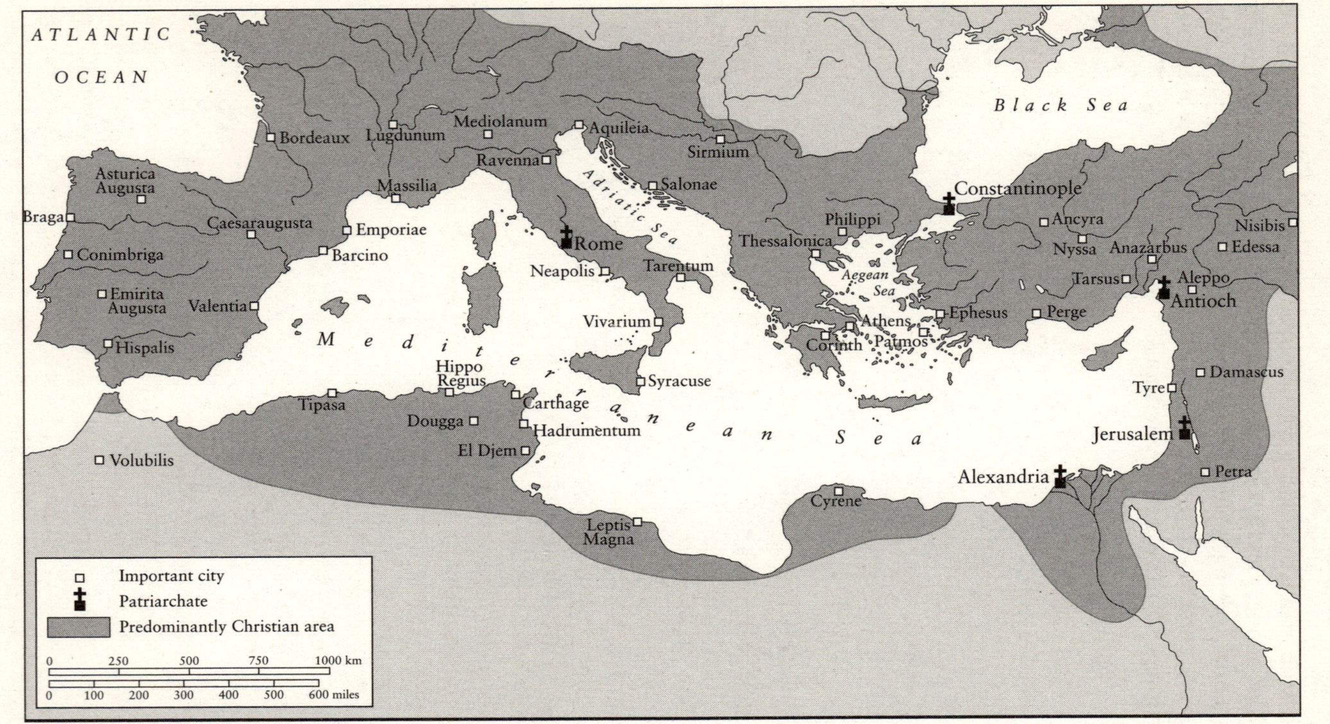

Map 1: The spread of early Christianity by the fifth century

2

NEW FAITHS FOR EUROPE

RECOVERING A CHRISTIAN EMPIRE FOR THE WEST

By the year 1000, Christian social expectations had transformed Western society. Children were routinely baptised as infants. The annual cycle of the Church's year gave an order to daily life. The clergy formed a powerful 'estate', the first 'order' in society, higher than the nobility, who came a mere second. The five early-medieval centuries had brought Christianity into most of Western Europe in way that decisively shaped almost everyone's lives. Christianity in the Greek-speaking East had a different though equally comprehensive impact, for there the Christian Roman Empire had not ended in the same way with the collapse of a civilisation. Byzantium's emperors succeeded one another until the fifteenth century. Their borders with the Middle East and their encounters with the new religion of Islam made theirs a different story, as we shall see. But there too Christianity dominated society and its arrangements and touched everyone's life. How did these changes happen?

The conversion of Constantine

Early in the fourth century, the repeated state persecutions Christians had suffered came to an end[1] when Christianity became the 'official religion' of the Roman Empire. Constantine (emperor from 306 to 337) became a Christian. He was probably looking first and foremost for military advantage when he did so. In 312, in a period of warfare over the succession amongst the offspring of previous emperors, Constantine was fighting his rival Maxentius for the imperial throne, and Maxentius was winning. Then Constantine assembled all his forces outside Rome, at the Milvian Bridge over the River Tiber.

According to Constantine's contemporary Lactantius (*c.*240–*c.*320) and the historian Eusebius of Casearea (260/5–339/40), Constantine had a dream or vision. Eusebius says that Constantine told him the story himself, setting his vision on a march rather than at the camp before the Milvian Bridge.[2] He saw a bright cross in the sky above the sun with an inscription, 'in this sign you shall conquer' (*in hoc signo vinces*). Eusebius says that God promised him victory if the shields of his soldiers were painted with the symbol of the Cross (*staurogram*). Lactantius's version describes the required 'sign' differently as the *Chi-Rho*, representing the first two Greek letters in the word *Christos*.[3] Constantine won the battle and Maxentius died in the river. That put an end to their rivalry and Constantine was able to enter Rome in a triumphal march. Grateful to the God he believed had given him the victory, he issued the Edict of Milan in 313, recognising Christianity as the official religion of the Empire.

Whether Constantine's own faith was real it remains impossible to know, but his mother Helena had been a Christian so he would have understood something of the Christian faith. Helena remained close to her son, and her own deep and lasting faith seems beyond question. She went on pilgrimage to the Holy Places of Palestine in her eighties. In the tradition at the time of deferring the cleansing of baptism until as late as possible in life, Constantine was baptised in 337, just before his death, by Eusebius of Nicomedia (d. 341), local bishop to the imperial court and connected by blood with the imperial family.

The conversion of the emperor radically altered the relationship of the Roman state authorities with the Christians. Constantine moved cautiously at first. He forbade the building of new pagan temples, though at first he allowed the continuation of sacrifice to the old gods. Later in his reign he became more repressive, commanding that the temples of the gods should be pulled down. His change of heart did not mean that all Constantine's subjects were personally converted too, but it certainly created a climate which encouraged it. Most importantly, it allowed those who were already Christians to flourish and to hold office.

The climate changed with the collapse of social order in Western Europe after the fall of Rome with the arrival of invading tribes. That upheavel left Roman Christendom in religious disarray. The task of the next few centuries was to reconvert as well as to convert. Conversion of a people by converting their leader was often the most practical way. Yet *cuius regio eius religio* ('the ruler's religion is the people's religion') was not to be framed as a theoretical principle for a thousand years.[4] It was simply taken for granted in the centuries after the fall of Rome. We shall see an example in the case of the conversion of the Anglo-Saxons at the end of the sixth century.[5] The method was to send a senior ecclesiastical figure or his representative to address himself to the leader of a people. Pope Gregory the Great sent his emissary Augustine (early sixth century to 604(?)) to Canterbury to persuade the king of Kent to become a Christian king.

For Christianity to penetrate down into the population – so that a largely uneducated people came to understand what they were expected to believe – was another matter. People continued to find it hard to part with old pagan loyalties and old pagan practices; it was natural enough to want to have it both ways. Martin of Braga (*c.*520–80) reproved the dogged superstitousness of uneducated people ('rustics'). 'They are still trapped in their former pagan superstition and they give more worship to demons than to God.'[6]

The rise of 'Arian' Christianity

The most important single factor in the changes to Christianity in Western Europe after Rome fell was the emergence of Arianism. By chance this coincided with the period when Constantine made it possible for Christians to be open about their faith, but it was going to divide Christendom for hundreds of years. 'Arian Christians' were followers of Arius (256–336), a Libyan by birth. Serving as a Christian priest in Alexandria, he had been preaching that Christ the Son is secondary to the Father, begotten before time began but not co-eternal with the Father, who is the one God.[7] Athanasius (296–373), then Bishop of Alexandria, responded vigorously, defending the principle that Father, Son and Holy Spirit are co-eternal and that there can be no subordination or succession or change over time in the Trinity.

The controversy became so divisive that a meeting of bishops of the whole Church was held in Nicaea in 325. This became generally accepted as the first 'ecumenical council'. It produced a statement of faith, the 'Nicene Creed', which – slightly adjusted by another such 'universal' council held in 381 at Constantinople – is still one of the fundamental confessional documents used in worship by Christians all over the world.

The division betweed 'Arians' and 'catholics' quickly became political as much as theological. Eusebius of Nicomedia (d. 341), who had been a personal friend of Arius, was a reluctant signatory to the confession of faith agreed at Nicaea. Always a skilful politician and courtier, he turned this concession into a compromise. He was in a position to ensure that influential persons at the imperial court had Arian sympathies. Then he ruthlessly brought about the exile of Arius's enemy Athanasius of Alexandria, even though, personally, the emperor held Athanasius in high regard.

By historical accident, Arius's influence on the history of Christian Europe reached a long way. Whole peoples identified themselves as 'Arians' as the migrating tribes already pressing on the Empire from the East became drawn into taking positions. Ulfilas (*c.*311–83) had been born in Cappadocia to a Greek family which had been captured and enslaved by the Goths. Possibly after he had spent some time in Constantinople and been ordained by Eusebius of Nicomedia, he became persuaded of the correctness of the Arian position. He settled in what was later part of Bulgaria and made a translation of the Bible into Gothic, adapting the Greek alphabet for the purpose. He may have taken Arianism to the Germanic tribes with missionary zeal, encouraged by Eusebius. In this account of events, Eusebius and Ulfilas may therefore together have been largely responsible for the Arianisation of the Germanic tribes, with its long-term historical consequences as far away as Spain. Another strand of evidence credits Fritigern (d. *c.*380) with the Arianisation of the Germanic tribes. He was a tribal leader among the Goths, who saw off a rival with the assistance of the Emperor Valens (r. 364–78), and then became an Arian Christian, in gratitude or coutesy, for Valens himself was an Arian.

Vast regions were taken over by the conquering 'Arian' tribes, defeating rival pagan invaders in the process. Ammianus Marcellinus (325/30–91) had a military career and became a historian with plenty of direct experience to write about. He describes the sudden 'whirlwind' arrival of a people who came down from the mountains destroying whatever they found.[8] These were the Huns, who seem to have come from Central Asia. The local people, who came to be known as the Visigoths ('Western Goths'), fled in terror to Thrace, roughly where Bulgaria, Greece and Turkey now meet, where the lands were fertile.

They thought they would be even safer on the other side of the Danube. Under the leadership of Alavivus, co-ruler with Fritigern, they sent emissaries to Valens (328–78), an Arian Christian who had become Roman emperor of the East in 364, and asked if they might become his subjects. Valens was more concerned to counter 'catholic' Christianity than to suppress paganism. These Goths were fellow-Arians. They promised to serve in the Roman armies if they were needed and otherwise to live quietly and be no trouble. Permission was given for them to settle south of the Danube in modern Romania. But it was not long before the settlers became disillusioned with the arrangements made for them in their place of refuge, and revolutionary leaders arose. Valens asked for reinforcements from the Western emperor Gratian to suppress them, and running battles continued until the Romans tried to take a firmer grip, but the decisive Battle of Adrianople in 378 left the Romans defeated and Valens dead.

Alaric the Goth (370–410), like others not Roman born, had early decided it was strategically wise to fight for the Romans not against them and joined the Roman army. He supported Theodosius (the last emperor to rule the whole Roman Empire, East and West, from 379 to 395). He helped to rescue the emperor from the challenge of a Frankish tribal leader who threatened his throne, but he did not receive the rewards he expected. He left the Roman army and became the leader of the Visigoths and a threat to Rome.

He first appears in that role in 391 in Thrace, as leader of an army of Goths apparently including different tribes. There the Roman general Stilicho stopped them. Stilicho was himself of partly Vandal extraction though well connected with the powerful of the Empire, being married to the Emperor Theodosius's niece. The Vandals too were migrant tribes, moving progressively into southern Europe. It was as leader of this motley army that Alaric sacked Rome in 410, giving the Romans their first serious shock of real fear that the whole empire might now be vulnerable to destruction by these invading tribes.

Ammianus Marcellinus's 'whirlwind' peoples came to be known as the Huns – a name apparently given them by Tacitus (*c.*56–after 117). These were not Christians of any colour, but pagan. They seem

Fig. 2: Book illustration, 1881, depicting the legendary fearsomeness of Attila, the fifth-century leader of the invading Huns

to have moved westward from Central Asia from the first century and had helped to drive tribes from the Caucasus still further west before them. Not everyone fled at their advance. They incorporated other tribes, including some that were Germanic and spoke Gothic languages. One way or another, the Huns and their allies, fighting as archers on horseback, had gained control of a good part of Europe as far as the Danube and the Rhine by the end of the fourth century.

From 434 to 453 their leader was Attila. He made an unsuccessful assault on Byzantium, laid waste the Balkans and got as far as Orléans in Gaul before he was decisively defeated at the Battle of the Catalaunian Plains. Then he turned his attention to Italy and had some success in the Lombard plain, though he did not capture Rome. This new military 'empire' did not survive Attila's death. It had not set about organising a continuing infrastructure to ensure adequate governance and the rule of law, and the Roman infrastructure struggled on into the sixth century, providing some system for such important matters as the distribution of grain, with the significant aid of the Church's own organisation. The letters of Gregory the Great when he was pope (590–604) are eloquent about the practical difficulties.

The Arian triumph did not last in Northern Europe, though it was to have its day in Spain under the Visigoths. In Northern Europe, the Ostrogoths and Burgundians and East-Germanic Vandals were conquered by adjacent tribes of 'Nicene' Christians by the end of the eighth century. Among the Germanic tribes only the Franks were converted directly from their original paganism to Nicene Christianity.

Gaul becomes France

The battering that Roman government received as the migrant tides flowed into the West did not wipe out Christianity in every part of the Western Empire. In some places, ecclesiastical organisation persisted. Gaul had a long Christian history. Christians had been persecuted in Lyons in the reign of the Emperor Marcus Aurelius (121–80)[9] and 48 martyrs were recorded, some of them slaves, some citizens. Some of the Christians in Gaul may have been the converts of missionaries who had arrived in Marseilles by sea and reached Lyons along the River Rhône. The historian Gregory of Tours (*c.*538–94), though writing long after the event, confidently describes one mid-third-century mission from Rome which he says sent seven bishops to Gaul to found bishoprics there, in Arles, Tours, Narbonne, Toulouse, Paris, Auvergne and Limoges.[10] A council held at Arles in 314 records the signatures of well over a dozen bishops of French sees.

By the fourth and fifth centuries there is evidence of the arrival of monastic communities, also apparently settling at first in the area of Marseilles. Martin of Tours (*c.*316–97) founded the abbey of Marmoutier. Cassian (d. 435) founded the Abbey of St Victor in the same area, to be a double monastery for men and women.

The opinion-formers of this Christian Gaul were a small aristocratic community who tended to know one another. Hilary of Poitiers (*c.*310–67) was born to pagan parents and had an excellent education. He was converted to Christianity and was baptised with his wife and child, and later made Bishop of Poitiers by popular acclaim. Ausonius (*c.*310–*c.*95) also had pagan parents but he too became a Christian. He taught rhetoric in what is now Bordeaux. One of his pupils was Paulinus (*c*.354–431), who seemed set for a political career until he also became a Christian and was made Bishop of Nola. Sulpicius Severus (*c*.363–*c*.425) was a friend of Paulinus. Gennadius of Massilia (Marseilles) (d. *c*.496) included Severus in his updated list of 'approved Christian authors'. This was a project begun by Augustine of Hippo's irascible contemporary Jerome (*c*.347–420) in his *De Viris Illustribus,* and kept up to date down the centuries.[11]

These leading Christians of Roman Gaul also became entangled in some of the the early controversies about the faith. Irenaeus (d. *c*.202), Bishop of Lyons, had been born in the Middle East, and had links to Polycarp of Smyrna. He was an able theologian and wrote a book against the heretics,[12] listing contemporary concerns. Gaul's Christian bishops in the third century played a part in the Novatian controversy over the unrepeatability of baptism and the restoration of the 'lapsed'. During the persecution of Christians by the Emperor Decius (249–51), many had apostatised, fearing death if they were known to be Christians. Novatius (*c*.200–58) and his followers insisted that apostates such as these could never be restored to the Christian community. Cyprian mentions them about 254. The Bishop of Lyons was against the Novatianists but the Bishop of Arles supported them.

So Gaul had had an impressive ecclesiastical organisation which made for a robust Christian continuity. Gaul first felt the impact of the 'barbarian' incursions in 407–10, as invaders swept through its territories into Spain from further east. Arian Visigoths arrived from Italy in 411 and settled across what is now the border between France and Spain until about 416. The Frankish tribes fought their way from Tournai to the Loire, finally driving the Romans out by the end of the fifth century. Early in the sixth they pushed the Visigoths south across the Pyrenees, except for part of the coast of the south of France. By 536 they had captured Arles and defeated the Burgundians.

Clovis I (*c*.466–*c*.511), founder of the Merovingian dynasty and a catholic Christian, was the first Frankish king who succeeded in unifying the Frankish tribes under one ruler. Gaul became 'France'. The Church continued to provide a remarkable degree of stability during the sixth and seventh centuries, holding frequent regional synods of its bishops. Christian France survived the transition from the late Roman world to the early medieval world without it being necessary for a fresh missionary endeavour to be made to bring back a lost Christian faith.

Fig. 3: *The Baptism of Clovis*, *c.*1500, painting by the Master of Saint Giles: Clovis, the fifth-century king who united the Franks, is shown being baptised by total immersion after his conversion to Christianity in 496

Spanish Christians: Arian or 'catholic'?

Roman Hispania had become Christian in much the same way as Roman Gaul had done, and it too enjoyed some continuity of Christian organisation throughout the collapse of empire and the tribal invasions. Like Gaul it had its share of eccentrics and prominent heretics among its leading Christian intellectuals. Notable among these was Priscillian of Avila (d. *c.*385), condemned for promoting extreme asceticism and encouraging his followers not to marry, thus, it was said, putting the future of family life at risk.[13]

The peninsula which Spain and Portugal now share remained a Roman province until late in the fifth century, when the Arian Visigoths arrived from southern Gaul. There they had been 'contained' since 418 as *foederati* or 'approved allies' of the Romans. This was a device astutely used by the failing empire to modify the impact of the invasions. Forced out by conquering Clovis, the Visigoths took their Arian Christianity onward into Spain, driving out the Vandals who had settled in parts of the territory.

Relations between 'catholic' (that is non-Arian) and Arian Christians in the region were evidently turbulent. The anonymous *Lives* of the Holy Fathers of Mérida were written at the end of the period of Arian dominance in Spain, *c.*630. They depict the Arian Visigoth ruler Leovigild as 'savage and cruel', and determined to force Masona, Bishop of Mérida, to abandon the catholic faith and turn Arian. An Arian, Sunna, was appointed as an 'anti-Bishop', who was to urge the people to rise up against their catholic bishop. Sunna is described as wild-eyed and hard-faced, a liar and depraved. He seized control of some of the churches and even tried to capture the basilica for the Arians. Naturally the catholic Christians resisted, so Sunna spread wicked rumours about them.

The king said there would have to be a judicial hearing to determine which was the true bishop. In preparation for the court, Masona spent three days in the basilica lying on the floor before the body of the holy martyr Eulalia; then he went home with a cheerful face. At the hearing, Sunna shouted and made wild accusations. Masona responded quietly and clearly and sweetly. Afterwards Sunna went on scheming and accusing till he got Masona sent into exile. The people protested indignantly in the streets as he was led away. The king arranged for him to be given a horse with a reputation for unseating every rider but when Masona mounted it, it behaved with miraculous gentleness.

He spent three years in exile in a monastery until St Eulalia appeared to the king in a dream and demanded his return, which the monarch granted out of fear of the consequences of not doing so.[14]

Towards the end of the sixth century, while Reccared was their leader (586–601), the Arian invaders converted to catholic Christianity. Meanwhile Spain's catholic bishops were busy seeking to impose both orthodoxy of faith and better standards of Christian life. At the Third Council of Toledo (589), 62 bishops condemned Arianism in Spain.

They also decreed that bishops should live chastely with their wives and forego sexual intercourse, or be degraded to the status of mere *lector*. Any women found to be acting as mistresses to unmarried bishops were to be sold into slavery and the price given to the poor. Bishops were to be expected to set an example in other ways too. In a bishop's household the Scriptures should be read at the bishop's table.[15] There should be no gossiping at mealtimes. As to the behaviour of the laity, idolatry in Spain and Gaul was to stop, so bishops should search for images and idols and destroy them, and ensure that idolators were shown the error of their ways.[16] There was also too much fornication, leading to the birth of too many children and the scandal of the growing number of infanticides. This too must stop.[17] Widows must be allowed to take a vow of chastity if they wished and not forced into a second marriage.[18] Penitents must not think they could go on sinning 'in a disgusting way' in the confidence that they could just confess and be absolved.[19] The general atmosphere was to be one of sobriety and good behaviour, with no dancing on saints' days.[20] Whether or not these decrees actually transformed behaviour, they seem to give a picture of the kind of society the catholic bishops wanted to see.

The decision to become catholic helped the Visigoths to integrate better with the local population in terms of government and trade. The Visigothic Code, completed in the mid-seventh century, was developed to provide a unified set of laws for the Visigoths themselves and the remaining 'Romans'. This integration did not, however, extend to the local Jews. The Sixth Council of Toledo (639) enacted Visigothic legislation concerning the Jews, dealing with relations between the two communities. Jews were not to be allowed to 'violate' the Christian faith.[21] Under the *Lex Visigothorum* 653, Jews were not allowed to testify in court, even if they became Christians and were baptised.[22]

Italian Christians after the fall of Rome

Christianity in Italy also faced its challenges after Alaric the Goth sacked Rome in 410. Alaric astutely sent bishops as emissaries to say he would leave Italy if the emperor would just provide grain to feed his army. This was a demand hard to meet in a time of famine and he was refused. So he captured the emperor's sister, Galla Placida. The stand-off showed every sign of escalating, until the Eastern emperor sent reinforcements to Ravenna, a token of the seriousness with which the Empire as a whole viewed what was happening. These troops provided a garrison for the walls of Rome while the Emperor Honorius clung precariously to power.

Alaric himself continued southwards, ambitious to reach Africa. But a storm wrecked his ships and he died on the way. The armies returned to the north and headed for Gaul.[23]

British Christians: Celtic or Roman?

Bede (672/3–735), the first historian of the English Church, went to some trouble to discover how the people of the British Isles had been converted to the Christian faith. There had been Christians in the British Isles during the Roman occupation which began in the middle of the first century, though this was probably never more than a patchy Christianisation, jumbled with the local pagan communities. Despite Bede's best efforts, the rechristianisation of Britain is still a confused story.

Bede thought the Irish Celts were the first to bring Christianity back into post-Roman mainland Britain. Patrick, the fifth-century hero saint of Ireland, is lost in legend. The story told in his 'autobiographical' life story, the *Confessio*, is that he was born on the British mainland and captured by Irish pirates as a boy, some time in the mid-fifth century. It is even possible that he grew up in Britain as a Christian. He escaped and returned to his family, later became a priest and went back to Ireland to covert it to Christianity. There he became Bishop of Armagh.

Though Bede himself never left Northumbria where he became a monk as a boy, he knew something about European current events. He dates the first Irish mission by the year when the Byzantine emperor Justinian was succeeded by Justin II, which was 565. Columba (521–97), Bede's first 'historic' Irish missionary, addressed himself to the Picts, in what is now Scotland. They had been Christians before.

Ninian, a fourth- or fifth-century missionary about whom almost nothing is known, was said to have converted them, but they had lapsed. Columba was granted the use of the little island of Iona off the west coast of mainland Britain, where he established a monastery. In due course, one of his monks, Aidan (d. 651), moved from Iona to lead another monastic community off the east coast of Northumbria on the island of Lindisfarne. There he set high expectations of regular serious study and hard living. Aidan was firm with the laity too, and spoke out fearlessly when the rich and powerful misbehaved.

Cuthbert (*c.*634–87), a local boy, probably got some education at Lindisfarne under Aidan. Bede says that on the night when Aidan died, Cuthbert had a vision. This persuaded him to become a monk, though he seems to have spent some time in a military career first. But once he entered monastic life he rose speedily and in due course became Abbot and Bishop of Lindisfarne.

Cuthbert became an inveterate missionary preacher. In his *Life* of Cuthbert, Bede describes how Cuthbert stressed the duty of Christians to live a good Christian life. Too many, he found, acted immorally and abandoned their faith in the creed in favour of 'idolatrous remedies' such as magic charms and amulets when they were ill or in trouble. To correct these errors, Cuthbert went out from the monastery on a horse or often on foot to preach to the nearby villages and those in out-of-the-way places. The people would gather round and listen.

The story of the Celtic missions is a tale of individual enterprise and the powerful influence leaders of monastic life could have. The conversion initiated from Rome at the end of the sixth century is another matter. It aimed to convert a people from the top down. The story was that Pope Gregory the Great, seeing some fair-haired slaves in a market in Rome, had asked where they came from. These 'Angles' looked like 'angels' he said. They ought to be Christians, the pope felt. He sent Augustine (d. 604) on a mission.

Landing on the Isle of Thanet with a party of 40, including Frankish interpreters to help him communicate with the Anglo-Saxons, this later Augustine began by trying to win over King Ethelbert of Kent. He sent him a message. He had come with 'good news'. The king told his visitors to stay where they were while he considered what to do. He knew about Christianity because his Frankish Queen Bertha was a Christian herself and the marriage settlement had included an agreement that when she was married she should be allowed to practise her faith, and should have in her retinue a bishop, Luidhard, who could ensure that this was properly respected.

After a few days the king came to the island, seated himself in the open air to protect himself from any hostile magic, and sent for Augustine to hear what he had to say. Augustine approached with the cross as his 'banner' and carrying a painted picture of Christ. His party sang a litany and prayed. He preached to the king. Ethelbert said he wanted time to think about what he was being told. Meanwhile he gave Augustine permission to preach to the people, and promised him and his companions sustenance and somewhere to live. He pledged that they would not be prevented from doing the work for which Augustine had been sent.[24]

The group established itself in a way of life designed as far as possible to replicate the way the early Christians had lived, spending time in prayer and vigil, fasting, preaching, accepting only the food they strictly needed and being ready to die for the faith if necessary. This brought several people to baptism, out of admiration for the example they set. A local church, St Martin's, dedicated to St Martin of Tours, probably a Roman church which had been repaired for the purposes, was already being used by the queen as a chapel for her own prayers. The missionaries adopted it and adapted it for worship, baptisms and celebrations of the Eucharist, until Ethelbert himself was converted and gave permission for the building of more churches. Bede says he too was won over by admiration for the example of holiness Augustine and his companions set, and the baptisms began to multiply.

Now that the mission was succeeding, Augustine wrote to the pope to ask for detailed instructions on a number of practical points. He got common-sense answers. Was he to destroy the shrines of pagan gods? No. Destroying the shrines would make the people hostile. The statues and images should be quietly removed and these places of worship familiar to local people should be made Christian by sprinkling them with holy water, and having altars set up in them and Christian relics placed there. Local people were used to the excitement of sacrificial slaughter and offerings at these shrines, so some Christian counterpart had to be provided instead. Feasting in honour of the saints and martyrs whose relics were placed in these shrine-churches was considered an appropriate way of doing this. Sacrifices became simply killing of the beasts to provide meat for the meal. A slow and steady changing of minds and expectations is the way.

Bede then describes the conversion of the northern kingdom of Northumbria in the time of another pope, Boniface V.[25] A second follow-up missionary group had been sent from Rome to arrive in Britain in 604, including the monk Paulinus. About 625, Ethelberga, sister of the king of Kent, was sent to marry King Edwin of Northumbria. Edwin was still a pagan, and Paulinus, now a bishop, accompanied the new queen. Bede says Paulinus arrived in Northumbria with a grander intention in his heart. He wanted to convert the people he was going to live among. On Easter Day in 626 the king's daughter was born. At Paulinus's suggestion, Edwin allowed his infant daughter to be baptised and – rather in the spirit of the Emperor Constantine – said he would become a Christian himself if his enemy was defeated. Soon after this, he won a battle.[26]

King Edwin was still slow to commit himself. He said he would take counsel with his court and then perhaps they could all be baptised together. Paulinus agreed to this and undertook the instruction of the court, conscientiously asking them individually about their response to the doctrine he was explaining to them. The chief of the pagan priests admitted that he found their existing religion unsatisfactory. No one had practised it more vigorously and carefully than he had, but he had personally prospered less than many others who had not done so. If the new teaching was more efficacious he would be happy to embrace it. Another of the chief courtiers agreed. So it was the prospective benefits which won them for the Christian faith.[27] The courtiers asked to hear more, especially about the promise of eternal life. They were keen to burn down the altars of their old gods straight away. The place where this dramatic action took place can still be seen, Bede says.[28]

When is Easter this year?

Easter is a moveable feast and different methods of calculating its date each year meant that Christians in different places celebrated Easter on different Sundays. This was seen not as a mere matter of difference in the calendar but as a division of the very Church itself. This Easter Controversy took on great significance throughout Christendom.[29]

In England the Roman and the 'Celtic' Christians observed different dates, and that could lead to discomfort even within a royal household with a king and his queen fasting for Lent and feasting for

Easter at different times. A synod was held at Whitby in 664 to try to resolve the matter. It was attended by representatives from both sides, Colman of Lindisfarne (*c.*605–75) speaking as an Irish bishop for the Celtic side, and the much-travelled Wilfred (*c.*633–709), who had studied at Lindisfarne as well as at Canterbury and in Gaul, speaking for the Romans. Wilfred was able to assure the meeting that he had observed for himself that everywhere else in Europe the Roman date was preserved.

NEW MISSIONS TO THE PAGANS, NEW MONASTERIES, NEW BISHOPRICS

Missions to Germany and Scandinavia

Within a generation, Christians coverted by the Roman missionaries to Britain were sending out missionaries of their own. The Anglo-Saxon missionary Boniface (*c.*675–754), probably born in the west of England, converted many of the tribes of those territories which now form part of Germany. His biographer Willibrord (*c.*658–739) was himself a missionary, particularly to the Frisians. These two give a glimpse of the speed with which a Christian and especially a monastic culture had coloured the life of Anglo-Saxon England.

Willibrord's *Life* of Boniface helped to establish some of the ground rules for outstanding saintliness which were later to be found everywhere in biographies of medieval saints. Typically they were said to have shown special holiness from childhood. Willibrord says that as a boy, Boniface imitated Jesus when he was found talking to the elders in the Temple (Luke 2.41–52), for when travelling priests came to his town he would 'converse with them on spiritual matters'. Soon he was begging his father to allow him to become a monk because his 'whole nature craved' for such a future. His father was furious and did what he could to tempt the boy with the 'promises of worldly success' because he needed him as 'heir of his worldly possessions'. Boniface stuck to his vocation and got his way.[30]

Willibrord himself had a father who as a recent convert to Christianity had given his young son to be a monk at Ripon Abbey. This gave him an entry into a world in which it was possible to climb in the ecclesiastical hierarchy and with luck get an excellent education and learn of interesting Christian adventures and projects. He met Wilfred, Bishop of York (718–resigned 732), who had been a

Fig. 4: *Saint Boniface*, modern engraving by A. Jameson: Boniface sails off on his mission to the European mainland with a group of monks to help him

former monk at Whitby under Abbess Hilda. Ecbert, an enthusiastic *peregrinus* ('wanderer'), encouraged Willibrord – whom he met during a period of study at the Irish abbey of Rathelmigisi – to travel with 11 companions as a missionary to the Frisians, a Germanic tribe then living along the mainland coast of the North Sea. This was only one of several missionary attempts instigated by Egbert.

Willibrord had a biographer too. In his *Life* of Willibrord, Alcuin (*c.*735–804), another student of Ecbert's – who rose to become educational adviser to the Emperor Charlemagne – described his mission in action. When Willibrord faced Radbod, leader of the Frisians, he found he was confronting a man who hated Christians. This was not the sort of cautiously receptive royal figure Augustine of Canterbury had encountered when he preached to the king of Kent. Willibrord built his argument on the threat that if Radbod went on worshipping the pagan gods he was worshipping the Devil and would find himself in hell. Radbod must realise, he argued, that he had an immortal soul and would live for ever, so it was clearly wise to be baptised and be cleansed of his sins and begin to lead a new life in the hope of spending eternity in heaven instead. This proved to be a powerful argument.

Fig. 5: *Charlemagne*, engraved portrait (*c.*1858) created by Gagniet after a painting kept in the Vatican: Emperor Charlemagne insisted on cathedrals running good schools for the clergy

The Christian Empire is revived

The title of Roman emperor was revived in the West with the coronation of Charlemagne (*c.*742–814) in 800. Charlemagne, a Frankish ruler, had conquered much of what is now France, Germany, the Netherlands and Belgium, adding the conquest of Italy in 774, assisting the pope to defend papal territories against the invading Lombards. This immense achievement of geographical unification was the first comprehensive settlement of a disrupted Europe since the fall of the Roman Empire in the West. Charlemagne also aspired to be a man of culture and brought together in his court learned men who stimulated a 'renaissance' there. To be fully established as Western Europe's ruler, Charlemagne needed to become a counterpart of the Byzantine emperor. He therefore accepted coronation as 'Emperor' by the grateful pope, Leo III (r. 795–816). Byzantium was resentful and resisted any claim that this was a continuation of the old empire of the West.

Yet here was a Christian emperor created by Christian authority, the first in Western Europe for 300 years. Pope Sylvester I had crowned Charlemagne and he was given a ceremonial sword to use for the defence of the Church. The idea of distinguishing the 'spiritual' and 'secular' swords came from the Gospel of Luke (22.38). When Jesus was threatened with arrest before his crucifixion his disciples brought him two swords. *Satis est*, 'it is enough', he told them, according to the 'Vulgate' Latin version. Controversy over the meaning of this passage ran on throughout the Middle Ages. Did Jesus intend that both 'swords' of power were to belong to the Church, with the secular 'sword' merely lent to an emperor or king at his coronation, making the Church the dominant authority? The evolution of the ritual of coronation raised a number of problems. It was not an ordination. The ruler would be crowned by a supreme ecclesiastical figure; he might be anointed with consecrated oil, but the king or emperor was not made a priest.

This revived 'Roman Empire' never extended across the whole of the ancient empire, even the Western part of it, and it does not seem to have been called the 'Holy Roman Empire' until the thirteenth century. Charlemagne's successors did not enjoy uncontested imperial sovereignty in the West until Otto I was crowned emperor in 962. But from Charlemagne's time, the new empire relied for its authority on its claim to have inherited the imperial powers of Rome's ruler.

Charlemagne's empire welcomed further Christian missionary endeavours. Ratramnus (d. *c.*868–70) of Corbie Abbey (founded about 660) sent advice to the monk Rimbert, when he was planning to become a missionary to Scandinavia.[31] Charlemagne's son Louis the Pious (778–840) had suggested the mission and it had been encouraged by the Archbishop of Rheims in the 820s.

Rimbert seems to have seen Scandinavia as the edge of the earth. He had heard that he might encounter beings who appeared only part-human, such as dog-headed people. Was he to try to convert these? Were they human, and did they have immortal souls? Ratramnus wrote him a letter about these 'Dogheads'.[32] He had read about them because Augustine of Hippo had discussed them and a comprehensive list of others: people with a single eye in the middle of their foreheads; those whose feet were attached backwards; hermaphrodites with one male and one female breast, capable of both begetting and bringing forth children; those without mouths who breathe through their nostrils only; pygmies; people with lifespans of only eight years whose women bear children at the age of five; people with a single leg who hop in rapid bounds and who use their single great foot as a sunshade in hot weather by lying on their backs underneath it; those without heads who have eyes in their shoulders.[33] Augustine's test was whether these strange creatures were rational and mortal.

Anskar (801–65) accompanied Rimbert on his mission and they had some success, without apparently encountering any dogheads or other dubious near-humans. In 864, Anskar claimed that 'the church of Christ has been founded amongst the Danes and amongst the Swedes and priests perform their proper office without prohibition'.[34] Rimbert wrote a *Life* of Anskar which he seems to have hoped would keep alive an interest in the missions to Scandinavia. His own life became the subject of an anonymous biography, the *Vita Rimberti,* written between 865 and 909.

Benedictine monasticism is founded

Whereas ecclesiastical settlement was ordered by the system of bishops and dioceses, monasticism had no comparable overall system. It remained experimental. The West had seen attempts at the monastic life at least since Cassian (360–435) had settled near Marseille, bringing with him some years of experience in living a monastic life in Egypt and Palestine. He wrote a series of 'Conferences'[35] or talks in which he tried to unfold for his monks the wisdom he had learned from the 'desert Fathers' with whom he had served his own monastic apprenticeship. Cassian also wrote a set of 'Institutions'[36] setting out a rule of life, including details about what to wear and what to eat as well as the order of worship to be followed day by day. These were widely circulated and became influential.

Among those who learned from Cassian's teachings was Benedict of Nursia (480–547). He borrowed from other sources too, among them the anonymous Rule of the Master, in designing a Rule[37] for the house he founded for a community of monks at Monte Cassino in southern Italy. This Rule established itself firmly as the one normally to be followed in monastic communities throughout the Middle Ages. (It was even adopted by innovatory monastic groups such as the twelfth-century Cisterians.) It was Benedict rather than Cassian who did most to create the style of monastic life which became characteristic of the Christian West, in which monks lived, ate and worshipped as a community, as opposed to the independent, individualistic and idiosyncratic manner favoured in Eastern monasticism.

Gregory the Great – the pope who sent the missionary Augustine to Canterbury – wrote the *Dialogues* in which he included a biography of Benedict and also accounts of the lifestyles and miracles of various monks of his times. These stories were intended to be 'examples'. They showed that the truly holy could do extraordinary things. Ordinary Christians were meant to learn from their behaviour. He tells the story of a monk of great virtue who had responsibility for the monastery garden. A thief began to steal the vegetables. The monk came across a snake and set him to guard the place where the thief was climbing in. The snake obediently stretched itself across the path and when the thief climbed in he saw the snake and lost his balance. The gardener-monk found the thief hanging upside down by his shoe. He dismissed the snake with thanks, unhooked the thief and showed him out, giving him the vegetables he had wanted to steal. He told him just to come and ask for them next time.[38]

Teaching the faith to converted peoples

This medieval missionary success tended to be recorded at 'headline' level. To 'convert' a ruler was to convert the ruled, but that really does not tell us how clear or detailed a grasp of the faith a converted population was likely to gain.

In what is now Portugal, Martin of Braga (*c.*520–80) wrote a letter to a local bishop on 'putting the uneducated right in their opinions' (*De correctione rusticorum*), making use of Augustine's 'On catechising the uneducated' (*De catechizandis rudibus*). Converts were keeping to pagan customs and loyalties. Martin suggested telling new Christians how God made the world; how his creatures 'fell' into sin and how he rescued them; then how everything will be resolved in the end at the Last Judgement.[39] They could then be challenged if they failed to honour the Lord's day but honoured Jupiter, Mercury, Venus and Saturn, whose behaviour encompassed adultery and magical practices and who were really mere devils. They should be asked why they lit votive candles at the shrines of the pagan gods at crossroads, why they continued with superstitious rituals, such as putting the right foot in front, throwing food and wine over the logs in the fire, dropping bread into a spring. Women who were Christians should be asked why they prayed to Minerva when they sat down at their looms to weave and insisted on getting married on Venus' 'day'? And why did they concoct potions to harm their enemies? This was all devil worship, Martin concluded.

Eighth-century missionaries took catechesis seriously.[40] In about 723–4, Daniel, Bishop of Winchester, wrote to Boniface the missionary with some pointers to the best way to convert pagans. He advised against trying to argue them out of their belief in false gods. Boniface should instead ask whether they wanted the mere benefits in this life on offer from such gods, or an eternal reward?[41] The monk and later abbot in Antwerp, Pirmin (*c.*700–53), in the 'Sayings of Pirmin' (*Dicta Pirmini*),[42] begins with a reminder to his 'dearest brothers' (*fratres karissimi*) that the Holy Spirit urges them through respected early Christian authors to preach the Gospel throughout the world. He is offering a brief memo to help them in this task.[43] His suggested method is to begin by telling the story of salvation. He describes the creation and fall of the angels,[44] and how after that 'ruin', God made man, moving on to man's fall and God's merciful decision to send his Son.[45] There follows the story of Jesus' life, crucifixion and resurrection.[46] The missionary may then explain about baptism. The person to be baptised is to be asked for his name and whether he renounces the Devil and all his works. He is then taken through the Creed and asked to assent to it clause by clause with the *credo* 'I believe'.[47] The new Christian must then learn to imitate Christ.[48] Pirmin lists the vices, including the worship of idols and eating items that had been sacrificed to them.[49] Then comes an encouragement to pay one's tithes and taxes. When facing death, the Christian should give alms generously, repent his or her sins, and pray.[50] Alcuin, who moved from York to become a mainstay of the educational establishment at the court of Charlemagne, wrote to Charlemagne in the late 790s with his thoughts about how best to convert the pagans of his growing empire. He referred him to Augustine's *De catechizandis rudibus* as still the best available guide.

CHRISTIANITY IN EASTERN EUROPE

East and West: the same and the different

By the sixth century the two dominant language communities of the Roman Empire, Latin and Greek, were increasingly separating, with fewer educated individuals able to command both languages.

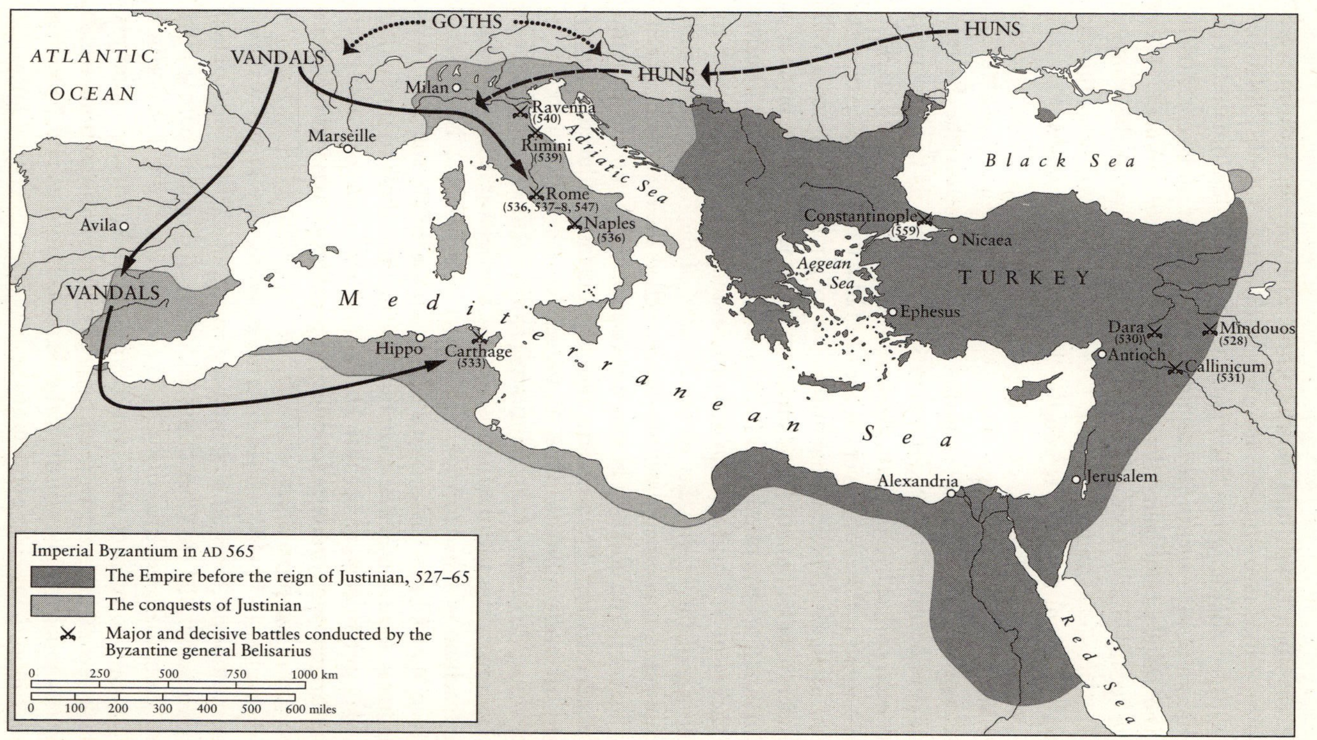

Map 2: Imperial Byzantium in AD 565

The theological writings of the Latin and Greek authors were diverging into two streams and two traditions.[51] Greek Christians were especially drawn to late Platonist ideas. 'Chalcedonian' Greek Christianity also set its face against development and kept closely to the beliefs established by the first ecumenical councils. They were regarded as recording changeless truth and what the Vulgate (1 Timothy 6.20 and 2 Timothy 1.14) calls the *depositum* (and the nineteenth century came to call the 'Deposit' of the faith).[52]

The Monophysite challenge

The most significant and enduring division to affect the Eastern Churches occurred at the Council of Chalcedon in 451. The council had been called by Marcian, Byzantine emperor from 450 to 457. Leo I, pope at the time, accepted the need to try to bring a resolution to the attempts of recent generations to explain what it meant to call the incarnate Christ both God and man. This became as important a controversy as the one begun by Arius and resolved by the Council of Nicaea in 325 and the Council of Constantinople in 381, with its querying of the co-equality of the Persons of the Trinity. This time the question concerned the humanity as well as the divinity of Christ.

That was the question before this council. It was an abstract and difficult question. Philosophers and theologians produced answers, many of great subtlety. One of these was the belief fostered by Nestorius, Patriarch of Constantinople from 428 to 431. He had been influenced by the anti-Arian theology of Christians at Antioch and by the teaching of Theodore of Mopsuestia (*c.*350–428). 'Nestorians' argued that Christ had a human body and a divine soul, and was thus truly *God*. But this explanation seemed to others to imply that he was not fully *man* because he did not have a human soul. The 'Nestorians' won quite a following especially in Syria and further east and in Egypt and further south.[53]

Eutyches (378–456), head of a large monastery at the walls of Constantinople, pressed a counter-argument, as early as the Council of Ephesus in 431. In Christ, he said, divine and human nature were fully combined, yet also distinct. The exact sense of either position is not easy to recover now even from the Greek, for contemporary Greek as well as Latin were struggling to clarify abstractions which were as much philosophical as theological. Eutyches and Nestorius both found themselves condemned as heretics.

The Council of Chalcedon agreed that Christ had two natures, being fully divine and fully human, in a single Person of the Trinity. Those believers in the East who could not accept this definition continued to assert that the incarnate Christ had only one nature, which was divine though possibly in some combination of the divine and the human. These became known as the Monophysite ('one nature') or Non-Chalcedonian Churches, and were concentrated in Egypt and Syria, though their view of things had a geographically wider spread. The Monophysite Churches continue today and are usually described collectively as the 'Oriental Orthodox'.

The gulf of opinion thus opened up, especially in the Middle East and the North African regions of Egypt and Ethiopia, threatened a dangerous division of the continuing Roman Empire in the East. Justinian, Byzantine emperor from *c.*482 to 565, was anxious to make his empire uniformly 'Chalcedonian' for political as much as religious reasons. He did not want a divided Christendom full of possible enemies of Chalcedonian Byzantium.

Armenia, geographically adjacent to Christian Cappadocia, had become Christian about 300 and there was a gradual increasing dominance there of Syriac Christian influence.[54] The Armenians had not been represented at the Council of Chalcedon; they were busy at the time resisting Persian efforts to impose the ancient Zoroastrian religion on them.[55] The Armenians tended to remain 'Non-Chalcedonian' Christians, and the Syriac Christians were divided on the issue. The Persian border with the Empire in the East also tended to be Monophysite, with the Arabian Christians there hostile to Nestorian Persian Christians.[56] The situation on the Persian border was complicated by the fact that Church organisation did not coincide geographically with the Rome–Persia borders.[57]

In time, Egypt as far south as Ethiopia became predominantly Monophysite.[58] Jewish influence was strong in Ethiopian Christianity through trade with Arabia.[59] When Islam was founded, and quickly began to spread into these regions, it was notable that, apparently satisfied on this key point of the oneness of God, Monophysite Christianity in Nubia resisted Islamic conversion though Islam seems to have been more successful in Egypt.

Discussions aimed at compromise failed, though it is unlikely that most faithful Christians in either camp fully understood their theological differences. By the late sixth century, Byzantium was in a settled position of formal opposition to the Monophysites.[60] 'Monophysite' and 'Chalcedonian' alliances influenced the outcome of various wars. In the reign of the Emperor Maurice (582–602), a confrontation emerged with the confederation of the Arabic 'Ghassanid' tribes, which had moved to the Levant from the Arabian peninsula in the third century and become Christian. Their leader, Al-Moundhir, was exiled by Byzantium for alleged treachery with the Persians. This war devastated much of Palestine and Syria and helped to create a situation where Christian monks feared the Arabs.[61] Persia took advantage of the situation to seize back the eastern provinces of Byzantium. They were helped by Jews and Samaritans and also by the Monophysites, for the Persians planned to allow the Monophysites to remain the majority religion in Syria, Asia Minor and Palestine if those were reconquered.[62] Persia duly reconquered Egypt from Byzantium in a war which included massacres of monks.[63] So for the Byzantine Empire the Monophysite controversy reached far beyond a fine point of theological difference.

Images, idolatry and iconoclasm

The great monotheistic religions have all been sensitive about practices which might seem to countenance polytheism. It might seem harmless to depict the Virgin Mary, or notable saints, in frescoes or mosaics or statues or paintings (icons) in the interiors of churches. But the nature of the respect to be shown to these figures, both the objects which represented them and the saints themselves, has been a centuries-long focus of concern. Were they really being worshipped? Could veneration of the saints lead to idolatry?

The first question was whether a given person was entitled to special Christian respect. How was the specially holy person who could be regarded as a 'saint' to be identifed? It all came to depend on indications of supernatural powers – usually that the candidate for sainthood had performed miracles while living or after death. Relics, clothing or miraculously undecayed body parts of the prospective saint might also be adduced in consideration of the legitimacy of such a candidacy. A hagiography or biography of the saint might be produced as testimony too. It would tell the story of a notably holy life, commonly including examples of miracles performed. In the Greek Christian East, a synod of bishops – or sometimes a bishop alone – would then, if satisfied, conduct a service of 'glorification'.

The 'glorified' were given a special day in their honour and listed on a Calendar of Saints. In the Christian West the process was known as 'canonisation' and involved papal approval.

Official approval was likely to follow behind popular acclaim. Prayers of the faithful would be addressed directly to the dead 'saint', asking for an illness to be cured or for some other special favour. Relics such as hairs, bones, objects touched or owned by the saint might become objects of veneration in themselves because they were believed to be numinous with the holiness of the saint. A Byzantine family might arrange for a portrait to be made of the dead, and that could be kept in the house as an icon to focus their prayers. A Western monastery might encourage pilgrimages to the shrine of a dead abbot.

High-level concern about the spread of popular enthusiasn for images and icons of saints first came to a head in the Christian East in Byzantium. Leo III (r. 717–41) was a Byzantine emperor with a strong interest in the defence of Christian orthodoxy. He scrutinised for heresy groups of Christians with apparently rather specialist ideas. The Paulicians, for example, appeared to him to have 'Manichean' views and to believe that Christ was 'adopted' by the Father and was not truly his divine Son. In the course of this active exploration of the religious preferences expressed in his empire, the emperor became convinced that there were dangers in the veneration of pictures and statues. Manichean circles in Baghdad were naturally hostile to the veneration of material objects, and their arguments had a good deal of sophistication.[64] Some of Leo's own bishops held strong opinions on the subject. Correspondence went on among bishops for and against icons. Theodore of Studion (759–826) even argued that images should be regarded as extensions of the divine act of creation.[65]

An Arabic-speaker from boyhood, the emperor may also have been influenced in his thinking on this point by contact with the multiplying adherents of Islam, an increasingly powerful presence in the Empire. Islam did not begin with the extreme views on images which later emerged. In the cultures of regions where Islam was to become dominant, where pre-Islamic polytheism existed, there were not many sophisticated images to be overturned or destroyed; more commonly the pagans overtaken by the early Islamic conquests merely practised veneration of numinous stones. Muslims were sometimes accused of giving Mohammed a status as a prophet which seemed to place him somewhere between man and God.[66] Yet Muslim antagonism towards icons was hardening in the eighth century.

Theology that defined the Islamic position on images seems to have been formed partly under Jewish influence in the seventh to the eighth centuries, at the period when the practical question of how to decorate mosques was being raised for the first time. Caliph Yazid II issued an iconoclastic edict against Christian as well as Muslim images in July 721,[67] though until the late eighth century some figurative representation was allowed.[68] So the actual position of Jews and Muslims on icons was perhaps more nuanced than the polemic suggests, and Byzantine iconoclasm had motives other than religious – for example, it saved money being spent on images during the construction of places of worship.[69]

By 730, Leo III was ready to make iconoclasm official policy in the Empire, against the resistance of Germanus who was then Patriarch of Constantinople. So Leo replaced him as patriarch with Anastasius, whose views better matched his own. It was decreed that there must be no worshipping of statues or other idols. Even the relics of Christian saints were regarded as dubious. Clerics who would not accept the new imperial ban might find themselves imprisoned. Rome was unenthusiastic about the new policy, so Leo cut off relations with the West as far as he could, with significant long-term consequences for the Greek churches in southern Italy and Sicily.

For decades afterwards, Byzantium was consumed by the dispute about idolatry. This first period of iconoclastic controversy came to an end in 787 with the second Council of Nicaea. At the meeting in October, Bishop John of Jerusalem, speaking on behalf of the Anatolian bishops, read a prepared statement which had been drawn up some years earlier. It gave an account of the way the 'subversion of images' had begun. He claimed that when Caliph Umar had died (720), his successor Yazin (720–4) had proved to be an unstable and frivolous character ('vain and easily distracted'). At that time the 'lawless Jews' had a ringleader, a magician and fortune-teller, who was being used as an instrument by demons. He was called Tessarakontapechys (meaning '40 cubits high'). This ringleader persuaded Yazin to begin – or continue – a campaign against icons by promising that if he did so he would rule for 30 years.

The new Caliph's campaign was to 'obliterate and overthrow absolutely every painting and image in different colours whether on canvas, in mosaics, on walls, or on sacred vessels and altar coverings, and as many such things as are found, in all the churches of the Christians, not to mention also everything of the same kind set up for the ornament and decorations of the forms of the various cities in your Empire'. This, complained John, had affected Christians, who had fled, and 'evil Jews and Arabs' came and 'effected destruction'. When John had finished reading, the Bishop of Messana took the opportunity to speak to confirm the accuracy of all that had been said. It was all true, the bishop claimed. He had been a boy in Syria, he said, when the Caliph of the Saracens destroyed the images. This can now partly be confirmed by archaeological evidence of Islamic destruction of Christian images in Egypt in 686–9, and also some early eighth-century examples datable before this edict.[70] Archaeological evidence also shows that images were destroyed in floor mosaics in Christian churches.[71] It is in this climate of hostility towards Islam that Theophanes the Confessor (758/60–817/18) called the Emperor Leo III 'Saracen-minded' (literally 'thinking like a Saracen', *Sarakenophron*)[72] because he appeared to agree with the Muslims about icons and the need for them to be destroyed.

The 'icon' Council of Nicaea (787) and the West

Pope Hadrian sent representatives to the council which met in 787 at Nicaea, Iznik in modern Turkey, to decide what to do about icons. This was later counted as the last of the definitive 'ecumenical councils'. It decided in favour of the veneration of icons. The Western representatives brought back to the West the record (*acta*) of its debates and decisions. Copies were given to the Emperor Charlemagne's English 'court scholar' Alcuin of York (*c.*735–804) and to Theodulph (*c.*750/60–821), later Bishop of Orleans, who was then a new figure in Charlemagne's circle and who relayed to the emperor in immense detail what had happened at this council.[73] There followed a period of 'briefing against', which is illuminating about the state of East–West political and Christian relations.

The study of the *acta* by the Council in the West will have required a Latin translation to be made.[74] This naturally provided an opportunity for diplomatic adjustment of the message by whoever did the translating. It was well known that Byzantine translators from the Latin could play games; it had even been necessary to issue a condemnation or *anathema* to discourage it.[75]

Which patriarch is primate of the whole Church?

Photios, a courtier and scholar, was Patriarch of Constantinople from 858 to 867 and again from 877 to 886. Photius's election to replace the previous Patriarch Ignatius, who was involved in a high-profile family scandal, took place at the instigation of the Byzantine emperor Michael III. Ignatius never got a chance to defend himself and Photius was still a layman when he was appointed. In 863 a synod in Rome purported to have deposed Photius and restored Ignatius, but the pope's interference in the affairs of the patriarchate was resented[76] In 867, Photius called a council which excommunicated the pope for the Western heresy of adding to the Creed the *filioque* clause, so that it said that the Holy Spirit proceeds from the Son as well as from the Father.

The context of this unusually public mutual hostility between the Churches of East and West was the recent conversion of Bulgaria. The question was whether Bulgaria should be regarded as a Latin or a Greek Church. The affair heightened tensions about papal claims that the Bishop of Rome had primacy over the other ancient patriarchates (Alexandria, Antioch, Jerusalem and the youngest, Constantinople, created when the Emperor Constantine became a Christian). That had never been resolved to general satisfaction.

Nor did the question of where the boundary was to lie between the Orthodox and Roman Catholic jurisdictions find a speedy resolution. The area now known as the Balkans has remained border country, with a mixture of Greek and Latin Christian affiliations. It was already turbulent, and the problems were political as well as ecclesiastical. In the mid-eleventh century, warfare in Eastern Europe involved the Holy Roman Empire in the West confronting threats from the federation of Slavic peoples in a state which was then known as Kievan Rus[77] during its heyday from the ninth to the thirteenth centuries. There were also political problems with the Baltic states, with Poland and with the Hungarians. Byzantium found itself in conflict with Croatia and Bulgaria, which was also fighting the Magyars attacking from the north.

Poland seems first to have encountered Christianity at the end of the ninth century. It turned for its allies to the Czechs rather than the Germans, but that still placed it on the Roman side of the division between Rome and Byzantium. In 965 the first Christian ruler of

Poland, Mieszko I (*c.*940–92), had married a Czech princess. In 966, after a full week's catechetical instruction with preparatory fasting, he was publicly baptised. Mieszko's plan was that this should set an example for his people. A missionary campaign followed, designed to get the population baptised too, though there was resistance from embedded pagan traditions. The pope created Jordan as the first bishop for Poland in 968. Mieszko formed alliances in the West, including with the Holy Roman Empire. Poland sent Christian missions into adjacent lands so the Christianisation of Poland was linked with its political expansion. In all these ways Mieszko positioned Poland to face West rather than East and provided it with a single dominant religion favoured by the state and the court. Lithuania was not 'converted' until 1386.

Christian Hungary too elected to face West towards Rome rather than East towards Byzantium. Hungary had had Christians from the third century but under successive waves of migration, especially that of the Huns, the faith had apparently more or less died out as it had elsewhere on the fringes of the old Roman Empire. There was no counterpart in Hungary to the determined official Christianisation which took place in Poland, but Hungary took up the same stance of deciding to be a Western not an Eastern European nation. Byzantine Christians had begun to make converts, but Géza (*c.*940–97), leader of the Hungarian tribes, favoured the missionaries who were arriving from the West. His wife was an Orthodox Christian but was said to be vague about her faith. He was himself baptised as a Christian but continued to take part in pagan rites.

Russia's conversion took a different early form. Photius proudly announced in 867 that the Rus people had taken to the faith which had been preached to them by the bishop he had sent. But their conversion does not seem to have lasted and they lapsed into paganism again. More effective – as elsewhere – was the conversion of a ruler, who created an expectation for his people. In the 980s, Vladimir the Great was baptised with his family and with the expectation that his people would follow.

The territories bordering the Black Sea which are now part of Ukraine and Crimea were Greek Orthodox in the Byzantine period, and Byzantine monasticism flourished there. They had been converted by the missionaries Cyril (826–9) and Methodius (815–85) who brought Christianity to the Slavs in the ninth century.

These two are thought to have been responsible for devising the Glagolithic alphabet, and their cultural influence on the Slavic peoples was immense.

Christianity reaches out to Persia and India

The Roman Empire had spread east as well as west. Christianity was well established in the Middle East from its earliest days. Eusebius of Caesarea reported that the Syrian monarch had been converted by one of the 72 (or 70) disciples mentioned in the Gospel (Luke 10.1–24). It was believed that this 'apostle to the Syrians' had been the apostle who became known as 'doubting Thomas' (John 20.24–29). There was a tradition that he had travelled far into Asia as a missionary to the Jews in diaspora – a legend said he met the Magi who had brought gifts to the infant Jesus on the way – and had baptised some Indians in AD 52, being put to death there by a lance. His remains were then brought back to Edessa in 232 by a pious merchant, with various miracles being noted on the journey. The Thomas tradition was strongly held in Syriac Christianity where the apocryphal *Acts of Thomas* were written. This must have been in use in the fourth century, because Epiphanius of Salamis (*c.*310/20–403) mentions it. It survives in Greek and Syriac versions, with some Gnostic traces edited out in the Syriac. Ephrem of Edessa (*c.*306–73), who arrived in Edessa as a refugee after Nisibis had been taken by the Persian armies, composed hymns describing Thomas's death in India and the translation of his relics to Edessa.

In the second century, Syria had translations of the Old Testament and the *Diatessaron* or 'harmony of the Gospels' of Tatian (110–80), and Edessa held a local Christian Council in 197. This flourishing early Christian community had its church buildings destroyed in a flood in 201, but there was soon a revival. Philip, emperor of Rome from 224 to 229, was of Arab stock, born close to the Sea of Galilee in a region where there was already growing Christian influence, partly as a result of outreach from Edessa, where Christianity was well established. Was this Arabic emperor himself a Christian? The historian Eusebius describes Philip's visit to a church immediately before Easter Day, where he was told by the bishop that he could not enter with his sins unconfessed.[78] Philip was killed by Decius who was to succeed him as emperor (249–51) and who initiated some of the fiercest of the imperial persecutions of Christians. The Bishop of Edessa was present at the Council of Nicaea in 325.

This link with the remoter East remained a live one. Christian missionaries from Edessa made converts in Persia and Mesopotamia. The Persian rulers of the late Roman period were tolerant of Christians and their Patriarch of the Church of the East, until Constantine was converted and officially sought Persian protection of Christians in 324. The Christians then became associated with an enemy state. Shapur II ruled Persia from 309 to 379 and was alleged to have written to his generals instructing them to arrest Simon, the Christians' leader, and to hold him until he signed an agreement to collect double taxes and tributes from the Christian community, because 'they live in our lands but are at peace with our enemy'.

Cyril of Alexandria (*c*.376–444) kept a nervous eye on the developments in Edessa where a highly successful 'School of the Persians' was running, attended by Christian students from Persia, but which, he feared, was showing Nestorian tendencies. The school was closed for a time in the middle of the fifth century and closed for good in 489, on the orders of the emperor as well as the Church. The Persian students moved to Nisibis where they laid the foundations for an enduring body of Persian Nestorians.

The Thomas Christians in India

The 'Thomas' Christians seemed to have formed a lasting community in India. These Indian Christians were first heard of in the West when the Emperor Constantius sent 'Theophilus the Indian' to Arabia Felix (roughly modern Yemen) in about 354. Theophilus was known as 'the Indian' because he had been sent to Rome in the reign of Constantine as a hostage from his Indian birthplace. The story is told by Philostorgius (369–439), an Arian Greek historian. He says that when Theophilus had completed his commissioned diplomatic task for Constantius, he took the opportunity to visit his home in the Maldives and then to travel more widely in India. There he encountered Christians on the west coast, in the region of Malabar. These were next mentioned about 535 by the Alexandrian trader – later monk or hermit – Cosmas Indicopleustes, who identifies Malabar as the place which grows pepper. The Christians he found there had a bishop who it was said had been consecrated in Persia. Gregory of Tours (writing before

590) decribes a conversation with a pilgrim called Theodore who had informed him that the bones of Thomas the Apostle had their resting place in India until they were removed to Edessa.

European contact with these Indian Christians probably faded during the Middle Ages but was revived with the Portuguese 'discoveries' from the end of the fifteenth century.

Christianity and Judaism from the end of empire: an uneasy relationship

The Emperor Constantine took the view that it would be a good thing to separate the celebration of Easter from the Jews' Passover celebration, on the grounds that the Jews had crucified Christ. This allegation was often used during the Middle Ages to justify harsh treatment of Jews, and as Europe became almost universally Christian the Jews remained misfits everywhere. Yet they were a widely visible presence and the strands of Jewish influence are woven through the fabric of medieval society in innumerable ways. After the disastrous outcome of their battles with the Roman authorities in the Holy Land, Jewish communities in exile settled in many parts of Europe.[79] Jews were living in Italy, Germany and France from the early fourth century and there were soon concentrations in Poland and Lithuania and generally in Eastern Europe. This sometimes led to violent attacks and pogroms.

European (Ashkenazi) Jews formed recognisable ethnic groups. Those in Germanic lands began to speak Yiddish, a language formed as Germanic words were added to Hebrew. In Slav areas, forms of the adapted language derived from Hebrew added local vocabulary, and something similar happened in Spain. These were indicators of the permanent settlement of Jews and also of a growing distinctiveness among the communities settled for generations in different parts of Europe.

In Spain, the Third Council of Toledo, in 589, decreed that Jews might not have Christian wives or concubines, or buy slaves for themselves as Christian masters were permitted to do. If there were children of mixed unions they should be baptised as Christians. Christian slaves of Jews should be freed and allowed to go back to the Christian religion without having to buy their freedom.[80]

In 610, Sesbut, the Visigothic ruler, tried to forbid the practice of Judaism altogether, but he did so ineffectually, so Jews began to return to Spain. The sixth Council of Toledo, in 639, included more Visigothic legislation about the Jews, again dealing with relations between Jews and Christians and distinctly disadvantaging Jews as citizens in comparison. Jews were not allowed to 'violate' the Christian faith[81] and were not permitted to testify in court, even if they were baptised.[82]

In Byzantium, the Emperor Theodosius I (r. 379–95) adjusted civil law to raise doubts about whether a non-Christian could be a citizen at all. The term 'Christian citizen' (*Civis Christianus*) came into use and Jews, like heretics and apostates, were to be treated as *alieni* and deprived of citizen privileges.[83] Emperor Leo III (r. 717–41) saw it as part of his imperial duty to enforce correct religious belief and practice. He may have been prompted to enforce the baptism of Jews as Christians because of the threat posed by a pseudo-Messiah from Syria, Severus, who claimed to be Moses or 'Jesus returned'.[84] In 722, Leo insisted that not only Jews should be baptised but also the Montanists, who had been accused of having Jewish sympathies.[85] (The Montanists' charismatic Christianity was seen as dangerously enthusiastic.) The Emperor Basil I in 873–4 had Jews baptised by force.[86] Jews were banned from public office by Basil, but in most reigns they did not suffer civil disabilities.[87]

Dialogue and disagreement

While Christianity was a missionary religion from the first, Jews never sought actively to convert non-Jews to Judaism, though they accepted converts. There was certainly enough mutual interest to get authors writing about the differences. The dialogue *Athanasius and Zacchaeus* was probably composed in Alexandria before 388. Zacchaeus the Jewish character is a teacher of the law (Torah). He challenges Athanasius the bishop to show how the doctrine of the Trinity is compatible with monotheism, both using the Old Testament texts as evidence.[88] In the end, Zaccheus declares himself convinced and asks what he must do to be saved.[89] Other dialogues survive from the centuries which followed, including the *Dialogue of Simon and Theophilus* (fifth century) and the *Dialogue of Timothy and Aquila* (sixth century).[90]

One of the oldest anti-Christian writings by Jews to survive is the *Toledot Yeshu* (*Life of Jesus*). It dates from the seventh century, though apparently it was still popular in later medieval centuries.

Its approach is to mock, taking the form of a parody of the Gospel story. At the end of the seventh century the *Book of Nestor the Priest* appeared, in which the arguments in support of Judaism are put by a former Christian priest who had been a Nestorian.

THE EMERGENCE OF ISLAM[91]

The Prophet arises

In 610, a middle-aged Arab living in the region of Mecca in what is now Saudi Arabia experienced a revelation. He was to become the Prophet of a new strictly monotheistic religion. We have already seen its impact on the Christendom of Eastern Europe during the iconoclastic controversy.

This, like Judaism and Christianity, was to be a religion of a book. Both the Qur'an itself and the record of Mohammed's life took written form over time. Early Muslims believed that the Archangel Gabriel had dictated the Qur'an to Mohammed over a period of more than 20 years. One tradition was that his companions had noted down his revelations as they were delivered and the whole had been compiled and organised after his death. There were early concerns about how to choose between conflicting versions, and Uthman (577–656), a trader who had been one of Mohammed's companions and first converts and became Caliph (644–56), tried to fix a standard 'authorised version'.[92]

Mohammed died in Medina in 632 and there followed a division among his followers, as has often happened when a great religious leader dies. This led to the separation of the majority Sunni from Shia Muslims, which still divides the Muslim world today. The Shia followed Mohammed's son-in-law in the belief that he had been appointed as Mohammed's successor.

The *Sira*, Muslim 'lives' of Mohammed including records of his sayings, were written in the eighth and ninth centuries, though the 'Life of God's Messenger' by Ibn Ishaq (704–68) does not survive in the original but only as material quoted by later authors. Christian biographers were not slow to appear. The *Istoria de Mahmet* is among the earliest rather hostile Christian accounts of the life of Mohammed, written about 850. It begins by explaining that Christianity in Toledo was flourishing when Islam emerged, which was said to be in Isidore's

Fig. 6: A modern photograph of the Holy Mosque in Mecca surrounded by praying pilgrims

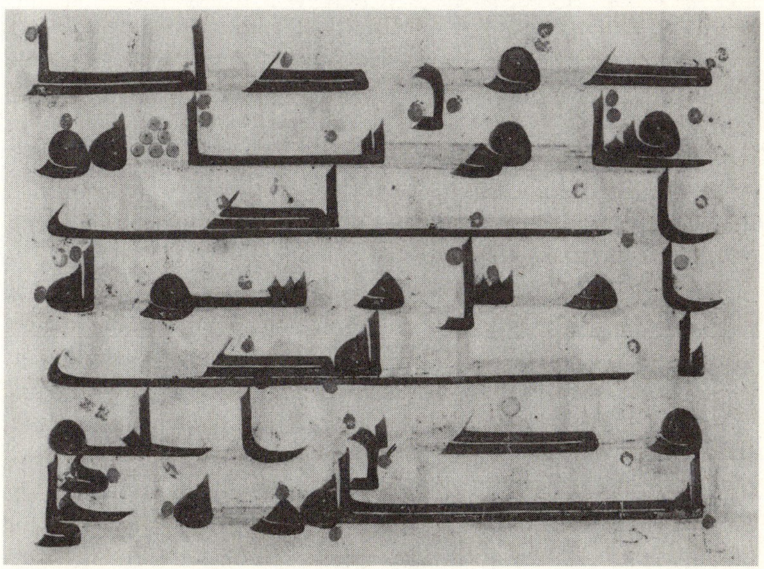

Fig. 7: A page of a manuscript of the Qur'an of the eighth or ninth century, Abbasid dynasty, Near East or North Africa

time. The young Mohammed is described as an 'avaricious usurer', who travelled on business and began to attend Christian worship out of interest, learning something of Christian ideas. Then 'the spirit of error appeared to him in the form of a vulture and, exhibiting a golden mouth, said it was the angel Gabriel and ordered Muhammad to present himself among his people as a prophet'. After that, he preached to 'irrational animals [...] so that they retreated from the cult of idols and adored the corporeal God in heaven'. Then he 'ordered his believers to take up arms on his behalf, and, as if with a new zeal of faith, he ordered them to cut down their adversaries with the sword of God'.[93]

Faced with the threat of a rival monotheism, both Christians and Jews expended a good deal of energy on the task of discrediting the Qur'an. In the ninth century, in *Against the Mohamedans*,[94] Nicetas of Byzantium argued that the Qur'an can claim nothing but human authorship.[95] It was not true that the Qur'an was inspired by God,[96] but rather, Islam, according to Nicetas, was a mere mixture of ideas from other religions.[97] Ridicule of the Qur'an often included reference to the popular legends associated with the life of Mohammed and and its alleged absurdities.[98] The Qur'an was claimed to contain grotesque errors: for example, Moses' sister Mary (Miriam) was not Christ's mother as it says – they were not the same 'Mary'.[99] It was a mere fable that God sat planning with his angels to create Adam.[100] It says in the Qur'an that Mohammed existed from eternity. Asked where he was before the world was made, the Muslim answers that he was hidden between earth and water. But before the creation of the world there was no earth or water. Who is the unbeliever here? Muslims should be ashamed to say such things.[101]

Among Latin authors, the Christian convert Bartholomew of Edessa, probably a monk, whose dates remains uncertain, wrote a *Confutatio Agareni* against the Muslim Agarenus.[102] Bartholomew claimed to know all about Islamic beliefs, but he had only recently become a Christian and was very ignorant about his own faith. He listed many 'false assertions' of Muslims about what Christians believed regarding the Trinity and Scripture, and expressed his low opinion of Islam's holy book: 'I have read in your Qur'an. It is full of nonsense.'[103]

Fig. 8: *Battle between Heraclius and Chosroes*: painting by Piero della Francesca (1415–92) of the Byzantine emperor Heraclius defeating the Sassanid Persian invaders in 622

Mission and conquest

Christian Byzantium and Zoroastrian Persia had been at war in the early seventh century, leaving both weakened. The Byzantine emperor Heraclius (610–41) could not resist the onslaught of the Arabs in Palestine and Syria when the new Muslim religion began to expand by missionary conquest. Arab armies also took control of Egypt after accepting tribute for a while to stay away.[104] The conquests moved on in a generation or two, along the coasts of North Africa and north into Spain.

The division of Sunni from Shia Muslims dominated the arrangements for ruling these new territories. In contrast to the established 'two swords' Christian tradition that secular and spiritual leadership must be distinct, the first Caliphs were simultaneously political and religious leaders, and seen as successors to Mohammed. The Sunni Rashidun Caliphs ruled between 632 and 661 and the Ummayad Caliphs from 661, first in the region of Damascus and extending in the mid-eighth century along the coast of North Africa and then into Cordoba (until 1031). The Abbasid Caliphs ruled Baghdad from 750 to 1258. The Abbasid and Fatimid Caliphates attempted to capture Byzantium. The resulting wars lasted from about 780 to 1180, with successes for the Greeks, who recaptured some of the territory they had lost. The Caliphs of Cairo (1261–1517) ruled North African and Middle Eastern territories. The Shia contested the Sunni claim to the Caliphates. The Shia Fatimids were

Caliphs in certain areas from 909 to 1171 and set about expanding Islamic dominance over a short period of time across Persia, Egypt and then along the coast of North Africa.

Byzantium and Islam

Muslims encountering Byzantine Christians were soon labelled 'Saracens', an older word connoting 'bandit' or 'robber'. Euthymius of Athos (*c.*955–1028), an Orthodox monk from Georgia, wrote a treatise on dogma, the *Panoplia dogmatica*,[105] in which he discusses the 'Sarakenoi' who, he says, are also called 'Ishmaelites' because they were descendants of Ishmael, Abraham's first son by a handmaid. His theory about the origins of Islam was that these people were pagans until a prophet arose amongst them called 'Moameth'. He says that Moameth encountered Jews, then the Arian Christians, then the Nestorian Christians, and framed a mixed religion taking parts of the belief systems of each.[106] The content of the Qur'an manifestly owed much to the Old Testament and the Christian Gospels, according to Euthymius, but it lacked the sacred authority of the Old Testament as far as Jews were concerned. For the Christian it was not an addition to the Bible and could not be counted among the approved early Christian authorities.[107]

Islam conquers Spain

The extension of the Islamic conquests was so speedy and so successful that by 711 an invading army under the Berber Tariq was able to cross the strait and land at Gibraltar. An invasion of southern Spain by Muslim forces now began. It was rumoured that Jews had helped the Muslims to invade Spain, because they thought they would have more peace and freedom under a Caliph than under the Visigoths. A chronicle apparently written about 754 by a Christian who lived in Andalusia described the Muslim invasion. He says that they burnt the cities and butchered the people. They terrorised the population until they accepted Saracen terms (which they later regretted and wanted to reject).[108] The Iberian Peninsula was brought under Muslim control in less than a decade; the Visigothic dominance of southern Spain did not last long once these Islamic armies arrived. In 711 or 712, the Visigoths were defeated at the Battle of Guadalete, though the Visigoth way of life was not entirely wiped out. Pelagius of Asturias won a victory against the

'Moors' in 722 and he was able to found a kingdom for himself, known as the Kingdom of Asturias. This helped to fix the boundary between Christian and Muslim areas of Spain during the succeeding medieval centuries until the Christian reconquest.

The invading army was probably largely made up of local North African Berbers, but the culture the invaders brought with them was Arabic. As early as 713 the Christian–Muslim Treaty of Tudmir (in south-eastern Spain) set out some ground rules for the settlement, the Muslims promising not to take prisoners or separate husbands from their wives or burn churches, so long as the Christians obeyed the terms set. These were that the Christians would pay the Muslim conquerors a dinar a year, and a quantity of wheat, barley, fruit juice, honey and olive oil. Christian slaves had to pay too, but only half the amount.[109] However, Islamic dominance in Iberia was not total. Its power was concentrated in the south of Spain, especially Granada and Andalusia, dividing medieval Spain roughly in half aross the middle, with a Christian north and an Islamic south. The active cultural and trading exchange between these areas was brokered partly by the Jewish population living in both Islamic and Christian lands.[110]

Christians ask why a Christian God allowed the Muslim invasion

For Christians, the question why God had allowed the Muslims to conquer Spain arose with much the same force as it had for Roman Christian Europe when it fell to 'barbarians'. Isidore, Bishop of Seville (*c.*560–636), wrote a history of the invasions of Spain in the form of a chronology, describing the 'ages of the world', of which this was the sixth.[111] A chronicle attributed to Alfonso III (*c.*848–910), king of Leon (and partly successful against the Ummayad Caliphs), was intended to be a continuation of Isidore's *History of Goths, Vandals and Suevi.* As he described it, in battle with the Saracens 'the power of the Lord was not absent. For when stones were launched from the catapults and they neared the shrine of the holy Virgin Mary [...] they turned back on those who shot them and violently cut down the Chaldeans.'[112] Al-Waqidi (*c.*748–822) and his secretary Mohammed Ibn Sa'd wrote detailed accounts of the early military campaigns which offer a different perspective.

The further spread of Islam into northern Europe extended a long way. The Islamic invasion would have carried on northwards into

France, but the invading armies were defeated at the Battle of Tours in 732 by Charles Martel, a Frank and a Christian. The Muslim invasion of medieval Christian Europe was subsequently reduced to instances of piracy in the Mediterranean from the Barbary (Berber) pirates of North Africa (with Christian pirates operating in the seas off Gibraltar making their own contribution to the threat to the shipping trade). Banditry by groups of Muslim robbers laying wait for merchants and other travellers in parts of Europe was also not unknown.[113] As late as 1179, the Third Lateran Council expressed concerns about the variety of fradulent and criminal activity going on, with even Christians providing Muslims with arms to attack Christians if there was money to be made or 'for gain acting as captains or pilots' in Saracen 'pirate vessels' to rob other Christians (24).

Practical compromises

The Mozarabs were Arabic-speaking Spanish Christians living in areas of Spain under Muslim rule – those who had learned the language of the conquerors. A delicate balance had to be struck here. Paul Alvarus, in his *Life of Eulogius*, *c.*859, describes some such Christians who chose not to practise their faith in secret but to do so publicly, only to be threatened with death by the Arabs. Among them was Eulogius, a leading Mozarab cleric in Cordoba. A young girl called Leocritia, of noble birth but 'begotten of the filth of the Muslims and born from the womb of wolves [was] baptised [...] by a Christian nun, Litiosa, who was of her kindred'. 'Secretly she blossomed in the Christian faith she had adopted, and knowledge of her spread abroad as a sweet odour.' Leocritia's Muslim parents tried to beat her into submission, but she appealed to Bishop Eulogius and he arranged for her to leave her home to attend a wedding, dressed in finery suitable for the occasion and pretending to have acknowledged Islamic authority. Eulogius and his sister gave her their protection. The parents made a fuss and there were arrests. Eulogius was martyred and four days later Leocritia was beheaded and thrown into the river. But her body remained miraculously upright and would not sink. The Christians recovered the body of Leocritia and buried her in the basilica.[114]

Ibn Shaprut (*c.*915–*c.*970), a successful diplomat, liaised with Christian rulers in this period. For example, Sancho I, son of the Princess of Navarre, had succeeded to the Kingdom of Leon in 956 and was dethroned by the nobles in 958, but Ibn Shaprut seems to have been instrumental in bringing Sancho and his grandmother to Cordoba where a coup was planned. Sancho was eventually reinstated by joint efforts of Muslim and Christian monarchs.[115]

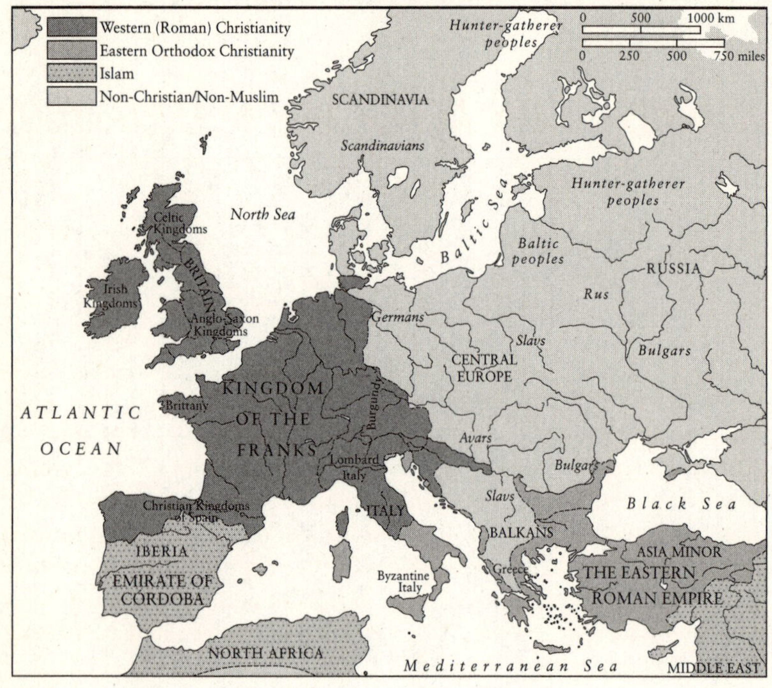

Map 3: Europe in the age of Charlemagne

3

CHRISTIANITY AFTER THE MILLENNIUM

FROM MISSION TO ESTABLISHED CHURCH

Ralph Glaber (985–1047) was sent off to become a monk as a young boy at the wish of a well-meaning uncle. To begin with he had a chequered monastic career. His bad behaviour led to several moves. Settled eventually at the monastery of St Germain in Auxerre, he took up the writing of history. In the rumour-filled times of the arrival of a new millennium he pointed to eclipses and famines as signs that the end of the world was near.

This expectation was disappointed. The world continued and by now, throughout most of Europe, it was a visibly Christian world. The establishment of dioceses and the spread of monastic houses were helping to map a more settled Western Christendom. Glaber writes of the whitening of the landscape as numerous churches and cathedrals were built.

Schism

Relations between the Church of Rome and Patriarchate of Constantinople (Byzantium) had been tense for some time when schism came in 1054. Disagreements ranged from the use of leavened or unleavened bread in the Eucharist and the Roman bishop's claims to primacy among the ancient patriarchs, to the Trinitarian question of whether the Holy Spirit proceeds from the Father and the Son or the Father alone. Greek churches in southern Italy and Sicily were pressurised to change to Latin or forced to close. In 1053, Michael Cerularius, then Patriarch of Constantinople, ordered that all Latin churches in Constantinople were to close. Pope Leo IX sent a legation led by Cardinal Humbert to negotiate for Byzantine help in a joint military expedition against the Normans who were invading southern Italy and Sicily. Met with a refusal, he excommunicated the Patriarch. Cerularius then excommunicated Humbert and his party. With mutual resentment and such largely political rather than theological disagreements, schism began, speedily reinforced by definitions of doctrinal differences. It has never been mended, though we shall see some medieval attempts to do so.

The sacraments in people's lives

The Church touched Christian people's lives directly through the ministry of the sacraments, beginning with the baptism of almost every baby in Europe except those born to Jewish and Muslim parents. The impact of the sacraments on the daily lives of ordinary Christians was to grow considerably in the medieval centuries, chiefly through the operation of an increasingly complex and burdensome penitential system.

The doctrine of the seven sacraments was thought through in its Western form only during the medieval centuries. A sacrament had been defined by Augustine of Hippo as an 'outward and visible sign of an inward and spiritual grace', a formula which had proved useful down the centuries. It recognised that people found it helpful to have something to see or hear or touch or taste or smell as an indication that they were receiving a spiritual benefit. The 'sign' might be words or the water of baptism or the bread and wine of the Eucharist. 'Questions on baptism' are listed by Peter the Chanter (d. 1197), a Paris scholar and precentor of the cathedral of Notre Dame at the end of the twelfth century. These 'questions' were the sort being discussed in the 'schools' that were in the process of becoming universities. He explained that 'a New Testament sacrament does what it signifies' (*sacramentum novi testamenti efficit quod figurat*).[1] The only 'words of the Gospel' (*verba evangelica*) on baptism, he explains, are that it should be carried out 'in the name of the Father, and the Son and the Holy Spirit'. So baptism takes effect through the use of these Gospel words (*ergo sacramentum effectum per illa verba evangelica*). Essential too is the use of water. But this was a questioning age in

Western Europe. If another person is baptised in the same water does it work, someone asks?[2] This approach was a considerable change in less than a century from that of Hugh of St Victor (*c.*1096–1141), who was still defining *sacramentum* simply as 'mystery'.

Only two sacraments had clear warrant in the New Testament. One was baptism, for Jesus himself was baptised (Matthew 3.13–17). The other was the celebration of the Eucharist (Mass or Holy Communion or Lord's Supper) in memory of the Last Supper Jesus celebrated with his disciples before his crucifixion (Mark 14.22–24), when he gave them instructions that they were to continue to celebrate in the same way in 'remembrance' of him.[3]

The doctrine of transubstantiation and the feast of Corpus Christi

The laity might have little idea what was happening before their eyes at a Eucharist. One knight said he would not go to Mass because he thought it just meant bringing offerings to the priest.[4] Some thought they saw a tiny Jesus held up before them when the priest lifted the consecrated bread or 'Host' (*hostia*). Some held the bread in their mouths and took it home to keep because they thought it had magical powers.

Fig. 9: Book illustration, 1860, of the feast of Corpus Christi being celebrated at Evian-les-Bains in south-east France, in the typical later medieval way, as an exciting local festival

Fig. 10: *Allegory of the Eucharist*, *c.*1480–1500: this fifteenth-century woodcut shows the consecrated bread becoming the actual body of Christ at the Mass

The question of what exactly happens in the Eucharist when the words of Jesus ('this is my body'; 'this is my blood', Luke 22.19–20) are spoken by the priest had caused dispute among Carolingian scholars. From the eleventh century the discussion of this problem grew more technical and sophisticated as a result of a renewed controversy. Berengar of Tours (*c.*999–1088), a famous grammar and logic teacher, insisted that the change was merely symbolic. Lanfranc (*c.*1005–89), abbot of Bec and later Archbishop of Canterbury, also an experienced teacher of grammar and logic, became prominent in a campaign to have Berengar condemned. He was twice forced to confess his 'error', in 1059 and again in 1079. The result was the formulation of the doctrine of 'transubstantiation'. This held that the 'substance' of the bread was changed though its appearance was not, reversing what would normally happen to bread, which could change in outward appearance by growing mouldy, though remaining bread in substance. This analysis depended heavily on the study of Aristotle's *Categories*, which sets out the principle that the substance of a thing may have a number of changing 'accidents', such as its quantity or its location.

From the point of view of lay understanding, the most important result of this clarification was the idea that the consecrated bread really was Christ in his human body. The laity were not offered the wine, which by custom only the clergy now received. The focus was therefore on the 'Body of Christ' and much lay and clerical speculation is recorded. If a crumb of the consecrated bread falls to the floor and a mouse eats it, is the mouse 'saved'? How can all those consecrated Hosts be Christ when their total volume is so much greater than a single human body?

Popular veneration of the consecrated Host led to the creation of a feast day for Corpus Christi, 'the body of Christ', held on the first Sunday after Pentecost. This feast seems to have appeared first in the thirteenth century at Liège, a prosperous merchant town, where an articulate bourgeoisie was to be found. Juliana, from a Beguine community of lay religious women,[5] worked as a volunteer at the local leper hospital run by the Praemonstratensian canons.[6] She had a vision in which appeared a moon with a bite out of it. She wondered what this meant, but Christ revealed to her that the moon represented the Church and the bit missing was a special day to mark the importance of the Eucharist. The Liége Dominicans[7] seem to have supported her campaign to establish such a day.[8] The papacy made the feast official in 1264, issuing the papal bull *Transiturus*. Enthusiasm for the establishment of such a feast was revived in 1313 at the Council of Vienne, during the papacy of Clement IV. 'Indulgences'[9] might be attached to the feast to encourage the people to take part.[10] The 1317 papal letter *Si dominum* gave the idea universal currency, and it was being fostered with some energy in England by 1318.

This early-summer celebration, whose date moved with the moveable Feast[11] of Pentecost, became quite a local event throughout Western Europe. In Milan in 1336, ecclesiastical dignitaries, members of all the religious orders and an archbishop, all riding white horses, joined in the procession. Such processions became popular[12] and Corpus Christi became an occasion for public preaching especially on the doctrine of the sacraments.[13] Richard FitzRalph, Bishop of Armagh, in his preaching diary for 1344–59 includes special 'popular sermons' for the feast. Corpus Christi also became one of the four official sermon days (*dies praedicabiles*) for the University of Cambridge, and both Oxford and Cambridge gained colleges named after the feast.[14]

Confirmation

The other five sacraments which touched lay people's lives in the Middle Ages were going to be rejected as true sacraments by most of the Protestant reformers of the sixteenth century. The first of them, 'confirmation', was needed as a consequence of the change from adult to infant baptism. That meant that learning Christian beliefs had to come after baptism and not before. The faith had to be taught to already-baptised children. They were then brought to the bishop when they were old enough to understand it and accept it for themselves. He laid his hands on them so that they could 'receive the Holy Spirit'. This might involve quite an 'event' for the parish when the bishop came to catch up with the local confirmations. But it left open the question of how, if baptism cleansed the sinner of both 'original' and actual sins, it could be supplemented by a further sacrament.

How much instruction was necessary? John Peckham, a Franciscan friar, became Archbishop of Canterbury (1279–92) and from that position of responsibility tried to insist that parish priests should give instruction to the faithful including the Ten Commandments, the

Fig. 11: Etching of children being brought to a bishop to be confirmed

Creed, the Lord's Prayer and the sacraments. Here was a 'syllabus'. Short texts could be produced which it was reasonable to expect people to learn in their own language and understand, though not perhaps small children. Archbishop Peckham's drive to educate the laity (1281) included the instruction that every priest must four times a year teach the people about the seven virtues and vices in the common tongue (*exponat populo vulgariter*). Lists of the vices and virtues lent themselves to the purposes of those who wished to encourage better behaviour.

Penance

Another consequence of the change to infant baptism was the certainty that everyone would go on to become a sinner and need to seek further forgiveness. That led to the evolution of an immense apparatus of penitential practice within the 'sacrament of penance'. In the early Christian centuries, only the great sins of apostasy, murder and adultery had required penance. During the Carolingian period a different practice grew up. Parish priests began to hear confessions, and their parishioners learned to confess even minor sins and to do

Fig. 12: A fifteenth-century (*c.*1460–70) woodcut of a repentant sinner confessing to a priest with a guardian angel looking on approvingly

it regularly.[15] The Fourth Lateran Council of 1215 decreed that this must happen at least once a year.

Confessors' manuals began to multiply from the twelfth century to help the parish priest, faced with the duty to hear these confessions and impose appropriate penances, act as 'physician' or 'judge' or a bit of both. Alan of Lille (d. 1202), in his *Liber Poenitentialis*, suggests questions for the confessor to ask the penitent, before stressing to him how important is true contrition. The book then helps the confessor to judge how heavy a penance to impose for sins of greater or lesser seriousness. Alan said he had relied on the *Corrector* of Burchard of Worms (*c.*950–1025) among other earlier sources in composing this manual.

Peter the Chanter in his 'Compendium of the sacraments and advice for souls' (*Summa de sacramentis et animae consiliis*) makes it clear that some of the problems a priest encountered might involve counselling rather than discipline. A pregnant woman who had previously had a miscarriage and was afraid it might happen again, asked whether a mother's faith can make her child be 'reborn' before it is born. The answer is that the aborted foetus will not go to heaven however hard she prays.[16] There would also be questions asked ahead of actually sinning. Wealthy local families may want to know whether they may

Fig. 13: A fifteenth-century (*c.*1480) woodcut of souls enduring their suffering in purgatory until they are fit to enter heaven, with a comforting angel hovering above

'buy' preferment in the Church for a son or nephew. Is it simony if someone buys something in which there is 'something spiritual' (*aliqua spiritualitas*)? Yes, this is definitely simony, says Peter.[17]

At St Victor in Paris, Robert of Flamborough published a *Liber Poenitentialis* between 1208 and 1213 to try to provide a system of classification of sins according to the types of sinner, such as married people or clergy. It considered the seven deadly sins and used a dialogue between the confessor and the penitent to enliven the learning process.[18]

Mainly a twelfth-century invention, 'purgatory' was an attractive idea in this climate of heightened concentration on the riskiness of dying in one's sins. It was generally accepted that whether heaven

Fig. 14: Mural by Ezra Winter (1886–1949) of Chaucer's Canterbury pilgrims on the west wall of the North Reading Room, Library of Congress, Washington DC

or hell awaited was fixed at the moment of death. The imposition of penances by the Church provided both a measurement of the amount a person 'owed' by way of reparation and the acceptance that getting to heaven involved making oneself worthy to go there. Few could be confident that they were sufficiently clean of sin to deserve to spend eternity in heaven. The emergence of the doctrine of purgatory was good news. There after death, in the certainty that one would eventually enter heaven, one could discharge the remaining finite penalties for one's sins.[19]

People naturally wanted to help beloved relatives or friends who had died to get out of purgatory as soon as possible. This opened up the possibility of praying for one's dead relatives or even paying, so as to shorten their time of waiting to enter heaven. Prayer to a saint in heaven with merits to spare was thought to assist those who were short of merits of their own, so the cult of saints became more important. These notions, of 'vicarious satisfaction' – making satisfaction on behalf of others – or praying to ask for the 'transfer' of good works which deserved reward, was to lead to an immense later medieval 'industry' of private Masses and of buying 'pardons' and prayers for the dead. It was mostly driven by popular demand.

The Church fixed and imposed the sinner's penances, so the Church had power to lift them if it chose. This was known as an 'indulgence'. Granting indulgences was not strictly part of the penitential system. It was considered an exceptional act and required a pope or at least a bishop to do it. Best of all would be a 'plenary indulgence', which would wipe out the consequences of all a man's sins of a whole lifetime. An early 'plenary indulgence' was offered in the preaching of the First Crusade, for all those who went on crusade and either died in the attempt or reached Jerusalem.[20]

Here, too, there was room for financial corruption to creep in, for it was an excellent means for the Church to raise money. St Peter's in Rome, for example, was built partly on the income from the sale of indulgences. Indulgences ceased to be rarities and became routine. For the sinner still alive or the deceased's relatives it became tempting to try to buy indulgences, and the sale of indulgences became a shameless late medieval industry.

If indulgences were for sale there would be criminals ready to peddle them. Travelling 'indulgence salesmen' known as 'Pardoners' appeared all over Western Europe. They carried holy 'relics' as tokens that they had something spiritually powerful to offer – though there could be no guarantees of their authenticity any more than of the genuineness of the indulgences they sold.

The 'Pardoner' who tells one of Chaucer's 'Canterbury Tales' is an example. He admits he is no cleric, yet he preaches, a jumble of commonplaces and lies. Some Pardoners were commissioned by Rome, while some were sent by hospitals and other institutions which were fund-raising; but some were simply frauds. It all became a racket and along with general abuse of the penitential system, the resulting plethora of theological confusions became one of the strongest reasons for reform of the Church in Martin Luther's opinion.

Another way of helping a dead relative into heaven more speedily was to pay for the saying of 'private' Masses. These were not ordinary celebrations of the Eucharist but special ones, in which the priest alone 'said the Mass' without a congregation, with the particular 'intention' of applying its effects to the deceased and thus shortening his time in purgatory. Such Masses became a significant source of income for 'Mass priests', and financial corruption was again a result. Moreover, the system presumed that a Mass could have the effect of helping to cancel out sin. And that in its turn seemed to some critics to diminish the completeness of Christ's sacrificial death on the Cross, because it allowed room for more sacrifices, every time the 'sacrifice' of the Mass was celebrated. It is significant that the word 'presbyter' gave way to the Latin *sacerdos* for 'priest' in the medieval West, with its connotation of the making of a sacrifice.

Marriage

It is likely that almost everyone who did not enter a religious order or become a priest in the Middle Ages got married. The extended family was the fundamental social unit, and the structure rested on the lifelong marriage of couples, with their children. The social order had a place for widows, and families could provide a place for their disabled children, but single people living independent secular lives did not 'fit'. Marriage, then as now, was fundamentally a contract between consenting parties. But in the Middle Ages it began to be counted among the sacraments and regarded as part of the Church's role in the life of the laity.

Preaching at a wedding in the thirteenth century, Hugh of St Cher (*c.*1200–63) begins in the traditional way with the marriage at Cana in Galilee, where Jesus performed his first miracle when he changed the water into wine.[21] Peter of Rheims, who was prior of Saint Jacques, the house of the Dominicans in Paris, at the end of the 1220s, preached a surviving marriage sermon in which Christ's 'marriages' are listed: to his human nature, to the souls of the baptised and again to the souls of penitents. Christ's marriage to the Christian soul is for ever and it is faithful. The soul wedded to Christ will not flirt with Satan. The children of the marriage are the good works of the soul which is Christ's bride.[22]

A parish priest must frequently have found himself giving instruction to those about to be married. Peter the Chanter explains that in every other sacrament there is conferred an increase of grace (*cumulus gratiae*). Marriage is the exception because it was instituted as a remedy (for lust) and not for the increase of grace (*ad remedium et non ad augmentum*), though Peter mentions authorities such as Bede who did not agree with this analysis.[23]

Peter the Chanter discusses what degrees of close kinship should prohibit marriage.[24] Then there is the question of secret marriages, for two people sometimes agreed to be 'married' without going through a public ceremony with the blessing of the Church. Is such secret marriage valid? Problems may arise about the legitimacy of offspring if that is not certain. There could be implications for inheritance, for example. You have to judge by their behaviour, suggests Peter. Do they seem to be living together faithfully, with the wife obedient to the husband, or not?[25]

Ordination

In the medieval West, clerical celibacy was expected of priests as well as of monks and friars who joined religious orders, so being ordained or entering the religious life was an alternative to marriage. But there was much to discuss with reference to 'orders'. Which orders required 'ordination' and which demanded celibacy? There was no clear difference between 'bishops' or 'presbyters' in the Bible. Both the words *presbyter* and *episcopos* are used in the Greek of the New Testament. Only in the case of deacons is there New Testament evidence about the specific responsibilities ministers were to have (Acts 6.1–6). The deacons were to make sure that the needy in the congregation, widows and orphans, were looked after. The apostles laid hands on them and so they were considered to have been ordained.

It was not long before the three roles became a ladder of ascent, in which a cleric first became a deacon, then a priest and finally perhaps a bishop, each with the allotted tasks and powers. The gifts of the Holy Spirit granted for each order of ministry were clearly identified. A deacon might not celebrate the Eucharist or grant absolution. A priest might do both but he could not ordain. Only a bishop could do that. There was little controversy about this development until the Reformation, when reformers began to campaign for the abolition of bishops and a return to what was claimed to be the 'presbyterian' New Testament practice of the community appointing 'elders' as its leaders.

By the Middle Ages, many lower orders came into existence, from sub-deacons downward, but ordination as deacon, priest or bishop was treated as sacramental, imposing an indelible 'character' on the person ordained.

Some monks were also priests, but taking monastic vows never came to be regarded as a form of ordination in itself. Instead, as reformers protested from the fourteenth century, taking monastic vows was sometimes seen as a kind of 'second baptism', making the religious see himself or herself as a 'better' or 'superior' kind of Christian. This was a way of thinking robustly attacked by John Wyclif and others as part of his campaign against the 'sects', as he called the religious orders.

The anointing of the sick and dying

One last practice came to be treated as sacramental in the medieval West. The sick were 'anointed' with oil consecrated for the purpose by a bishop, and the seriously ill received a final anointing ('supreme unction') at the point of death. The practice lacked obvious scriptural warrant, but it could be comforting to the sick and dying and to their families. This was probably another example, like much penitential practice, of a development led by popular demand and only afterwards given theological rationalisation. Some theologians said it formed part of the teaching of Jesus that was not recorded in the Gospels. Some suggested that the apostle (James 5.14) had described the practice when he said that the elders of the community should visit the sick person and pray over him or her, anointing with oil in the Lord's name.

The ministry of the sacraments and getting to heaven

For the ordinary medieval man or woman, the contact with the sacraments during a lifetime would be quite frequent, in person and through family members, with baptisms, confirmations, weddings, annual confessions and episodes of illness. However, the question of whether it was possible to get to heaven without these sacramental aids from the Church naturally arose. Augustine of Hippo thought there could be 'no salvation outside the Church' (*nulla salus extra ecclesiam*), but he allowed that God could save anyone he chose by grace even if he or she had not been baptised or had sins forgiven.

EXPERIMENTATION IN MONASTIC LIFE

By the year 1000, Benedictine monasticism dominated the monastic life of Western Europe.[26] For a long time, infant admissions to the life were common. Child 'oblates' were given by their parents and brought up and educated in the monasteries to become monks and nuns. Whether they had a vocation or not could be discovered only when they grew up.

A few of these children came from peasant families and were left at the door of the monastery either because the family could not afford to bring up another child or because the parents wanted it to have opportunities they could not give it. For monastic life could be a means of upward social mobility. Most of those given in this way came from wealthier and more influential families, well aware of the career opportunities that might be available, especially to a boy, who might even rise to become a bishop. A girl might be intended to be abbess in a convent to which her family had been a major donor, a boy to be abbot on the strength of belonging to a noble family with especially firm links with the house. That way lay potential for corruption of Benedict's principles, for it could create abbots with no regard for their vocation or spiritual state, or even their suitability to lead such a community.

This exercise of influence had a long history and showed early potential to blur the distinction between ecclesiastical and secular power and foster corruption. Dunstan (909–88) came of an influential family in Wessex. His paternal uncles were bishops of Winchester and of Wells (later Archbishop of Canterbury) and he had a pious mother. His parents sent him to school with the monks at Glastonbury, but he seems to have chosen of his own free will to become a monk there.

However, Dunstan was not simply left to live the life he had chosen. Athelm, the uncle who became Archbishop of Canterbury in the early 920s, saw him as a promising young man and called him into his own service. From there he entered the royal service where he encountered jealousy and allegations that he was practising witchcraft – he was even beaten up and thrown into a pool of sewage, but climbed out and sought refuge with his other episcopal uncle, Aelfheah, Bishop of Winchester. It was suggested that Dunstan should become a monk, but legend has it that he was persuaded to return to Glastonbury, where he lived as a hermit in a tiny cell. He had musical and artistic talents and became well known as an illustrator or 'illuminator' of manuscripts.

After his father's death, Dunstan inherited a considerable fortune and he found himself once more drawn into life in royal circles under King Edmund, and once more the object of jealousy and attacks. But the king narrowly escaped death after a life-threatening incident, when he had prayed for his life and promised God to do something for Dunstan if he survived. Edmund kept his promise and took

Dunstan to Glastonbury where he was made abbot by the simple but unorthodox method of placing him in the abbot's seat in the abbey church. Dunstan now saw his way to leading a reforming campaign. He restored the life the monks were leading at Glastonbury to proper Benedictine standards and then set to work to reform English monasticism more generally. It badly needed it.

An analogous process of reform took place at the abbey of Cluny in the tenth century. Cluny itself was a relatively young foundation, begun in 910, a creation of Duke William of Aquitaine. But by the mid-twelfth century the Cluniac Order had become Europe-wide and, thanks to reforms mainly by Odo of Cluny (878–942), a by-word for the living of a severe and exemplary Benedictine life. Only by the later eleventh and early twelfth century did it become more widely fashionable to become a monk as an adult,[27] retiring late in life from a marriage (usually with one's spouse's consent) or from military or academic life. For example, Herluin, the founder of the very successful monastery at Bec, was a knight who had discovered he had a vocation. This element of personal choice was still chiefly available to the well-born, but it began to disrupt the settled pattern.

Whole new orders began to appear, founded by independent effort. The Cistercians followed the Benedictine Rule but had a fresh vision of what the latter order originally intended. They set out to avoid acquiring wealth and influence in high places and chose remote sites for their houses where such things were less likely to become temptations. The Cistercians quickly became rivals to the Cluniac 'reformed' Benedictines and were even accused of poaching young monks from them. There was much mud-slinging. A lively correspondence on the subject survives, between Bernard of Clairvaux (1090–1153), the great Cistercian leader whose charismatic personality had proved so attractive to recruits, and Peter the Venerable, Abbot of Cluny (*c.*1092–1156).

Grown-up monks could become challenging and dangerous figures if they went wrong.[28] Henry of Lausanne seems to have been a monk at Cluny in the first half of the twelfth century. Then he left monastic life to go preaching. He was said to be tall and impressive, with long hair and a beard, and he went about dramatically preceded by a man carrying a rod with a cross at the top. Henry arrived in Le Mans and asked for permission to preach there, which, while the bishop was away, he was unaccountably allowed to do. But Henry had too much popular impact for the comfort of the ecclesiastical authorities. He preached the idea, already attractive to the populace, that the clergy were corrupt and unworthy. He thus made himself a threat to the Church. Bernard of Clairvaux mentions him in Letter 241 as a man possessed by the Devil, suffering from 'Jewish blindness' and leading ordinary people astray by discouraging them from baptising their children.

Other experimenters won ecclesiastical approval in the end. Robert of Arbrissel (*c.*1045–1116) was the son of village priest in the Breton diocese of Rennes. He may have followed his father as local priest there,[29] although in later life he campaigned vigorously against simony and in favour of clerical celibacy, to the point where he made himself thoroughly unpopular. He probably studied in the cathedral school at Laon, so he would have had a good theological education.

About 1095, in a period when experiments in monastic life were fashionable,[30] Robert made a decision to live as a hermit, though he had a companion, the Bernard who became the founder of Tiron.[31] Local people seem to have been drawn to hermits in the Middle Ages, as they had been in the first Christian centuries, as a living and visible focus of holiness from which spiritual nourishment could be drawn. Robert's special theme was the life of poverty.

His attractiveness to his followers, some of whom seem to have been the disadvantaged and undesirables such as prostitutes and beggars, was heightened by his own obvious dedication to living as an example himself. Women seem to have been particularly susceptible, though the story was told of a woman who arrived with a gift of three eggs, which Robert refused to accept because he said she had stolen them. He was quite right. They turned into three frogs, until she took them back to their owner when they became eggs again.[32] Robert must have made a more widespread name because he gathered enough followers to found a monastery. He eventually became founder abbot of Fontevrault. In 1096, Pope Urban II showed his approval, by commissioning Robert as a wandering preacher.

The canons

There were new twelfth-century orders of 'regular' canons (canons living under a Rule) too, the Victorines, whose house was at St Victor in Paris, and the Praemonstratensians, also called Norbertines after their founder Norbert, a friend of Bernard of Clairvaux. Canons were priests who were not, like the Benedictines or Cistercians, expected to spend their lives in the house where they first took their vows. They could do active work in the world, especially preaching.

The anonymous treatise 'On different orders' (*De diversis ordinibus*) was written in the mid-twelfth century[33] in a worried attempt to take stock of the proliferation of monastic experiments. This proliferation caused concern in high places. There was too much room for disorder and corruption and what might now be described as 'mission creep'. The Fourth Lateran Council of 1215 (13) tried to call a halt to so much religious experimentation, with a 'prohibition against new religious orders': 'Lest too great a variety of religious orders leads to grave confusion in God's church, we strictly forbid anyone henceforth to found a new religious order.'

There was a variety of financial corruption and abuse of influence. The Third Lateran Council (10) tried to end the practice of monks paying to enter a particular monastery and ignoring the vow of poverty so as to keep money of their own: 'Neither priories nor obediences are to be handed over to anyone for a sum of money.' Some monks were not living with communities but individually in towns and were therefore not necessarily keeping to their Rule.

The Fourth Lateran Council (59) tried to stop another undesirable practice:

> [N]o religious, without the permission of his abbot and the majority of his chapter, may stand surety for someone or accept a loan from another beyond a sum fixed by the common opinion. Otherwise the convent shall not be held responsible in any way for his actions, unless perchance the matter has clearly redounded to the benefit of his house. Anyone who presumes to act contrary to this statute shall be severely disciplined.

This sort of interaction with lay financial affairs had other faces. Lateran IV (61) tried to stop regular canons from being given livings like secular clergy 'without the bishop's consent'.

Monasticism and the ecclesiastical authorities

There was rivalry for power between 'secular' clergy and monks. Abbeys liked to claim to be subject directly to the jurisdiction of the pope and not to that of their local bishop. Some abbots intruded upon actions which belonged to bishops only. The Fourth Lateran

Council of 1215 (60) warned that abbots were 'not to encroach on episcopal office': 'From the complaints which have reached us from bishops in various parts of the world, we have come to know of serious and great excesses of certain abbots.' These abbots were 'hearing matrimonial cases, enjoining public penances, even granting letters of indulgences and like presumptions. It sometimes happens from this that episcopal authority is cheapened in the eyes of many.'

The military orders

The Hospitallers and Templars, two orders founded to provide protection for pilgrims and crusaders in the Holy Land, fell into corruption too. The Hospitallers had begun in the eleventh century, running a hostel-hospice-hospital of St John in Jerusalem to meet the needs of the growing numbers of pilgrim-tourists. The Templars, who gained recognition in 1118, had a different mission: to protect pilgrims from robbers and bandits and try to give them safe passage to the shrine they wanted to visit. The Templars' first 'house' was on the site of Solomon's Temple. Bernard of Clairvaux wrote a treatise 'In praise of the new soldiery' (*De laudibus novae militiae*)[34] to remind them that they were members of a religious order as well as fighting men.

In 1179 the Third Lateran Council sounded a warning. These anomalous Orders had begun to behave like other 'religious', as though they did not owe obedience to the ecclesiastical hierarchy. Canon 9 protested that episcopal authority was 'being disregarded':

> [W]e have learnt from the strongly worded complaints of our brethren and fellow bishops that the Templars and Hospitallers, and other professed religious [...] have often disregarded episcopal authority, causing scandal [*scandalum*, meaning 'stumbling block'] to the people of God and grave danger to souls.[35]

A lengthy list of their offences is given.[36] There is too much bending of rules 'on the occasion also of the brotherhoods which they establish in many places'. 'They weaken the bishops' authority.' They let in anyone who wishes to join and they allow recruits to keep personal property.[37]

Mendicants

The Orders of 'mendicant' ('begging') friars came into being in the early thirteenth century. They were beggars because their idea was to

Fig. 15: Painting, *c.*1470, by Agnolo degli Erri of a Dominican friar preaching to a large congregation

live by travelling and preaching the Gospel, expecting to enjoy the hospitality and generosity of those who heard them (Matthew 10.10–14). This new trend was led by the Franciscans and Dominicans. They had in common a preaching mission and a preference for urban centres for their houses, for they needed to be where people were most numerous. The Dominicans were founded by Dominic, a Spanish priest, who had a calling to try to rescue the Albigensian heretics of northern Spain and the south of France from their error. The Cistercians had been trying but were considered to have failed in this objective. The Franciscans were the creation of Francis of Assisi, a young nobleman who felt drawn to try to live the life Jesus had taught to his apostles, living in apostolic poverty and preaching the Gospel. These innovative religious orders gained the approval of Pope Honorius III in 1216 and 1219 respectively.

Their differences were soon eroded, for this was also the time when the first universities were emerging and preachers needed a good education. So the two orders quickly became rivals for academic leadership in the universities of Paris and Oxford and soon suffered the same decline into wealth and corruption as had afflicted the Benedictines, Cistercians and orders of regular canons over time. But the mendicants risked corruption in an additional way. Because they were free to leave their houses – indeed they had to do so as wandering preachers – they came to be popular as personal 'confessors' to the nobility. That gave them the ear of powerful figures and the temptation to interfere in secular and ecclesiastical politics.

Mutual indignation mounts

The Church's high-level anxieties about the failings of the religious orders continued into the fourteenth century. The Council of Vienne (1311–12) took place during the period of the papal exile in Avignon which lasted from the early fourteenth century until 1377. The 'exile' began with the election of the Frenchman Clement V as pope in 1305. He was not willing to move to Rome because of the history of conflict between the French monarchy and Boniface VIII, his last predecessor but one, which remained unresolved. Clement therefore did not rate higly his chances of survival in Italy. The exile was ended only when Pope Gregory IX decided to return the papacy to Rome in 1377.

The Council of Vienne could not take the title of a Lateran Council if it did not meet in Rome. In any case, it seemed a pale shadow of its predecessors. It attracted many fewer bishops, but nevertheless issued some significant decisions.

The council regretted (30) that 'complaints, loud, frequent and incessant come to us from certain religious that very many prelates – bishops, their superiors and others – unjustly disturb in many ways the peace of the religious'. Conversely (31), the religious were intruding on the work of the bishops and priests. The council condemned those

> religious who presume to administer the sacrament of extreme unction or the eucharist to clerics or lay people or to solemnise marriages, without the special leave of the parish priest, or to absolve those excommunicated by canon law.

The same council (37) reproved the Franciscans for offering a sacramental ministry to 'brothers and sisters of the third order' during a period of Interdict, causing scandal to those who were excluded because it seemed to undermine the force of ecclesiastical censure. If the friars continued to do this they would find themselves 'under automatic excommunication'.

The Council of Vienne went so far as to 'suppress' the Knights Templar,[38] whose behaviour was growing ever more scandalous, with reports coming in to the pope from all over Europe:

> Indeed a little while ago, about the time of our election as supreme pontiff before we came to Lyons for our coronation, and afterwards, both there and elsewhere, we received secret intimations against the master, preceptors and other brothers of the order of Knights Templar of Jerusalem and also against the order itself.

The king of France had also received similar reports, and the council pulled no punches: 'Not slight is the fornication of this house, immolating its sons, giving them up and consecrating them to demons and not to God, to gods whom they did not know.' It decided not only to suppress the order but to reassign its 'property to the use for which it was intended', by handing it over to the Hospitallers. The transfer included

> the house itself of the Knights Templar and the other houses, churches, chapels, oratories, cities, castles, towns, lands, granges, places, possessions,

> jurisdictions, revenues, rights, all the other property, whether immovable, movable or self-moving, and all the members together with their rights and belongings, both beyond and on this side of the sea, in each and every part of the world, at the time when the master himself and some brothers of the order were arrested as a body in the kingdom of France, namely in October 1308.

SPEAKING TO THE FAITHFUL IN THEIR OWN LANGUAGE

The problem of the language barrier

The need for vernacular versions of Latin teaching became obvious in the West of Europe not long after the end of the Roman Empire, as classical Latin began to give way as a vernacular to the versions which eventually became the modern romance languages. Speakers of Teutonic languages, such as the Anglo-Saxons in England, were even more at a disadvantage. King Alfred of Wessex (849–99) wrote to Bishop Waerferth of Worcester regretting how standards had slipped from the good old days and deploring the diminishing numbers able to read authors in Latin. He suggested that it would be a good idea to translate some of the books which really ought to be more widely read into the language everyone could understand. Young men of sufficient wealth to have the leisure really ought to make the time to read them, Alfred asserted, for he knew that many who could not read Latin could read in English.

King Alfred decided to set an example. No doubt on advice from his senior clergy, he chose as a book for translation the *Pastoral Rule* (*Regula Pastoralis*) of Pope Gregory the Great (*c.*540–604). This had been written to guide bishops in the decaying Roman world where the Church had become the only authority which kept up a structure capable of ensuring supplies of essentials such as grain for the local populations of Europe. Alfred's England was a different world and he himself was no scholar; in fact as a Latinist, he was something of a beginner.[39]

The first chapters of the *Regula Pastoralis* concern government and the bishop's duties of 'oversight' in his diocese, but soon Gregory moves on into practical suggestions for the way the pastor should teach ordinary people. In Chapter 24, he says that men should be admonished in one way, women in another. Men will rise to a challenge, so be severe. Women need to be flattered if they are to behave better. Similarly (Chapter 25), the young should be admonished in one way, the old in another: the ruler should admonish the young and coax the old. Chapter 26 dealt with admonishment of the rich and the poor, recommending that the ruler should frighten the rich – who may be arrogant – and console the poor. Chapter 27 explains that the happy should be admonished in one way, the sad in another: warn the cheerful that their satisfaction may not last, but comfort the sad that things may improve. Chapter 28 suggests that rulers should be admonished in one way, subjects in another. This balancing act continues, to cover masters and servants, the foolish and the wise, the proud and the humble. The aim was to maintain good order, in which everyone knew his place.

Further on, Gregory, with King Alfred and presumably his helpers patiently translating, comes to the ruler's guidance to be offered in the context of the spiritual welfare of the people for whom he is responsible. Those who repent the sins they have actually committed should be admonished in one way, the repentant of things they have merely intended but not actually done, in another. There is instruction (Chapter 25) on how to speak firmly to exhort someone who suffers many evil temptations.[40]

Though Latin was still a living and developing language throughout the Middle Ages and beyond, it was hence to become the language of the educated, which now meant clerks trained as notaries and civil servants, and the clergy. The Bible in Western Europe was read in Latin, in Jerome's Vulgate version. That presented a barrier of access to a laity few of whom were literate even in their own language. That did not mean that the laity were fools, though there were clergy who believed that only the ordained were full members of the Church. But it is difficult to enter into the detailed thoughts of ordinary lay people who were not in a position to leave many records of their ideas and experiences in their own words.

Even for those in search of glimpses of the patterns of daily life, evidence such as parish records gives limited information beyond names and dates. Wills can sketch a family's possessions and relationships and indicate the importance attached to paying for prayers to be said for one's soul, but the reader is left with a frustrated sense that there must have been much more undocumented: family discussions, the widening viewpoints of an expanding bourgeoisie, reflections during worship in the parish church, questions for the priest during a confessions of sins, or the fun of putting on mystery plays telling the Christian story from the sin of Adam to the life of Jesus.

Schooling in the faith

How were children to learn about the Christian faith in a medieval Europe where few lay people went to school? Some monasteries ran schools which outside pupils could attend, like the school at Bec under Lanfranc (1005/10–89), but mostly the teaching of young monks-to-be was likely to have been a strictly internal affair. Guibert of Nogent (*c.*1055–1124) had an ambitious mother who arranged a schoolmaster, who taught him on the principle that a child learns best if knowledge is systematically beaten into him with a rod.[41] John of Salisbury (*c.*1120–80) says he went to school with another little boy though their master was rather too fond of magic to be a reliable teacher.[42]

For the most part, people must have had to depend on the parish church and its local priest for teaching. Parish churches might have frescoes on the walls or statues to provide visual instruction, but how 'instructive' the visual interior of a place of worship could be made might very often depend on the generosity of a patron. There was no formal qualification for being ordained and many local clergy would themselves have struggled with the Latin, of Scripture and liturgy alike.

For children there were no 'Sunday schools' yet, and catechism classes before confirmation were probably rare. By the fourteenth century, John Thoresby, Archbishop of York (d. 1373), was following the example of Archbishop Peckham and trying to make provision for adequate teaching of the Christian faith to lay people in full recognition of the problem of the language barrier. He commissioned John Gaytryge to write *The lay folks' catechisme*[43] in both Latin and English.

Teaching by preaching

Augustine as Bishop of Hippo would preach a series of sermons lasting an hour or two each, working his way steadily through a whole book of the Bible. Gregory the Great did the same. In the medieval parish, sermons were likely to be much more modest in scope and length. There was no general expectation that there would be a sermon every Sunday, but there is evidence that sermons might be preached in the language of the people, usually with an emphasis on encouraging good Christian behaviour rather than teaching detailed theology.

One anonymous collection of sermons in English from the tenth century includes not only a series for the seasons of the Church year, but also stories and saints' lives, all aiming to give moral guidance.[44] The sermon would take a text of Scripture as a theme, perhaps adding little bits of 'information' likely to be interesting to the curious. In the story of Mary and Martha (Luke 10.38–42), Mary the sister of Martha was often confused with Mary Magdalene who broke the vessel of precious ointment over Jesus' feet (John 12.3). In one homily on the time the sisters entertained Jesus and Mary left all the work to Martha, listeners were told that the ointment 'Mary' used had 18 herbs in it. Our own numerous good deeds should be like Mary's anointing oil with its sweet scent.[45] A medieval preacher liked nothing better than a number on which he could hang a series of points.

Sometimes a particular preacher emerges vividly as a person. Aelfric (*c.*955–*c.*1010), abbot of Eynsham, was a born teacher. He wanted the listener to feel the nearness of even the highest and most respected of Christian writers. The human authors of Scripture are men like us, he stresses. St Paul wrote a letter to sinful men admitting that he was a sinner too.[46] When he preached to an uneducated audience, Aelfric kept to the literal meaning of his chosen Scriptural passage if possible, so as to make it easier for his hearers to understand.[47]Aelfric's messages are simple and designed to stick in the mind. In a sermon for the Feast of John the Baptist (Sermon XXII), there is a discussion of the Gospel text (given in Latin) which speaks of the 'voice of one crying in the wilderness' (John 1.23). We are 'in the wilderness', he explains, when we turn from God, are disobedient and think more about earthly pleasures than heavenly delights. The Lord 'cries to us' and we behave as though we were deaf.[48] The appeal of Aelfric's homilies meant they continued to be used and imitated for the next couple of centuries.[49]

Alan of Lille (d. 1202) was one of the first to design a published handbook for preachers, an *Ars praedicandi* or 'Art of preaching'. He modelled it on the classical art of public speaking, which taught the orator to memorise 'topics', that is examples and illustrations and ready-made arguments to drop into a speech to enliven it and bring arguments home. He arranged these materials for special imaginary congregations, one composed entirely of widows, another composed of princes, another made up of virgins and so on.

Alan died just as the first universities were emerging, and the Franciscans and Dominicans were being founded as orders of specialist preachers. Soon the tradition of the 'university sermon' began, always in Latin. From about 1230, more *artes praedicandi* appeared, together with various new aids and handbooks, such as dictionaries of words in the Bible to help a preacher make cross-references, and more collections of stories to put into sermons to illustrate certain points.

The friars often carried notebooks of such *exempla*,[50] for they became the professional preachers *par excellence* of the late Middle Ages. An ideal of the apostolic life understood as the life of a dedicated and selfless man called to preach was fundamental to their vocation. It is summed up by Pierre de Reims, prior of the Dominican house at Paris, Saint-Jacques, from 1227 to 1230. The apostolic life, he says, has a twofold mission. It is a life of preaching for the good of one's neighbour and it is a life of contemplation and the exercise of the virtues.[51] The success of the friars depended partly on the lack of a regular preaching ministry in the parishes and dioceses of Western Europe.

The friars were highly educated 'university' men, but they were trained to communicate well with simple people.[52] There was no need always to say something new: a preaching friar could use the same sermons again and again as he travelled. His impact was likely to be heightened by his local novelty-value. Here was a different voice from that of the parish priest the people usually heard, if he preached regularly at all.[53] The Franciscan historian Salimbene di Adam (1221–90) says Berthold von Regensberg was so successful in frightening people with his descriptions of the Last Judgement that they begged him to stop because they could not bear any more. Popular taste evidently favoured a good story, preferably involving miraculous powers or magic.

Preaching is the sowing of seed, says Pierre de Reims, prior of the Dominican house in Paris between 1227 and 1230. The seed bears fruit when it moves people's hearts to repentance and confession. The friars developed their own handy portable reference books for use when they heard the confessions their sermons prompted.[54] Indeed, it was not long before the hearing of confessions became a regular mendicant task,[55] and one where the nobility and the mendicants alike took full advantage of the special relationships of high-level influence that were possible.

The friars quickly caught on to the fact that people of all classes enjoyed a good story and would be more likely to remember what they were taught if it was enlivened in that way.[56] Étienne de Bourbon (d. *c.*1261) became a Dominican, studied at the University of Paris and became a noted collector of good stories.[57] Caesarius of Heisterbach (*c.*1180–1250) wrote a popular *Dialogue* full of stories that could be employed in sermons.[58]

Jacques de Vitry (*c.*1150/60–1240), a former student of theology at Paris, became a campaigning leader in the Church who applied his preaching skills against the heretics and in support of crusading ventures. He preached in support of the Albigensian crusade and actually led an army to Toulouse in 1214. In the late 1220s he was again preaching against the Albigensians. He also preached in support of a crusade against the Saracens, and was rewarded by the pope with the bishopric of Acre. Jacques was made Patriarch of Jerusalem shortly before his death. He said it was vital for the preacher to make extensive use of good stories to keep the attention of the congregation or it may grow bored and fall asleep.

Some of Jacques's stories[59] had a long Christian heritage, originating from as far back as the first hermit monks of the early Christian Egyptian desert, perhaps by way of Cassian's discussions (*Collationes*) with his monks in Gaul. In one such story, a young man is tempted by the flesh to leave the desert, but is sharply reproved by a desert 'father'. On his way back to the world he meets a holy abbot. The abbot prays that the desert father will learn what it means to be tempted. The desert father duly suffers the temptations of the flesh himself and decides to return to the world. But he too meets the holy abbot on his way back to the world and the abbot reproves him for being so harsh with the young man.[60] God can rescue any situation and turn it to good, claims Jacques de Vitry, giving an example from his own times. A certain knight is captured by Saracens on pilgrimage to the Holy Land along with some Templars. The Saracens hate the Templars and consider they are entitled to kill them. So they do so and when the knight explains that he is just a pilgrim, they refuse to believe him and kill him anyway. But he still counts as a martyr in the eyes of God.[61] The Devil was also employed in stories, giving an opportunity for topical satire which suggests that congregations may well have been up to date with current events. For example, in one story, the Devil writes to some Sicilian bishops to thank them for sending on to him all those entrusted to their pastoral care.[62]

Stories about corrupt clerics seem to have been enjoyed by a population only too ready to criticise the powerful, privileged and wealthy, especially if they abused their power or were involved in financial corruption. One story tells of an avaricious priest who refuses to bury a young man's mother unless he is paid; but the young man is too poor to pay. So the boy puts his mother's body into a bag and takes the bag to the priest and tells him it is wool which his mother had spun and worth a good deal. The priest opens the bag and is overcome with shame. He then buries the boy's mother for free.[63] In another tale, a priest is told by his bishop to chose between his mistress and his parish. The priest chooses to give up the parish, but the woman leaves him because it was a rich parish and now he is poor. He gets what he deserves.[64]

Sometimes a cleric is the hero of these stories, setting the right example. Here, clergy are depicted taking a firm line. For example, some Dominicans hear the confessions of nuns in various convents and consider all nuns were probably just as shocking, so they use them as examples in their sermons and cause general scandal.[65] Another tale is of a parishioner who always donates debased money or does not pay his tithes at all. The priest puts one of his bad pennies into his mouth at the Eucharist, and the parishioner is so upset that he makes his confession to the priest.[66]

Stories about confession and penance and the importance of cleansing before death are common, sometimes depicting the tussle between a cunning Satan and a just God. One such is of a man with a serious sin to confess but who is too ashamed to do so until he is near to death. Then the Devil, who was looking forward to taking him to hell, pretends to be a priest and hears his confession. He tells the man that the sin is so serious it might cause scandal if he told it to anyone else to discourage him from making confession to a real priest and getting absolution. Then the man dies and the Devil claims him because he had never confessed to a priest. The man's guardian angel objects and says that his intention had been good and the Devil should not profit from his fraud. God agrees and the man goes to heaven.[67]

Animal stories with morals could be engaging. In one, a crow dresses in borrowed plumage but this king of the birds has all his feathers pulled out so he is left naked and ugly.[68] In another, a wild goat's mother taps the ground with her foot and tells the kid to stay while she goes to find food. He is so obedient that he allows himself to be captured rather than disobey his mother.[69]

The Virgin Mary was reportedly particularly helpful in putting right the consequences of sexual sins. In one story, a monk and a pious lady were often seen talking together in church, on religious topics only, it was insisted. But the Devil was jealous of their virtue and tempted them until they fell in love and planned to run away together, with money the woman intended to steal from her husband and treasure the monk schemed to steal from the church. The woman's husband and the defrauded monks set off in pursuit, captured the fugitives and threw them into prison. The miscreants repented and the monk and the woman both began to pray to the Virgin. Then the Virgin appeared to them, very angry. She could ask her Son to forgive them, she said, but what was she to do about the scandal they had brought upon the religious orders? In the end, she called upon the demons who had seduced the pair to put things right, and they undid the deed. The angry husband found his wife at home at prayer and the monks found their treasure where it had always been, in a still-unbroken container. The wife and the monk appeared to be still in prison but suddenly they revealed themselves as demons in disguise. The demons admitted what they had done and the scandal was undone, for the people believed that the misdeed had never really happened and it had all been the work of demons in the first place.[70]

Vernacular preaching and the 'licence' to preach

The pulpit is where the Church spoke to laypeople.[71] The rule was that a person ordained as bishop, priest or deacon (even a sub-deacon) was allowed to preach, with a licence from the local bishop, but normally only if he had 'cure of souls', a parish full of people for whose spiritual welfare he had responsibility.[72] The friars broke new ground when they began their travelling ministry and caused offence by preaching in other people's parishes.

The Church needed to control the right to preach if it was to ensure that popular rabble-rousers did not multiply. In the south of France in the later twelfth century a group of dissidents appeared, known as 'the Poor Men of Lyons' (also called the Waldensians after their founder Waldes or Valdez).[73] These seem to have represented a new 'middle class' of businesspeople or traders in the emerging urban centres. The Waldensians found some sympathetic clergy with whom they discussed the content of Scripture, becoming so proficient that when the Cistercians came to preach against them as 'heretics' they were able to trade quotations and argue back.

Literate laymen were also to be found in north Italy, where sophisticated urban life had survived the fall of Rome better than it had in northern Europe.[74] Jacques de Vitry mentions *laici litterati*,[75] some of whom may have been graduates of the law school at the University of Bologna, a precursor of the modern business school. It may be that the confraternities[76] – associations of lay people with 'vocations' – and families and businesses who did not actually want to become monks or friars included lawyer-laymen.[77] There is evidence too of merchants employing clergy or graduates as private tutors for their sons.[78] In later medieval Flanders, an education was to be had for members of the merchant classes, who would need at least to be numerate.[79]

Medieval life offered little in the way of formal entertainment for the rural laity and not much even in towns. In that context, a local sermon became an exciting event, the more so if it was delivered by someone without a licence, who might have rabble-rousing and controversial things to say. We shall come to these dangerous demagogues in a later chapter.[80]

What of Christian women?

Women had a voice among Christian people in the Middle Ages, but only unusual women. They might be untypical in breaking free of social expectations or in their wilder imaginings. Christina of Markyate in the twelfth century made her name by escaping from sexual abuse by a bishop, then from a forced marriage, to live as a nun or recluse. Her biographer describes how she was visited by demons in her hiding place, bulls with threatening horns and glaring eyes, and how her cell was invaded by toads.

Marjorie Kempe (b. *c.*1373) was 'just a housewife' until she felt a call to pray for the souls of other Christians. The normal way to do this would have been to become a nun or perhaps a hermit. But she found she wanted to be out in the world, travelling on pilgrimage and telling people about her experiences. The birth of her first child was difficult and dangerous and it prompted her to send for a priest so that she could confess her sins. But he handled the moment badly and she did not tell him everything. She then describes what sounds like post-natal depression, a period of more than half a year when she seemed to see devils grinning all about her, threatening her and trying to devour her. She bit her own hand so hard that the scar never healed and she tore at herself with her nails and had to be restrained with ropes. Marjorie confesses that she slandered her husband and her friends and behaved wickedly. Then Jesus appeared and sat on her bed in a purple cloak and she was instantly sane again.

Marjorie's neighbours did not know what to make of her. Some supported her. Some said she was mad or a fraud or a heretic or simply showing off. She certainly seems to have liked to live with a swagger and dressed conspicuously and in fashion, with 'gold pipes on her head and her hoods with multicoloured tippets' so that she should be admired. It could well be that her very ignorance and lack of social status (though her father became mayor of what is now King's Lynn and an MP and an alderman of the local guild of merchants) meant that she was not inhibited by a sense of what was possible for her. She struck a bargain with her husband that their marriage should henceforth be celibate. Marjorie made visits to friars and hermits to discuss her growing sense that she had a special calling. Then she went on pilgrimage to Jerusalem, where she nearly fell off her donkey so overwhelmed was she by the sight of the blessed city, a foretaste of heaven. Her conversion was completed by the strong sense she had as she visited the pilgrim-tourist sites that she has been there with Christ at each of them, including at the very Crucifixion. These experiences were dictated to an amanuensis and so were passed on to posterity. If Marjorie was alive today, she would probably be an avid user of social networking.

Julian of Norwich (*c.*1342–*c.*1416) became a hermit and a mystic and the author of the famous assertion that 'all shall be well', for God will bring good out of a still inevitable suffering.

The German nun Mechthild of Magdeburg, too, wrote of life as exile in a foreign land. Her special tasks in her convent at Helfta included teaching the novices and leading the singing, so that she was known as the community's 'nightingale'. In a vision on Quinquagesima Sunday, she felt herself singing with the angels at a heavenly Mass. Singing in worship was antiphonal, a musical dialogue, and that seems to have prompted her to write in the form of dialogues with Christ. Her thoughts were recorded by Gertrude the Great, apparently directly in Latin, and translated into English as the *Booke of Ghostlye Grace*. Mechthild describes penitents carrying their sins on their back to lay them down before the feet of God. There, in an alchemical reaction, they are transformed into shining gold. In Book1.26–31 she writes longingly of heaven in terms of both visual and auditory delights.

Mechthild's conversations with Christ were set in the context of the Mass, when she heard Christ address her 'with a full private sweet speech of love'. This seemed to be a conversation of equals in which she did not feel overwhelmed. When she bowed at his feet, Christ said, 'Rise up my friend, show me thy face.'

Other women of note as Christian writers, such as Gertrude the Great, another product of the rather learned community of women at Helfta, will have their place in this chapter, along with the Anglo-Saxon abbess Hilda who was able to preside authoritatively over a double monastery, including a community of monks.

Here are insights into the minds of uneducated or partly educated medieval women of strong faith and powerful emotionality. Among them were some accused of heresy, as we shall see when we come to the Beguines. Prous Boneta of Montpellier, a Provençal Beguine, in her *Confession* of 1325, which mingled Catharism and Joachism, thought she was the incarnation of the Holy Ghost for the new age and also an angel from the Book of Revelation, the one with the keys. She imagined a new crucifixion, in which she herself would hang from the Cross.[81]

SAINTS, MIRACLES AND MAGIC

What is a saint?

Medieval people were not surprised if a saint (even a dead saint) was said to perform miracles. In his first letter, Paul told the Corinthians they were 'called to be saints' (1 Corinthans 1.2), and his second is addressed to 'the church of God that is in Corinth, including all the saints throughout Achaia'. *Sanctus* (Latin) and *hagios* (Greek) simply mean 'holy', but Paul did not mean to suggest that these Corinthian Christians were all outstandingly holy. His letters reproving them for bad behaviour make that quite clear. The idea that some Christians were 'saints' in a higher and holier way emerged only gradually as the Greek and Latin Churches designed a process of formal recognition or canonisation by the Church.

It was probably popular pressure which gradually created a demand for 'saints' in the stronger sense of the 'especially holy'.[82] The notion that saints might have special influence with God, or so much virtue that there was merit left over when they had 'deserved' to get to heaven, helped to provide a bridge from reliance on the assistance of the pagan gods to having, still, something less high and remote than the one God to turn to. The bones of a saint or pieces of his or her clothing or even a place associated with the saint were thought to contain some of the power of special holiness, which could be 'applied' to meet the needs of a person who prayed to the saint for help.

As early as the fourth century,[83] Christian Constantinople seems to have begun the practice of dismembering the bodies of saints. That created multiple 'relics' of each saint. These numinous objects were placed in containers in which they could be carried on the person as talismans, or in processions, or displayed in churches. The containers were ornate, often made of precious materials, in honour of the saint within. The saint might be honoured simply by visiting him in his casket, or by touching or kissing the container. He might be asked for help or healing.

In Anglo-Saxon England, Bede included many stories of miracles brought about by relics in his *Ecclesiastical History*. He describes how the bones of the saintly Oswald of Northumbria were brought to Bardney Abbey by Oswald's niece and her husband, King Aethelred. She chose the abbey because she was its patron and had done a great deal to enrich it. The bones arrived in a cart or carriage towards evening. But the monks were not pleased to see them, for although they knew that these were the remains were of a saint, Oswald had belonged to another Anglo-Saxon kingdom which had attacked their own; they hated him even in death. So the vehicle was left outside all night with a cover over its contents. And all night long a great column of white light, visible for miles, stretched upwards from the carriage to heaven. By the next morning the monks had changed their minds and were eager to receive the bones with honour.

The bones were appropriately displayed in the church and after they had been washed, the water was thrown away in a corner of the cemetery. For ever afterwards the soil where the water had been thrown had the power to drive out devils if a body was placed there. Occasionally some of the soil was sent to other places to effect a cure. For example, one abbess took some back to her abbey, which stood near a monastery where her brother was abbot. One night a guest in the monastery was seized by a devil and thrashed about in a fit until the abbess arranged for some of the soil to be brought. As soon as it was brought into the porch, the possessed man lay still in a quiet sleep. When he awoke he testified that it was the arrival of the soil that had rescued him, so he was given a tiny amount of the soil as a prophylactic for the future and had no more trouble with possession by devils.[84]

Preparation of a saintly body for burial in the twelfth century is graphically described by the author of the *Life of St. Hugh of Lincoln.* He himself had washed the body and found it astonishingly clean and white. He dried it and dressed it in the dead bishop's episcopal vestments. His body was placed in the church and the vigils of the dead were sung all night. The next day it was decided that because the body had to be taken a long way to be buried, the bowels should be removed. They were found to be miraculously clean, as clean as if someone had already carefully washed and wiped them. They were put into a leaden casket and buried under a marble slab in the Temple Church, ready to be reunited with the rest of his body at the Resurrection.[85] On the way to Lincoln the body performed several miracles, and more were reported once it arrived there. The local people became excited and tried to cut off pieces of the vestments as the body was carried to its burial.[86]

In Orthodoxy the cult of the saints had consistently been strong and central. The distinction of ordinary Christian *sancti* from the specially holy seems to have been made 'official' in the West only in 993 when Pope John XV 'canonised' Bishop Ulrich of Augsburg. Enthusiasm for creating 'saints' grew, and when the Italian-Norman Lanfranc became Archbishop of Canterbury in 1070 one of his first projects was to conduct a clean sweep of dubious Anglo-Saxon 'saints', after making careful enquiries as to their authenticity.[87]

From the late eleventh and twelfth century a special cult of the Virgin Mary developed in the West, encouraged by Anselm of Bec and Canterbury in his *Prayers*, and by Bernard of Clairvaux in his sermons. There was growing popular enthusiasm for prayer to local saints and even local statues and images of the Virgin. This simple trust, redolent of the instincts of the worshippers of pagan gods in Roman times, was natural enough. The Church continued to countenance it because the shrines of saints brought in useful income from pilgrims. But towards the end of the Middle Ages it was challenged by dissidents and reformers. Christ was the only mediator between God and man, they said. He had done all that was needed to save the fallen human race. There could be no place for the alleged 'treasury' of saintly merits, uncertainly based on Jesus' words about laying up treasures in heaven (Matthew 6:19–20).

Miracles and the laws of nature

The educated medieval Christian recognised that there are divinely-appointed laws of nature, which nature faithfully observes. For example, an acorn grows into an oak tree not an apple tree. Common experience taught everyone how the natural world works, spring following winter, harvest the sowing of seeds.

The laws of nature could be changed only by the God who established them. If he caused something to happen that did not accord with the laws, it was not a breach of the laws: it was a miracle. Medieval observers accepted that sometimes God performed a miracle through a holy individual and that when that happened it was a testimony to the holiness and deserving of the saint, who acted as God's instrument and with God's permission in apparently overriding the laws of nature. Caesarius (*c.*1170–*c.*1240) was a Cistercian monk at Heisterbach and the author of a penitential manual written in dialogue form between the Novice and the Monk. In this manual, each topic has a miracle story to illustrate the point.[88] These offer a mine of information on contemporary underlying assumptions about sin and God's response to it. Nowhere was the priest confronted so directly with popular ideas on the subject as in the confessional.

The result of all this was a hybridisation of the rules of natural law with the extraordinariness of miracle. Natural remedies were still to be seen as God-given, but they might be enhanced by prayer. Monks and nuns would treat their colleagues and there might be a *medicus* in the abbey who would also treat local lay people, but even physicians might ask for a saint's help in effecting a medical cure. Healing miracles often begin with tales of the steps the sick took to heal themselves before turning to the saint. The patient might be recommended to offer a saint a candle with a wick as tall as the patient in order to improve the chances of a cure.[89]

God might intervene directly to make a miraculous event edifying for observers as a token of his approval of the Christian heroism of the saint. Abbo of Fleury wrote about the 'martyrdom' of St Edmund, who had been king of East Anglia during the period of the Danish invasions in the late ninth century. The invaders were prompted by the Devil, says Abbo. They came in their ships and slew men, women and children, harassing innocent Christians, and demanded that Edmund should hand over gold and treasure and become a mere vassal-king. Edmund sought episcopal advice and the bishop counselled giving in. The king refused and said he would rather die for his country.

Edmund faced the advancing marauders unarmed, because he wanted to imitate Christ when he faced his own accusers. He was tied to a tree and insulted and beaten, just like Jesus facing Crucifixion. Then the Danes shot arrows at him till he looked like St Sebastian who had been executed on the orders of the Emperor Diocletian in a rain of arrows. Last of all Edmund's head was cut off and thrown into the bushes. An eyewitness hidden nearby was able to report all this in detail later, the storyteller explains.

The local people came to see what had happened and began to search for the head. God ensured it was safe by appointing a wolf to guard it day and night. As the people called out for the head, it answered them until they found it between the paws of the wolf, who was very hungry by then but would not eat it. The people took the head away, praising God for the miracle, and the wolf came too, until they neared the human settlement, when it quietly went away.

Aelfric of Eynsham had many edifying tales to tell when he preached a sermon on a saint's day. The day for celebrating saints Julian and Basilissa fell on 9 January. Aelfric related how Julian wanted to remain a virgin and Christ gave him a wife who felt the same. On their wedding night the bride-bed was filled with the scents of lily and rose and all desire for his wife left Julian. They lived chaste and almsgiving lives and founded religious houses, but were martyred around 300. According to Aelfric, the whole story was very long and too dull to tell in full, so he relayed an abbreviated version.[90]

The writing of the *Lives* of saints soon became quite a medieval industry in the West, and a natural place to look for the especially holy was a monastery. From the late eleventh century it was even possible for a monastery to hire a professional hagiographer such as Osbern of Canterbury to write a 'saint's life' or hagiography of a deceased abbot, in the hope that he would be canonised. In his biography, the dead abbot would be credited with all the signs of sanctity the genre expected, such as a vision by his pregnant mother, a decision to give up secular learning or a secular position, miracles performed and so on. If canonisation ensued, the monks could expect a lucrative pilgrimage trade, at least from visitors in the locality. If the saint was more prominent, pilgrim-tourists might come from a much greater distance. This was worthwhile because a well-written *Life* could help towards canonisation, and canonisation could bring local people and even long-distance tourists on pilgrimage, furnishing wealth for the monastery by way of gifts and the purchase of souvenirs.[91]

Some of these cults were comparatively short-lived, but other saints venerated in the West endured in the religious imagination of people distant from their places of origin.[92] Saints in the Greek East were and remain still more central to local popular veneration. Those seeking the healing help of the Virgin still hang small depictions of the affected part of the body near the icon, praying perhaps for an eye or an elbow to be mended or healed.

Magic and devilish deceptions

Belief in magic persisted alongside this comforting conviction that if something happened in breach of natural laws it was God's will and intended to be instructive and edifying. Devils had magical powers. They were fallen angels and had not lost their high spiritual abilities when they sinned against God. But now they used them to frighten and upset and to seduce souls from the love of God to join them in hell. There are innumerable tales of such devils' work in medieval literature, intended to be as vivid and compelling as the stories Augustine had related when discussing the same phenomenon in Book VIII of *The City of God*.[93]

A medieval saint had one function which sharply distinguished him or her from an old pagan god. Saints were not merely spiritually powerful; they were good. Christians would do well to emulate them. But they would also do well to be alert to the Devil's cunning attempts to pervert Christians' attempts to imitate the saints. In one story a certain monk lay prostrate in prayer before the altar. God made him so full of contrition that his tears soaked the ground. But the Devil was watching and he put it into his mind to feel rather proud of this achievement. The monk congratulated himself and wished people could see how wet with his tears he was making the ground. So he lost all the spiritual benefit of his contrition through his vanity.[94]

It did not follow that Christians should try to test the authenticity of devilish activity. A certain knight asked for a demonstration of necromancy ('black magic'), for he questioned whether demons really existed. He was warned that it was horrible and dangerous to see a demon but the knight insisted that he wanted to see one called up. He agreed to be tied up to keep him safe. Then he saw herds of pigs and high winds heading his way, followed by a horde of cunning temptations. When it was all over he was left very pale. He has never recovered his former colour, but now he believes in demons.[95]

The desire to test stories of the wonderful was often treated as something to be punished.

> I will tell you a true story of something amazing which really happened. Some young students of nigromancy from Swabia and Bavaria at Toledo in my time hearing stupendous and incredible things from their Master went to him and said they wanted a demonstration. The Master drew a circle round them and instructed them to stay in it and not come out on pain of death however they were tempted. The Master summoned some demons with chants and they appeared ready armed in military formation and surrounded the students. They used every military trick to coax them out. Then they turned themselves into beautiful girls who sang and danced to tempt the boys out. As the dreadful consequences unfold the Master protests that this was none of his doing; the students had forced him.[96]

As fallen angels, demons were able to take many forms.[97] In one tale, a demon had been busy tormenting a man horribly. One of the bystanders asked whether this devil would not prefer to go back to heaven. He answered that he would rather, if he had the choice, take one deceived soul with him to hell rather than return to heaven. His vocation was now to capture souls for hell.[98] The belief was that demons were not happy in their wickedness, any more than humans.[99] In another account, a demon had been tormenting a woman, without success, and was challenged by a junior demon who thought it might be preferable for the two demons to try to get back to heaven themselves. The senior demon, aware that there was no hope of heaven for himself, preferred to concentrate on tormenting a human soul.

It is not difficult to see why exciting stories about demons and their doings were so popular. In one case, that of ‘a well-known woman’, the devil who had taken possession of her was said to have done so at the invitation of her husband.[100] This was the stuff of modern popular newspapers, the medieval equivalent of celebrity scandal.

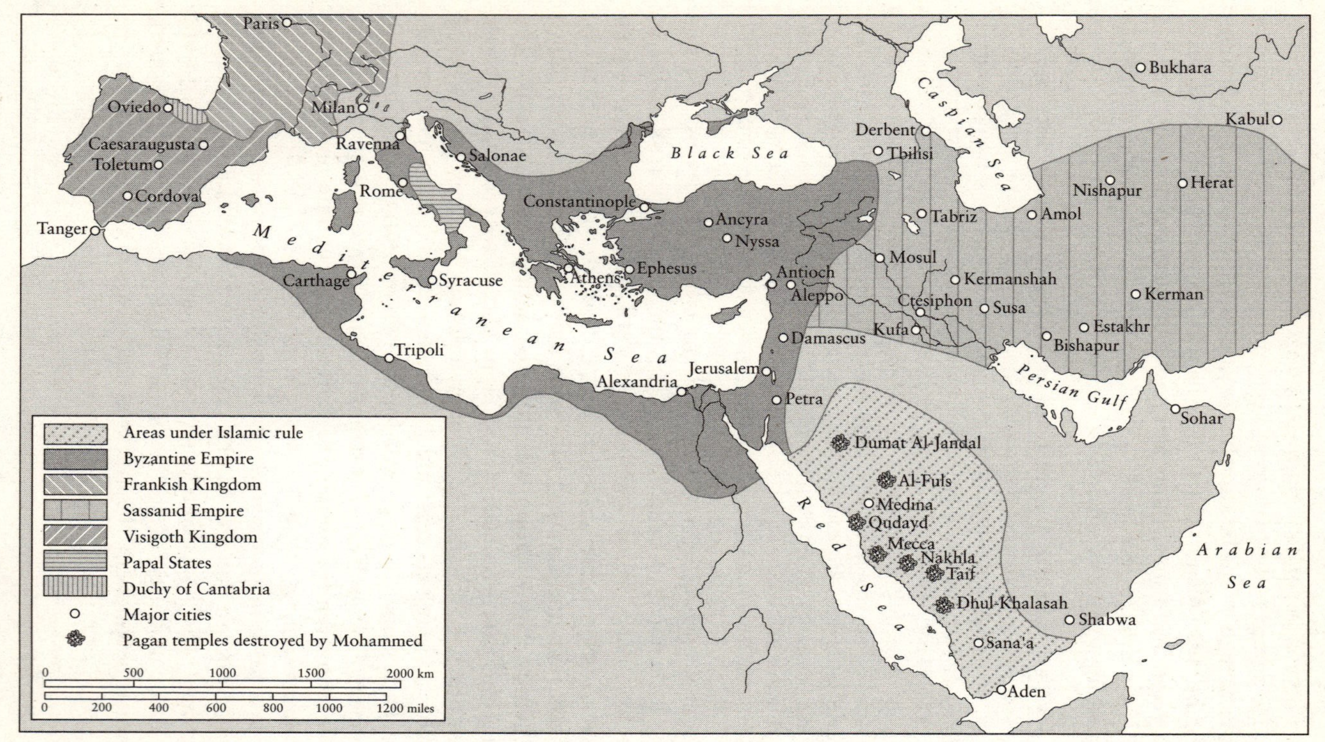

Map 4: The spread of Islam up to AD 632

4

CHRISTIANS, JEWS AND MUSLIMS

A MULTI-FAITH WORLD

THE SPANISH MELTING-POT

How were medieval Christians to live and work in societies where there was a substantial Muslim minority or even a majority and a community of Jews? The resulting arrangements did not derive from any clearly articulated principles of equality or ideals of 'human rights'; such notions would have been anachronistic. Jews lived in a pragmatic accommodation with Christian and Muslim societies alike. Muslim communities were present in Spain and parts of the Byzantine Empire and areas of the Middle East and North Africa where it was not necessarily the case that the Christians were in the majority or in control. The relatively short-lived crusader Middle East had only a limited effect in 'Christianising' the birthplace of the Christian religion.

Medieval Spain probably went further than any other part of Europe in arriving at practical arrangements to accommodate the multicultural realities of the mixed 'faith' populations of both Christian and Muslim territories. The Charter of Jaca (in north-east Spain), dated about 1077, contains rules to govern the good behaviour of citizens, protect property and maintain good order. This was a Christian not a Muslim city. Christians involved in disputes were allowed to seize a neighbour's Saracen servant (man or woman) as a pledge. The Saracen must be held in the palace and given food

Fig. 16: Cathars being expelled from Carcassonne in 1209

(bread and water) and treated as a human being (*homo*) and not left to starve like a beast.[1]

Further south it was Muslim territory and there, too, rules of conduct were enacted, intended to make for civil order in a multicultural society but reflecting different priorities. In early twelfth-century regulations for the Seville market, eating truffles near the mosque was forbidden because eating truffles was a sign of a dissolute person. There were rules on hygiene to prevent people unknowingly buying rotten food. Grocers and apothecaries were not to make and sell medicines, only physicians. No one serving as a bath attendant, masseur or barber should walk about the baths half-naked (i.e., without appropriate clothing). Drunkards must not be flogged while drunk; the authorities must wait until they are sober again. Catamites must be driven out of the city.[2]

The contribution of the Jews

The Jews had valuable skills to offer to both Christian and Muslim governments.[3] The picture of Jews as high-powered 'facilitators' in Christian–Muslim relations in Spain contrasts oddly with the story told elsewhere in this book[4] of widespread medieval Christian hostility to the Jewish people in their diaspora communities throughout Europe. In the Iberian Peninsula, Sephardi Jews, settled from about the year 1000, evolved a language derived from Old Spanish and Hebrew with some Aramaic elements known as Ladino. This took place without the community losing sight of its Hebrew heritage. Hispanic Jews with an intellectual bent had their own *yeshivot* schools for studying the Talmud, where they could learn Hebrew grammar, law, sciences and philosophy.[5] This made them the more useful as professional assets to the Christian and Muslim rulers of Spain.

The law forbade Christians from usury, particularly from charging their fellow-Christians interest. Muslims had similar restrictions. The Jews could provide financial services that were needed and also had useful skills as notaries, in law, medicine and diplomacy.[6] Medicine was a common profession for medieval Jews and there was always a need for court physicians. There is evidence that Jews were also involved in what would now be called the pharmaceutical trade, selling medicines in markets as well as supplying them to the wealthy valetudinarian.[7] 'Barber-surgeons' who practised blood-letting as well as cutting hair and shaving, having sharp blades for both purposes, included Jews.[8] Jews offered high-level management skills too, to the point where they themselves might even employ Christians, when in high office or working for the authorities in Muslim territories.[9] Jews with positions at court could become powerful figures in local politics and society. Ibn Shaprut (*c.*915–*c.*970), a Jewish courtier to the Spanish Caliph, seems to have exported some of the ways and style of court life into his local Jewish community. Cultural patronage of Jewish learning could imitate the Caliph's patronage of Muslim learning.[10]

Societies evolved in the Iberian Peninsula, under both Muslim and Christian rulers, which fostered the creation of 'Jewish areas' where Jews tended to live close together, though not necessarily in ghettos (though in parts of Western Europe the Jews clustered in a town 'quarter' that was essentially a ghetto). But at the same time, Christian traders did business in Jewish areas as the Jews did in the parts of towns where the residents were mainly Christians.[11] Some

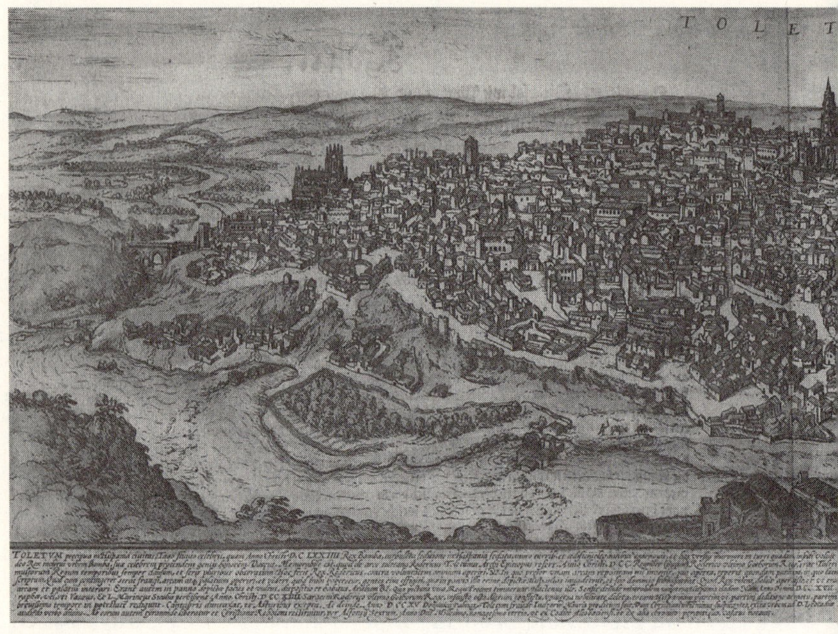

Jews chose to become Christians and there was some intermarriage with local people. That could interrupt the matrilineal descent which, strictly speaking, was necessary to make children Jewish.

This working relationship between Spanish Jews and Christians and Muslims had its ups and downs. Many Jews moved from Muslim to Christian Spain as a consequence of the twelfth-century Almodad persecutions. The reconquest by Christian rulers of Cordoba in 1236 and Seville in 1248 shifted the balance of power between Muslim and Christian rulers. As the Christian kingdoms of Portugal, Castile-Leon and Aragon became dominant and flourished, Jews found they could make a good life for themselves as artisans, merchants and even courtiers in Christian Spain as they had done in Muslim Spain.

CHRISTIANS BEGIN TO READ THE QUR'AN

Why Toledo?

Toledo was taken by Christian forces in 1085, the first Christian reconquest of a significant Moorish city in the Spanish Peninsula.

Fig. 17: A picture-map of hilly Toledo as it looked at the end of the Middle Ages, from Braun and Hogenberg, *Civitates orbis terrarum* (1589)

For a century, Toledo remained a Christian town within a Muslim region.[12] The city, on its strategically placed hill in central Spain, proved to have staying power as an important centre of government, trade and the cultural influences that trading activity brought with it. It had been notable in trade and government since Roman times, and after the Empire fell, it remained important as a Visigothic capital. Then when the Moors entered Spain and conquered the region, it became part of the Caliphate of Cordoba.

A series of challenges beginning in the eighth century eventually fitted it peculiarly well to become a polyglot centre in which Catalan, Basque, Arabic, Hebrew and Latin were all spoken, as well as the late Latin Mozarabic language spoken by Christians living in Muslim territory. In the early tenth century, a Basque Emirate had been formed by a group apparently descended from both Arabic and Visigothic families, before the area was conquered for the Cordoba Caliphate.

Toledo became a notable centre for Arabic and other library collections. It had the largest Jewish community in medieval Christian Spain, and many had a command of Arabic as well as Latin and the local vernacular.[13] The Jews had established a learned community studying Greek science and philosophy.

Here was a place where Christian scholarship could now flourish and where it could draw on both the thought of the ancient world and the sacred books of Islam. For Arabic was the exception to the rule of Roman times that there were two languages for educated men in Europe, Greek and Latin, and in the West in post-antiquity, in reality only Latin. The Arabs were ahead of the medieval Latin-speakers – by several centuries – in translating many of the ancient Greek philosophical and scientific texts into their own language. The motives for this seem to have been political as much as scholarly. The Arabs needed to be able to challenge the claims to civilisation of the Persians and the Byzantines and demonstrate that they too were 'learned'.[14]

The translators brought together and organised by Al-Kindi (*c.*800–*c.*870) are likely to have been Byzantine or Syrian Christians. They provided him with texts for the task of interpretation and synthesis designed to win cultivated Arabs to the view that they could learn from Greek thought and that it was potentially acceptable to Arabic theologians. For this was also a period of energetic debate about Islamic theology.[15]

Greek philosophical works – with the exception of Aristotle's logic, two books of which Boethius (*c.*480–524) had translated – meanwhile remained largely lost to the West until the late twelfth and thirteenth centuries. Western access to most of Plato only began in the fifteenth century. Avicenna (980–1037) produced in his encyclopaedia, the *Kitâb al Shifâ*, a comprehensive handbook to subjects that were of growing interest to the eleventh and twelfth century West, including astronomy, cosmology, medicine and mathematics.[16] It was not an easy book to translate. Between 1151 and 1166, Ibn Daoud made a literal translation of part into Castilian, and Dominicus Gundissalinus (fl. mid-twelfth century), Archdeacon of Toledo, turned that into Latin – more successfully than might have been expected. Then he translated the *Metaphysics* with the help of an Arabist called John, possibly Ibn Daoud himself after his conversion to Christianity.

So a 'school' of translators emerged in Toledo where highly-educated speakers of Latin, Arabic and Hebrew were all to be found. Early discussions about how to translate from one language to another had suggested doing it 'word for word', *de verbo ad verbum*. That does not work very well for rendering abstract ideas. Latin, the local Catalan vernacular of the time, Arabic and Hebrew (both Semitic languages) differed not only in vocabulary but also in grammatical structure and in idiom.[17] But much was achieved just the same, as Jews, Christians and Muslims explored together the common ground of ancient philosophy.

Under Raymond of Toledo (Archbishop 1126–51), the cathedral library of Toledo became a veritable translation centre. For some time, the most energetic of the Toledo translators was Gerard of Cremona (*c.*1118–47), an Italian cleric. He arrived in Toledo in 1167, still ignorant of Arabic but looking for a copy of Ptolemy's book on astronomy, the *Almagest,* which he had heard of. To begin with, he relied heavily upon the help of Arabic speakers. Eventually he seems to have translated nearly 90 works of Arabic philosophy and science, many already translated from the Greek into Arabic and the subject of commentaries and analysis by Arabic scholars.

Among the few Westerners competent to translate directly from the Greek to the Latin was Dominicus Gundissalinus (fl. 1150), who may have been a baptised Jew. He was possibly the first to head the Toledan school in its mid-twelfth century heyday. Until he learned enough Arabic, he seems to have relied for translation from philosophical works originally written in Arabic, such as those of Avicenna (*c.*980–1037), and on the collaboration of John of Seville (sometimes called John of Spain) (fl. 1135–53). Mark of Toledo also rendered medical works of Hippocrates and Galen from the Greek.[18]

Michael Scot (1175–*c.*1232) found his way from Scotland to Oxford, then to Paris, Bologna and Palermo and at last to Toledo, where he was able to learn Arabic and read Arabic philosophy as well as new works of astronomy. He too joined the translators. Hermann of Carinthia (*c.*1100–60) was another of the principal figures in the Toledo 'school' of translators. Rudolf of Bruges, a student of Hermann of Carinthia and a friend of John of Seville, also joined the translation team. His special interest lay in astronomy and he translated at least one Arabic work on the Astrolabe, which he dedicated to John.

Robert of Ketton (*c.*1110–60) was an Englishman, born in Rutland, who had studied in Paris and who travelled in 1134–8 with Herman of Carinthia in the East, both learning Arabic. He seems to have settled in Spain by 1141. Robert's great interest was in the

Arabic scientific and mathematical materials. Of Peter of Toledo's life less is known, though it is thought he translated the Apology of al-Kindi.

Ibn Daoud (*c.*1110–80), a Jewish philosopher who also wrote in Arabic, was a forerunner of Maimonides (1135/8–1204) in that he regarded Aristotle as 'the Philosopher' and had a high regard for the work of Arabic philosophers on Aristotle's texts, particularly Alfarabi (872–950/1) and Avicenna (Ibn Sina) (b. *c.*980). He encountered some of the problems Christian thinkers faced in the early thirteenth century when the philosophical and scientific works of Aristotle entered the new universities of Europe for study in Latin translations, and it was realised that on the creation of the world and the origin of the soul there were contradictions to be resolved between Christian teaching and these newly accessible 'authorities'.

Did a pilgrimage prompt the idea of translating the Qur'an?

Where did the idea of adding a translation of the Qur'an into Latin come from, making use of all this expertise and enthusiasm? There were numerous Christian visitors to medieval Spain from other parts of Europe, some on business in Arab territory, some on Christian pilgrimage. Since the ninth century, one of the principal shrines of medieval Europe had been that of the legendary burial site of the Apostle James ('Santiago') at Compostela.

An account survives of the Santiago pilgrimage, as it would have been taken about 1140, probably written by a Frenchman who had recently made the journey. Some chapters claim to be by Pope Calixtus or Aymericus the Chancellor, but medieval authors were fond of putting famous names to their compositions as 'authors' in hopes of impressing their readers. The narrative offers practical guidance for the pilgrim and a glimpse for the modern reader of the uneasy multicultural mix of the time as it looked to contemporaries. There are comparisons of clothing and descriptions of the appearance of the Basques and Navarrese, who are said to wear similar garments though the Basques have paler skins, are 'repulsively dressed' and eat and drink in a disgusting manner. All classes in a household 'eat all their food mixed together from one pot, not with spoons but with their own hands [...] if you saw them you would think them dogs or pigs [...] Their speech is utterly barbarous.' It is alleged that they expose their private parts to one another and practise fornication with animals. They are rumoured to be descended from those Julius Caesar sent to Spain to conquer the territory and make sure Roman tribute was paid, namely the Nubians, the Scots and the Cornish people with tails.[19]

These debased human beings are said to have had criminal tendencies. The narrative gives further helpful guidance and colourful details of rivers the pilgrim will encounter, with a note of those which are safe to drink from. In some places local people lurk close to the river with sharp knives with which to skin the horses of travellers, if any are foolish enough to drink the water and die.

Translating the Qur'an

It may have been in connection with such a pilgrimage to Compostela that Peter the Venerable, Abbot of Cluny from 1122 to 1156, hit upon the idea of organising a translation of the Qur'an into Latin, with the purpose of enabling Christian apologists to understand the Muslim faith. That there was such a need is clear from the still highly abbreviated notion of Islam to be found in the *Contra haereticos* of Alan of Lille (d. 1202). This has four 'books', dealing successively – and in progressively less detail – with two categories we shall meet again later: the contemporary dualists (such as Albigensians and Cathars) and the rival contemporary anti-establishment dissidents known as the Waldensians. Then come the Jews and finally the Muslims (*Pagani seu Mahometanos*). The Muslim section is by far the shortest of the four.[20]

Peter the Venerable went to Spain himself only once, probably on pilgrimage, in 1141–3. Did he go to get a better sense of Islamic thinking or did the meetings he had on the journey prompt the project to get the Qur'an translated? He took his journey in fairly leisurely stages it seems, for as Abbot of Cluny he could take the opportunity to stay at Cluniac abbeys on the way, visits that were also official visitations. Peter seems to have had an invitation from Emperor Alfonso VII of Leon-Castile to a meeting on Spanish soil.

When Peter arrived at Santa María de Nájera, one of the chief Cluniac houses in Spain, it seems very likely that he met, or was able to begin to bring together, four individuals who could form a team for translating from the Arabic, including Robert of Ketton, Hermann of Carinthia, whom we have already met, Peter of Toledo and Mohammed the Moor.[21] These were not Cluniac monks so it is hard to guess why they might be staying in a Cluniac house (if indeed they were). Robert was soon going to be made Archdeacon at Pamplona, so were they bringing manuscripts from Toledo to Pamplona in order to provide themselves with library resources? The others were probably mainly interested in mathematics and science, but Peter of Toledo would have had an interest in Christian apologetic and the Qur'an translation project. There are indications that the group may have gone on with Peter the Venerable towards Compostela. On the way back, if they accompanied him, he could have dropped off Peter of Poitiers and Robert of Ketton. But whose idea was it to translate the Qur'an?

The commission was quite a tall order. The team translated a series of texts about Islam into Latin, not only the Qur'an, but also the account of Mohammed's birth and upbringing (*De generatione Muhamet et nutritura eius*) and the doctrine of Islam (*Doctrina Muhamet*). The completed task included a collection of other useful materials to arm the Christian to counter the 'heresy' of the Saracens, the *Collectio Toletana*.[22] Peter the Venerable's long letter to his rival monastic leader, the Cistercian Abbot of Cîteaux, Bernard,[23] contains versions of two works of Peter's, the *Epistola de translatione sua* and the *Summa totius haeresis Saracenorum*. It seems uncertain whether the Abbot of Cluny could afford to pay his translators well. Cluny was financially embarrassed and he may have been seeking to raise funds for the abbey on this journey.[24]

Peter of Poitiers, who became a loyal 'personal secretary' to the Abbot of Cluny, kept copies of Peter the Venerable's correspondence with Bernard of Clairvaux. He seems to have developed a special interest in the translation work and could perhaps have been one of the originators of the whole project, drawing Peter's attention to the idea and its importance. He wrote the introduction to the *Contra Sarracenos* and helped with the Arabic translations.[25]

Peter the Venerable mentions in Letter 111 to Bernard of Clairvaux that he is sending a new translation containing a discussion of the 'execrable heresy of Mahomet'. He says he has had it translated by Master Peter of Toledo who knows both languages well, but Arabic better than Latin, so he has also involved 'our brother and son Peter [of Poitiers], who serves as our secretary', to help him. He has made corrections and supplied notes. The word 'Alcoran', if it is translated literally, signifies the 'collection of precepts which that wicked man

Mahomed pretended were revealed to him from heaven bit by bit'. He had also enlisted Ab'dia, a certain Jew, and others of his faith, to translate and assess the fables which they said were 'the dreams of a madman'.

MEDIEVAL JEWRY AND THE BLOOD LIBEL

In 1144 a boy was found stabbed to death in some woods in Norfolk and the Jews of Norwich were accused of ritual murder. The child, whose name was William, was canonised and his life story was written by Thomas of Monmouth (fl. *c.*1149–72).[26] Thomas enhanced his tale by claiming that the Jews of Europe met every year to choose the country in which the child sacrifice of that year was to be carried out. They do this, he said, because they believed a prophecy that this annual sacrifice would eventually lead to their return to the Holy Land.

Medieval Jews may have been found immensely useful as secretaries and courtiers in areas where such careers were open to them, but they also faced claims that they practised the ritual murder of Christian children and used their blood in worship. These ideas may have come from a garbled understanding of the story of Abraham and his willingness to sacrifice his son Isaac (Genesis 22.2–8) and from the use of the blood of sacrificed animals in Old Testament rituals. In 1171, Jews were accused of committing ritual murder in Blois, prompting a lynch mob to set upon a Jew accused of murdering a child together with his Jewish supporters; the Jews were beaten, tortured and then burned alive. A purge of Jews followed in this locality and some of those who would not convert to Christianity were killed. Many examples survive of episodes of local violence against Jews in English towns in the twelfth century, involving burnings and killings.

Children rumoured to have suffered at the hands of the Jews might even be made saints, as happened to Hugh of Lincoln (d. 1255) and later to Simon of Trent (d. 1475). Hugh's case became famous enough to be mentioned by Chaucer. *The Prioress's Tale* tells the story of a child in an Asian city who sings a Christian hymn as he walks through the Jewish quarter of his home town. Satan tempts the local Jews to murder him and throw his body onto a dungheap. His grieving mother finds his body, and it begins to sing the hymn and goes on singing all through the Mass intended to be the boy's

Fig. 18: A miniature from the *Grandes Chroniques de France* of Jews being expelled from France in 1182

requiem. The offending Jews are dragged through the streets tied behind wild horses and then hanged. The story ends with a mention of Hugh of Lincoln, for his story seemed similar, except that his body was found in a well belonging to a particular Jew, and the king became involved in the matter. Ninety-one Jews were said to have been taken to London where many of them were executed over that affair, though some were reprieved at the request of the Franciscans.

This all reflected – and heightened – a popular Christian suspicion of the Jews which both Church and state reinforced in various ways in the West during the high Middle Ages. In 1215 the Fourth Lateran Council decreed that Jews should wear distinctive clothing (a badge or a pointed skull cap, the *pileum cornutum*) so that they could be distinguished at a glance from Christians. This requirement was further enforced in Vienna in 1267. In 1229, King Henry III of England imposed a tax on half the property owned by Jews. They were also required to worship very quietly in their synagogues so that the sound would not upset passing Christians, and were not allowed to employ Christians as servants.

Louis IX (1214–70) expelled the Jews from France, as did Philip IV (1268–1314) and Charles IV (1294–1328). In 1290, Edward I expelled the Jews from England. Many set off for France but some were thrown overboard by ship's captains on the way. Medieval kings were not averse to seizing the property of the Jews when they wanted to raise money. During the Black Death of 1346–53, Jews in France and Spain were accused of causing the pestilence by persuading lepers to poison the wells with their disease. Pope Clement VI tried to intervene by issuing two Bulls during 1348 insisting that this rumour was the work of the Devil, but many Jewish communities across Europe were disrupted by popular revenge. In 1385 the German emperor Wenceslaus arrested Jews living in Swabia, seizing their books, and expelled the Jews from Strassburg after a 'community' or popular debate. In 1391 the Archdeacon of Ecija began a campaign which – it was said – led to the death of 10,000 Jews as it spread across much of Spain, wiping out whole Jewish communities. Synagogues were taken over and turned into churches. A moratorium was attempted by Pope Martin V in 1422 when he issued a Bull to stop the Friars inciting Christians to hostility against Jews, but he withdrew it only a year later.

A more complex picture

This broad-brush picture of anti-Jewish Christian attitudes is not the whole story. Jews and Christians were living in proximity all over Europe and their relations were in reality far more complex, and not only in Spain. Judah al-Harizi (1170–1235), in his *The book of Tahkemoni,* says he was with a group of Jewish friends one day when they met a newcomer to the city who claimed to be a popular astrologer. The astrologer attracted a crowd of citizens and put on a showy performance of being able to tell the future. The Jewish friends then agreed to ask him 'When shall salvation come to the sons of our scattered nation?' The actual form the question was to take was 'When shall the Fallen one [meaning Israel (Amos 5.2)] be restored?' The astrologer did his calculations and then said 'You are of the accursed Jewish race.' Then the watching crowd dragged the group of Jewish friends through the streets, spitting on them, and threw them down before the magistrate of the city and accused them of treason. The magistrate imprisoned them overnight for their own safety and then set them free.[27]

Stories told by Caesarius of Heisterbach indicate this complexity of social attitudes to Christian–Jewish relations in the thirteenth century. In one anecdote, a beautiful Jewish girl was desired by a young clergyman, who seduced her and slept with her, but they were discovered in bed together by her father.[28] From the priest's point of view it seemed that sexual misconduct with a Jew might be regarded as less serious than the same act would have been with a fellow Christian. Other stories were told of clergy sexually abusing Jewish girls.

Despite such unedifying instances, it was thought important for Christians to be careful about the impression they gave to Jews and Muslims. An elderly abbot, himself a humble man, found himself on a proud horse which whinnied and capered about and would not let him come near the Emperor Frederick. The emperor was offended and the abbot backed away, blushing with embarrassment, and tried to get the horse under control. The moral drawn from this story by Caesarius of Heisterbach is that we should be conscious of the impression we may give – our reputation before other people is easily damaged. Arrogant behaviour by Christians may lead Jews and Muslims to blaspheme against Christ in disgust.[29]

'BOOTS ON THE GROUND': PILGRIMAGES AND CRUSADES

Pilgrims before armies

The medieval Christian invasions of the Middle East entered a Holy Land which already had an understanding of Christianity. This was where Christianity began, and where latter-day Christian communities flourished, including many that were Monophysite. These territories also had recent extensive experience of pilgrim tourism, in which the spiritual journey relied on paid practical assistance, transport, tour guides and opportunities to buy souvenirs. Popular enthusiasm for visiting the places where saintly holiness lingered led to the emergence of pilgrimage routes across Europe and into the Holy Land.

The development of veneration of the saints[30] had its commercial side not only in the Holy Land itself. The Fourth Lateran Council of 1215 (62) deplored the damage to the reputation of the Christian religion when traders pretended to be selling relics of saints using forged documents testifying to their authenticity. The council declared that this practice was to stop. Relics should be kept reverently in the proper containers ('reliquaries') and clergy with responsibility for churches and cathedrals should not allow these merchants to enter the building to peddle their wares. If it was claimed that a 'relic' was newly discovered, it was not to be venerated unless it had the authentication of papal approval.

There was money to be made because popular enthusiasm for relics fed a 'pilgrim trade'. This became the 'mass tourism' of the Middle Ages. A pilgrim might expect to enjoy a holiday adventure as well as a spiritual experience, with the added bonus of an improved hope of heaven or perhaps a cure for an illness. Smaller local shrines attracted fewer pilgrims than the most famous ones, but we have already seen that by the late eleventh century it proved well worth an abbey hiring a professional hagiographer to write a *Life* of a deceased abbot with a view to getting him canonised and making money out of the resulting pilgrim visitors to his shrine.[31]

The great pilgrim sites of the high Middle Ages were Jerusalem, where Jesus was crucified and rose again from the dead; the shrine of the apostle James, who was believed to be buried at Santiago in northern Spain; and Rome, whose first bishop had been the apostle Peter. Pilgrimages to Canterbury did not come far behind in popularity after Thomas à Becket, then Archbishop of Canterbury, was assassinated in Canterbury Cathedral in 1170 in an attempt to please the king, who was embroiled in a bitter dispute with the Archbishop about the respective jurisdictions of Church and state, and the murder sent shock waves across Europe.

Geoffrey Chaucer (*c.*1343–1400) was an author who successfully bridged the gap between an articulate middle class, which lacked an academic education and did not think naturally in Latin, and the intellectuals of the day, who did. Chaucer's *Canterbury Tales* tells the story of a pilgrimage to Canterbury two centuries after Archbishop Beckett's 'martyrdom' there, during which a series of mostly 'worldly' pilgrims tell their own often risqué tales to pass the time on the journey. He could expect to please a readership who recognised the sharpness of the satire, perhaps from their own pilgrimage experiences. Chaucer understood very well that pilgrimage had its social as well as its spiritual context.

Chaucer was not alone in his time in writing pilgrim tales, though others did so in a more pious and less satirical spirit. Some made the story into a fictional 'moral pilgrimage' representing the life of man.

In Guillaume de Deguileville's fourteenth-century *Pilgrimage of the Lyfe of the Manhode*,[32] an allegorical pilgrimage is presented in which the dreamer, having seen the heavenly city, the celestial Jerusalem, in a dream, conceives a desire to reach it. The poem describes the whole of a soul's life on earth. He is born, experiences the sacraments in baptism, and sets out with a pilgrim's scrip and staff. He encounters friends and foes – especially the fearsomely armed Seven Deadly Sins, and later both Satan and Heresy. Early on he is dressed in armour as a knight – as if the journey is to be a chivalric quest with battles – but he finds this too heavy and awkward, so Grace allows him to remove it and set out as a simple pilgrim. There is a shift here from military symbolism, with the soul at first protected by the symbolic armour of God, to a more passive concept: the soul can do little for itself and needs the help of Grace and the Virgin Mary on its journey. Tossed on the sea of life, the Dreamer finds safety by entering the Ship of the Church. At the end of his dream the soul, at death, leaves the body and flies up towards heaven. The Dreamer then wakes up and finds that he is at his monastery in Chalons.

The history of veneration for relics in the Greek East offered parallels with the Western experience. Those who went on lengthy pilgrimages to the shrines of saints, or who brought their requests to their local shrines in Byzantine territories, often sought healing, as can still be seen in Orthodox churches where little pictures of the affected part of the body are hung around the image of a chosen saint. The supplicants sought protection from the temptations of the Devil and wanted a way of getting in touch with God and help to get their needs heard. People have long believed in the efficacy of numinous and holy objects such as relics and the places where they resided. They believed too that prayers to saints could be persuasive.

John of Hildesheim, a Carmelite friar of the mid-fourteenth century, offers an account of the pilgrim process which crosses the East–West division and underlines the essential unity of approach. His story was probably written because Rainald of Dassel had brought the bodies of the Three Kings of the Bible to Cologne in 1164, having taken them secretly from Milan with the aid of a local nobleman, and donated three fingers to the cathedral of Hildesheim. It was suggested that they had reached Milan (where they were found in 1158) from Constantinople, through the agency of Eustorgios. He had persuaded the Byzantine emperor Manuel to give them to

Milan when he was made bishop there (343–*c.*349). They had got to Constantinople because they had been brought there from different places by St Helena. The Three Kings were very popular as saints in the West (though not especially in Byzantium) and a lot of detail had been 'discovered' about their names and lives. John said he had used Eastern (Byzantine) sources in his account.[33]

The Crusades

At the end of the eleventh century an urgent call for help reached Western Europe. It came from the Byzantine emperor Alexios Comnenos (r. 1081–1118). He was fearful at the Turkish invasions threatening his empire, but as it turned out had little understanding of the Westerners' different style of Christian civilisation and the fact that for them the 'Crusades' which followed would trigger fresh encounters with an Islam of which they could know very little unless they lived in Spain. Western Christians did not understand the Byzantines any better than the Byzantines understood them. The schism of 1054 between the Churches of East and West was only a generation old and Urban was shortly to hold a Council at Bari (1098) at which one of the topics for discussion was to be an attempt to mend the divide.

The chroniclers who told the story of what happened bring sharply to life the idealism and impracticality of the crusading ventures, the waste of life, the hungry seiges, the uselessness of Western weapons and heavy horses against the more mobile Arabs with their much faster horses. The chroniclers are less frank about the mixed motivation for the Crusades. For alongside an honest if naïve eagerness to rescue the Holy Land for Christianity, there was also an admixture of baser motives such as the desirability of acquiring new estates in the Middle East, when a noble family's lands in the West had become too subdivided amongst its heirs.

Pope Urban II (1088–99) launched the First Crusade at the Council of Clermont in 1095. Christians in the East were in need of Western help, he said. Byzantium had been attacked by Turks and Arabs, who had conquered as far as the Hellespont. If they were not stopped, all Christendom would be at risk. The bishops, said Urban, must persuade all their people – peasants and nobles, poor and rich, foot-soldiers and knights – to go to the aid of these threatened Christians. It would be disgraceful if these 'worshippers of demons' should succeed in conquering God's people. A 'just war' was recognised by Augustine of Hippo as a war only to defend against attack and restore order. A military campaign to defend a part of Christendom being attacked could certainly be regarded as 'just'. A 'holy war' (*bellum sacrum*) would be something new. The pope gave a promise of heaven to those who reached Jerusalem or died in the attempt.[34] That set the seal of divine approval on the proposed war. There need be no difficulty in putting an army together. Feudal northern Europe was, after all, organised as a military society.

The historian Guibert of Nogent (*c.*1055–1124) was also present at the Council of Clermont, recording his impressions of Urban's speech, in which the pope emphasised that the Holy Land was the Christian's special inheritance even before Jesus walked there and much more so since. In Jerusalem, Jesus died and was buried and rose again. The Church of the Holy Sepulchre in Jerusalem is the most holy place of all for Christians.[35] The Maccabees fought to defend the Temple.[36] You are willing enough to fight ordinary wars, Urban pointed out, so why not this one which is a Holy War? Your enemy is Antichrist, who is not going to attack the Jews or the Gentiles. His very name tells you that he is 'against Christ', so he will attack Christians.[37]

Robert the Monk wrote an account of the council more than two decades later. This too gives a vivid picture of the evils of the 'pagan' foes. A cursed race, separated from God in its hearts, has been invading Christian lands (Byzantium) and the Holy Land itself, burning, desecrating, pillaging, taking and torturing captives. Details of the torture were provided: Christian captives were forcibly circumcised and their blood poured into the baptismal fount. They were cut open and had their intestines pulled out and tied to a stake. Then the captives were flogged until they fell to the ground, or were bound to posts and had arrows shot into them. The women were raped. How could a Christian not wish to avenge these horrors?[38]

Archbishop Balderic of Dol (*c.*1050–1130) also emphasised the sufferings of Christians at the hands of these 'infidels'. Christian blood had been shed and must be avenged. Base and bastard Turks were now in control of Christian lands and had imposed their own superstitious beliefs in place of the Christian faith. Christian property had been seized and Holy Jerusalem polluted, the very Sepulchre in which Christ was buried now pillaged and the offerings left there stolen. Make a little effort, face a little suffering, and your reward in heaven is sure he promised.[39]

Fig. 19: Stained glass window in the Cathedral of St Michael and St Gudula (Brussels) depicting the First Crusade and Godfrey of Bouillon

Setting off

In December 1095, Pope Urban sent a letter to the crusaders who were assembling in Flanders. He announced that he had appointed Adhemar, Bishop of le Puy, to be leader of the expedition on his behalf. The armies were to obey him[40] and were to set out on the day of the Assumption of the Blessed Virgin Mary in August.

The Crusaders included a number of future historians. The cleric Fulcher of Chartres (1059–*c.*1128), who may also have been an eyewitness to the pope's speech at the council, travelled east himself with the crusading nobles Robert of Normandy and Stephen of Blois. He later became chaplain to Baldwin of Boulogne, who settled at Edessa when the Crusade proved successful, so by the time he wrote his history he had first-hand knowledge of crusading.[41] The description of the First Crusade in *Gesta Francorum* ('The Deeds of the Franks') was written by an unknown author apparently attached to the party of another crusading leader, Bohemond, a nobleman from southern Italy, who was already experienced in warfare against Byzantium.[42]

The eager crusaders, not all of the knightly classes, were consciously imitating the Gospel call of Jesus to the disciples to 'deny themselves', 'take up their cross' and follow him (Matthew 16.24). Moved by the preaching they heard all over Europe, they began to sew crosses onto their right shoulders, ready to go. A group led by Peter 'the Hermit' (*c.*1059–1115), a priest from Amiens, was the first to leave. It was made up of a rabble of idealistic but untrained people, apparently mainly peasants and bourgeoisie. Byzantium viewed their progress and arrival with disquiet. They ignored attempts to persuade them to stay and wait for the main army to join them, but were easily eradicated by the Turks who lay in wait for them near Nicaea. A few months behind them came a French contingent, under the leadership of Hugh of Vermandois, another of Italians and another led by Normans.

Anna Comnena, the highly-educated daughter of the Byzantine emperor Alexios Comnenos, wrote his life story in her *Alexiad*.[43] She witnessed the arrival of the crusading parties. They seemed to her mere barbarians, but Bohemond she describes with some admiration as spirited, aristocratic, bold and courageous, though a cheat and a liar. The crusaders were provided with accommodation in Byzantium while attempts were made to ensure that they would fight for the Byzantine good and not for Western benefit.

Anna's father unsuccessfully attempted to persuade the nobles among the crusaders to swear personal oaths of fealty to him, thus becoming, under the rules of the feudal system, in effect his subjects.

Some crusaders attack European Jews instead

As they left France in 1096 some crusaders were diverted into attacking local Jews in the towns and cities of the Rhineland. To the Crusaders' way of thinking, the Jews were just as much non-Christians as the Muslims who had captured the Holy Land. They were also believed to be wealthy, and the crusading armies needed money to pay for supplies. Peter the Hermit presented a letter purporting to come from French Jews at Trier which begged the Jews encountered on the journey to be generous in their financial support for the crusaders. One of the mid-twelfth-century Jewish chronicles, by Simon bar Simson, says this sense of crusader 'entitlement' terrified the local Jews,[44] and not without reason, for some crusaders invited Jews they met to be converted, and if they refused felt justified in seizing their wealth and killing them.

One of the surviving Hebrew chronicles of the First Crusade by an anonymous Mainz author[45] describes a massacre of the Jews as the crusaders passed through the city. Eliezer bar Nathan gives a graphic account (*c.*1146) of the terror local Jews experienced when they heard reports that the crusaders were saying that they might as well attack the Jews too. The Jews prayed and fasted, but it did no good: the army attacked them in their homes, destroying the houses and pillaging and plundering as well as murdering, women and children as well as men. They tore up and trampled on copies of the Torah, laughing and sneering.[46]

Eliezer bar Nathan adds details of Jews killing themselves and their friends and families rather than be massacred by the crusaders.[47] Women even killed their children. Once this had begun, other Jewish communities imitated the behaviour, inspired, says the chronicle, by the courage of those who had died. Mothers and their children, even their newborn babies, were dashed to pieces. Fathers killed their sons, who willingly offered their necks, and then they killed themselves, falling upon the bodies of their sons as they died. The chronicle also says that a French rabbi recited the blessing used in the ritual slaughter of animals before killing himself and dying 'before the Lord'. Some stood and faced the crusading fighters and killed one or two before being cut to pieces themselves. Those too elderly to fight back, sat and awaited their deaths with courage and dignity. This is a response to the massacre which is loosely linked in the chronicle with a notion of martyrdom, though Judaism did not share the Christian (or Muslim) belief that to die for the faith was an act of martyrdom deserving reward in heaven.

The Archbishop of Mainz accepted payment from the local community in return for protecting Jews, giving them refuge in the bishop's palace. A similar attempt to protect local Jews by the Bishop of Trier was not successful. Faced with the fact that the local townspeople did not support him, the bishop told the Jews that he could do nothing for them unless they converted and became Christians. In Cologne, some of the local people took pity on the Jews, offering them shelter in their homes.

The First Crusade arrives in the Holy Land

Moved briskly on as they passed through Byzantine territory, the crusaders made their way south. Their method of warfare was to lay siege to towns and cities in the hope of capturing them. It became tempting to stop at that point and establish little Christian kingdoms in the captured places. Baldwin of Boulogne and his troops gained control of Edessa early in 1098 and he stayed there, treating it as his own. The crusaders then won control of Antioch in the summer of 1098 and lingered nearby for many months. They were in some disarray because Adhemar of Le Puy had died and they lacked a papal legate to lead them. Bohemond seemed satisfied to stay at Antioch and keep it for himself as booty.

Raymond of Toulouse decided to attempt a seige of his own and set off for Maarat. The others, a mixture of knights, junior soldiers and infantry, always at risk of becoming a mere rabble, began now to talk of advancing to Jerusalem without senior leadership. But after Christmas, Raymond decided to turn south and Tancred – Bohemond's nephew – and Robert of Normandy agreed to follow him, which necessitated their becoming his vassals to make it clear who was in charge.

Meanwhile in Jerusalem it was known that the crusaders were coming. The Shia Fatimids, who then ruled Syria, made some overtures towards peace, but the crusaders were not interested. The Christians living in Jerusalem were expelled in preparation for the coming conflict and the wells were poisoned, posing a problem for a besieging army which would itself need water. The crusaders gained the city after some failed attempts once they had a source of supplies from Genoese ships and had obtained the wood to build mobile siege towers, catapults and engines. One siege tower was destroyed in the attack but the other enabled the crusaders to get across the wall and take the city. Massacres followed, with the Muslims and Jews the chief victims. Historians described the victors wading in blood. But there was also much taking of captives. Tancred seized the Temple and its surroundings for himself.

After the capture of Jerusalem, Godfrey of Bouillon took the title of Defender of the Holy Sepulchre (*Advocatus Sancti Sepulchri*). He would not call himself king, for he said he could not wear a crown of gold in the city where Christ died. Raymond of Toulouse would not accept a title at all and set off on a pilgrimage.

The Westerners wanted to establish a local leader for the Church, and Arnulf of Chocques was chosen to be the first Latin Patriarch. He soon claimed to have found the relics of the Cross on which Jesus died. For the army this was a powerful sign and the Cross was carried victoriously into battle at Ascalon in August.[48] Around the Kingdom of Jerusalem, other Western fiefdoms were established. The County of Edessa (1098–1149) was led by Baldwin, while the Principality of

Fig. 20: The Church of the Holy Sepulchre in Jerusalem

Antioch (1098–1268), first ruled by Bohemond, was regarded as St Peter's city, where he had first been bishop. The creation of feudal structures, in which vassals of the new feudal lords were granted land in return for loyalty and military service, was not without its problems. For example, King Fulk faced open revolt from Hugh of le Puiset in 1134. The Kingdom of Jerusalem lasted from 1099 to 1291, when the city of Acre fell.

The Second Crusade and beyond

In 1144, after a series of attempts, some partly successful, Muslims recaptured Edessa, the most exposed of the new crusader states, and a Second Crusade was called. Massacres of the Jews loomed again, when Rudolf, a French monk, claimed that they were not contributing to the cost as they should. Peter the Venerable argued that the Jews should pay for the Second Crusade, for 'the Jew is rolling in wealth and luxuries' (*pinguescit* [...] *et deliciis affluit Judaeus*). He could afford to pay,[49] Peter argued; furthermore, the Jews were blasphemers and far worse than the Muslims: *longeque Sarracenis deteriores Judei*. They had got rich by dubious means: *fraudulenter lucrati sunt*.[50]

King Louis VII of France expressed an interest in leading an army in 1146, and then emperor Conrad III of Germany and Frederick Barbarossa his nephew said they wanted to do the same. The absence of these rulers potentially left their kingdoms dangerously exposed to invasion and disruption. Some Germans, Poles and Danes were keener to fight the Slavs than the Muslims.

Pope Eugenius asked a reluctant Bernard of Clairvaux to preach in support of the new Crusade. Bernard thought he ought to be devoting his sermonising energies to reforming Christian Europe, but once persuaded to preach for the Crusade, his advocacy was so successful that the supply of crosses to be sewn onto shoulders was soon exhausted and clothes had to be torn up to make more for those rushing to enlist as he spoke. Pope Eugenius issued the Bull *Divina dispensatione* in March 1147, in which he declared that participation in this Second Crusade would entitle those who participated to the same eternal reward as the first crusaders. He also permitted those who preferred to fight the Muslims in Spain to do so, with the same rewards on offer.

Crusader numbers bound for the Holy Land this time were comparatively small. It has been estimated that the French brought about 700 and the Germans perhaps 2,000 knights to the Second Crusade. The crusading kingdoms in the Holy Land itself probably furnished a few hundred each. There would have been foot soldiers too, and many camp followers, but it was the knights who represented a more or less professional soldiery. The Westerners did not all favour the same style of combat. One chronicler reports that the French preferred fighting from horseback wielding spears, while the Germans liked to stand on their feet and fight with swords in hand-to-hand combat.

Again, the Byzantines moved the crusaders on, once they had all trickled into Constantinople after King Louis and his men. Manuel, now emperor, tried to extract an undertaking that any conquered lands would be given back to Byzantium. The crusaders were shipped across to Asia Minor, but Manuel refused to add Byzantine troops to their number, as his empire had troubles of its own – Roger II of Sicily had seized this moment to invade the Peloponnese and he would have to be repulsed.

The Western venture quickly became a muddle. The crusader rulers of Jerusalem had held a meeting near Acre on 24 June 1148 to decide what the crusading armies should do next. It was agreed that the greatest threat lay in Damascus, so it was decided that it should be laid siege to. The Muslims ambushed the crusaders when they arrived at Damascus in late July, forcing them to retreat to Jerusalem and harassing them most of the way.

At the beginning of Book II of his five books *On Consideration* (which he began as guidance for the unsatisfactory Pope Eugenius III who had once been a Cistercian monk), Bernard of Clairvaux broke off to review the failure of the Crusade he had preached in support of – against his better judgement. Bernard's *apologia* ran along the following lines. The call to Crusade came from God, but his armies displayed such pride and bad behaviour that they deserved to fail. God has chastised the crusaders. As Bernard himself said ruefully, it is not for us to query God's decisions just because we do not understand them. The crusaders could hardly expect victory if they were always turning back. It was as though Moses had led his people out of Egypt only to find they kept wanting to return there.[51]

Towards the Third Crusade

Yusuf Saladin (1137/8–93) was of Kurdish origin. He proved a considerable military strategist. Ultimately he was to dominate a Sultanate that stretched from Egypt to Syria and which included much of Arabia and some of North Africa. One of the results was a unification of Muslim leadership in the region. Saladin defeated the armies of the Christians occupying the Holy Land at the Battle of Hattin in 1187 and then steadily captured most of the lands of the crusader states, leaving in Christian hands only Antioch, Tripoli and Tyre. It was all done with scrupulous attention to good manners. Foreseeing that Westerners might yet arrive to support the Christian rulers, he had agreed that 'if any king or great noble arrived they were free to give him assistance and the armistice should be renewed on his withdrawal'.[52] Saladin needed to protect trade routes and to take account of the presence of the 'crusading castles' built on the Western European model.

By now, Byzantium was ready to adopt a realist approach to its position and make a secret deal with the Muslims about how to deal with a future crusading venture. They would no longer support the crusaders in order to guarantee their own safety from Muslim attack. The response was inevitable. A Third Crusade (1189–92) was led by kings Richard I of England and Philip II of France. Emperor Frederick Barbarossa of Germany intended to join them, but he was drowned crossing a river on the way. The French and English kings, mutually suspicious, each tried to avoid setting off first in case the other took the opportunity to invade his kingdom.

It was a disastrous expedition, hampered by famine and disease in the Christian and crusading camps. The Crusade ended in some face-saving: in return for agreeing to allow the Muslims to keep Jerusalem, Richard won a concession from Saladin allowing free access to the city for pilgrims and even merchants so long as they were unarmed. A *Life* of Saladin written by one of his staff, Baha al-Din, gives a closer and more personal account of the way a Muslim might regard the Christians.[53] The author came from the educated notary or civil servant class, something of a novelty in Muslim lands, but roughly equivalent to the class now being educated in the Christian West to service the needs of Church and state alike. He described Saladin's nervousness about making peace with the Westerners because he did not trust them.[54]

The Fourth Crusade

After the failure of the Third Crusade, Innocent III, elected as pope in 1198, was anxious to launch another attempt at once, and preaching for a Fourth Crusade began.[55] This Crusade (1202–4) did not attract kings to lead it, but the chronicler Geoffrey de Villehardouin (1160–*c.*1212) emphasises that the noblemen who joined in were very high and powerful persons. Among the French noblemen who took the cross was Simon de Montfort, who developed such a taste for crusading that he later took part in the Albigensian Crusade (1209–29) against the heretics in the south of France.[56]

During the year 1200 there was much conferring about transport, and six envoys were chosen and authorised to enter into agreements if they could find sufficient ships to hire. They arrived in Venice to make arrangements early in 1201 and went to see the Doge. Venice was prepared to build the necessary ships and provision them, in return for a fee for each man and each horse to be carried. Venetian ships would accompany the crusader expedition, and the spoils of any conquests were to be divided equally. The envoys came before a great assembly of the Venetian people in St Mark's Square and affectingly pleaded in tears for the help they needed to rescue the Holy Land.

The crusaders borrowed all they could but found themselves still 34,000 marks short to pay for the Venetian ships they needed. The Doge proposed a solution: the crusaders should lend their military strength to assist the Venetians in recapturing lands taken from them by the king of Hungary, giving the crusaders a chance to win spoils that would enable them to pay what they owed. To encourage them and as a sign of good faith, the Doge took the crusading vow himself.

Meanwhile, in the imperial family of Byzantium a murderous family quarrel was afoot. Alexius, son of the dethroned and imprisoned Emperor Isaac, fled seeking help. His sister was married to Philip of Germany but on his way to take refuge with her he encountered crusading forces assembling to leave. It was agreed that if Philip would support their venture the crusading armies might go to Constantinople and set about recapturing the lands he claimed had been wrongfully removed from him. In return for the crusaders restoring Alexius to his rightful position as heir to the emperor of Byzantium, he would hand over Romania and provide the crusaders with 200,000 marks for their expenses.

The crusading armies were divided about this plan. Some said there was no alternative if they were ever to get to the Holy Land, but others argued that this was not the war they had left their homes to fight. Break-away groups set off for Syria independently, but many died on the way. Some of the leaders joined forces with the king of Hungary, Simon de Montfort among them, and the crusading army became still further depleted.

With its purposes now hopelessly confused, the Venetian fleet with its crusaders set off in spring 1203 and paused at Corfu before continuing the journey to Constantinople. Some went ahead to Acre while the main body stopped off to capture Constantinople. In 1204 the crusaders sacked this Christian city, involving widespread and shameless plunder and rapine. A Latin Kingdom of Constantinople was established, with Baldwin of Flanders crowned as its first emperor. This Latin Kingdom would last until 1261 when the Byzantine Empire reasserted its control, but it was never a success. It quickly fell victim to the stresses of the endless warfare in the Balkans. In reality it was never likely to bring Greek Christianity under the jurisdiction of Rome.

Innocent III was reluctant to leave it there, with the Holy Land itself still under Islam. At his wish, the Fourth Lateran Council of 1215 – very much Innocent III's personal venture – attempted to raise a fresh expedition 'to liberate the holy Land from infidel hands': 'Crusaders are to make themselves ready so that all who have arranged to go by sea shall assemble in the kingdom of Sicily on 1 June after next.' Those nobles who did not propose to fight in person 'should contribute, according to their means, an appropriate number of fighting men together with their necessary expenses for three years, for the remission of their sins'. There was a promise to relieve embarrassed debtors as an additional enticement: 'Their creditors shall be compelled [...] to release them from their oath and to desist from exacting the interest.' The council helpfully added a threat of excommunication to discourage the pirates who were now regularly 'capturing and plundering those who are travelling to and from' the Holy Land. Anyone engaging in trade with them was to be ostracised. Any current wars were to cease until the Crusade was successfully completed. It never was.

This was not, however, the end of the 'crusading movement'. A series of later Crusades was attempted, but the simple clear purpose of the first attempt – to rescue the holy places of Jesus' life from Muslim control and install a Roman Christian jurisdiction – never again came into military focus in the same way. The Western Christians had learned the hard way something the Byzantines already understood regarding the political complexity of the Balkans and the Middle East.

5

SOME HARD TALKING

UNIVERSITIES AND COUNCILS

AN ARGUMENTATIVE CULTURE: THE NEW ACADEMIC WORLD

In 1211 Robert Courson (b. 1160/70), a former student in Paris and Oxford, became Chancellor of the still-new University of Paris. He struck the pope as the right person to head a commission to look into the 'errors' which were being taught there. He tried banning books: a broad range of the new Latin translations of the scientific and philosophical works of Aristotle which had proved hard to reconcile with Christian teaching. He also tried banning modern commentaries on them by such authors as David of Dinant (*c.*1160–1217) and attempted to fix the content of a 'safe' syllabus for Christians to study.[1]

The provision of 'higher education' had previously fallen to monasteries, the aspirations of whose schools depended on the quality of 'schoolmaster monks' they had in the community, and to the cathedral schools. Charlemagne had given instructions that each cathedral should run a school of sufficient quality to ensure that the priests who were canons were sufficiently educated. A number of notable 'Carolingian' scholars was the result, some of whom we have already met,[2] and including Hildebert of Lavardin (1056–1133) who conducted the cathedral school at Le Mans and eventually became its bishop (1096). Odo (*c.*1050–1113), later Bishop of Cambrai, taught in the cathedral school at Tournai for a few years from 1089 until he became a monk at St Martin Tournai.

In the eleventh century it became fashionable for students to travel independently in search of independent 'masters' with whom to study. Masters were 'found' by reputation if they were themselves peripatetics, 'wandering scholars' travelling at will, often settling for a time in cathedral cities where fee-paying students were to be had – for students also congregated to hear notable masters if they were teaching in cathedral schools. Peter Abelard (1079–1142) began as a 'wandering scholar', doing some logic teaching here and there, making his name and attracting fee-paying students. But lecturing in theology carried much more fame and respect, so he went to hear Anselm of Laon lecture at the cathedral school there, declared he could teach theology just as well himself, and lectured the very next day on Ezekiel, one of the most difficult books of the Old Testament.

There were no 'academic jobs' as such at this time, so aspiring intellectuals got their living where they could, with their students often paying fees. At some time between 1110 and 1116, Petrus Alfonsi was teaching astronomy in England. According to one manuscript of Alfonsi's *Disciplina clericalis* ('Clerical instruction'), he served for a time as royal physician to King Henry I of England (r. 1100–35).

Alfonsi tried to produce a Latin version of al-Khwārizmī's *Zīj al-Sindhind*, a set of astronomical tables with accompanying 'canons' or explanatory texts. Walcher of Malvern (d. 1135) and Adelard of Bath (*c.*1080–*c.*1152), two more leading mathematicians, were among his English students. Walcher composed a text on how to predict eclipses, based on the teachings of Alfonsi, and Adelard revised and improved Alfonsi's Latin version of al-Khwārizmī's text. In the 1120s, Alfonsi seems to have been in France. He could be combative and irritable, and his interpretations of the Qur'an and Talmud seem to be suffused with Hispano-Arab religious polemics.[3] He also wrote an open letter of complaint, *Epistola ad peripateticos in Francia* ('Letter to the peripatetics in France'), expressing annoyance that he did not have as many students as he would like, mainly because they did not appreciate the study of astronomy and only wanted to learn grammar and logic.[4]

The driving force in education was not solely intellectual curiosity. Ambitious students might be aiming for careers in the secular or

Fig. 21: Petrus Alfonsi in an interfaith dialogue with Moses the Jew, as depicted in a thirteenth-century Belgian manuscript

ecclesiastical civil service as notaries or perhaps ultimately for high office in the Church. A school at Bologna founded at the end of the eleventh century resembled an early business school in offering training for such careers. John of Salisbury is an example of a student who made his way to high office through a civil service career, spending his years of study in Paris. He describes in his *Metalogicon*[5] the dozen years he seems to have spent lecture-tasting, and what he thought of some of the masters whose lectures he heard. He became a senior civil servant to the Archbishop of Canterbury, mixed with the great and the influential of Europe at the papal and the royal court, and was eventually made Bishop of Chartres.

The basic curriculum of study adopted in this inchoate system of higher education had its roots in antiquity. The 'seven liberal arts' began with the study of Latin textbooks of grammar and logic, proceeded less thoroughly to the set books of rhetoric, making up the *trivium* or 'three ways'. The other four subjects – arithmetic, music, geometry and astronomy – formed the *quadrivium* or 'four ways', though they often got still shorter shrift. A collection of the standard classical and late-antique Latin textbooks still used in the middle of the twelfth century in the cathedral school at Chartres[6] shows at a glance that the gloss and commentary is far more detailed for the grammar and logic books and tails off noticeably as the syllabus continues through the available textbook on the other five subjects.

Wandering scholars join forces and universities become institutionalised

The first 'universities' of Europe were an invention of the late twelfth and early thirteenth centuries. They formed spontaneously in a few cities where there was a critical mass of independent scholar-masters who discovered a common interest in benefiting from attracting a substantial community of students to teach. They formed themselves into guilds or 'corporations' (*universitates*), Paris and Oxford among the first. The medieval craft guilds operated a process of admission on which the universities naturally modelled themselves. The undergraduate students counted as the 'apprentices', Bachelors of Arts were the counterparts of the partly qualified 'journeymen' in other guilds, while the masters of a higher education guild became Masters of Arts. These masters 'approved' successful students by examination and awarded degrees (*gradus*) accordingly.

Universities soon began to multiply and even specialise throughout Western Europe, though they did not spread into the Byzantine Empire. In Italy and elsewhere the institutional model was different to the *universitas* guild of Northern Europe. At Bologna, students as fee-paying customers set the syllabus requirements and even employed or dismissed the lecturers. Montpellier and Salerno gained a particular reputation for medicine, and Bologna developed its 'business school' for law. 'Higher degrees' began to appear, in law, medicine and theology, involving lengthy additional periods of study leading to doctorates. These were 'taught' not 'research' degrees.

There were no admissions requirements for would-be students. The student simply registered with a chosen master in a chosen university and might move elsewhere at will. In this sense the world of higher education was open to all but the requirement of literacy and a sufficient command of Latin to enable the student to follow the lectures presented a practical barrier.

Aristotle challenges Augustine: a problem for Christian doctrine

The issue of 'dangerous' literature now became a potent one. The emergence of the universities coincided fairly closely with the arrival of the 'new' Aristotle, in the form of Latin translations of his philosophical, political and ethical works. This was partly the result of the efforts of the Toledo translators[7] working mainly from Arabic translations from the Greek, and partly a consequence of the work of a few individuals such as James of Venice competent to translate into Latin directly from the Greek.[8]

This new material proved controversial as it became apparent that Aristotle and the Bible often disagreed. Masters teaching the 'arts' course added some of the novel philosophy to the traditional syllabus, and fell into dispute with those teaching the 'higher degree' subjects of law, medicine and theology, especially the theologians. For example, the study of the soul and its origins (Aristotle, *De anima)* was potentially both a philosophical and a theological topic, as was the question of whether the world was eternal as Aristotle said in *On the Heavens and the Earth*, or had had a beginning as described in Genesis.

The new works of Aristotle had been condemned in 1210 in an attempt to stop them being studied in the University of Paris: 'Neither the books of Aristotle on natural philosophy nor commentaries upon them are to be read at Paris publicly or secretly.'[9] The condemnation had no long-term effect, as Robert Courson found a generation later. The attraction of these newly available books was too strong and what they said too exciting. Even when academic censors focused on listing unacceptable opinions and banning them, debate continued.

COUNCILS: WARNING SIGNS OF THE NEED FOR REFORM

The early ecumenical ('general' or 'universal') councils were regarded as having assembled the bishops of the whole Church in order to make decisions binding everywhere. In reality they were far from comprehensive, with the churches of Western Europe rarely as well represented as those of the Greek-speaking East. This sequence of councils came to an end in the eighth century, though the churches of the Greek East always adhered firmly to their findings and would accept no later council as ecumenical in the same way.

At that first spontaneous 'council' reported in Acts 15 it was the 'apostles and elders' who made the decisions. It became the custom for the people of God to entrust the task of 'meeting and deciding' to their leaders. By the Middle Ages the right to vote at a council was limited to bishops. Ordinary people were also excluded from the discussions. In an era when travel was difficult and roads were dangerous it would hardly have been practical to do anything else. The majority of councils (or 'synods', derived from the Greek term) were relatively local, but even so they could not include all the congregations of a province in person. In any case, local councils did not claim to make decisions binding on the whole Church. They concerned themselves mainly with matters of discipline and rites in the dioceses represented at the meeting, and hardly ever with the great questions of faith.

After the schism which divided East from West in 1054, the idea of holding general councils came back into fashion in the West. And whereas the early ecumenical councils could be summoned and dismissed by an emperor, these 'general' medieval Western Councils tended to be called by popes. In the case of the Fourth Lateran Council there is evidence that Pope Innocent III had written the decrees before the council met, and that the role of the assembled bishops was to agree rather than to debate and decide.

Nevertheless, the series of Church councils held in the West during the Middle Ages, some including 'observer' delegates from the Greek churches, provided a useful overview of what was worrying the leaders of the Church. Often it was a problem raised in one way or another by ordinary Christians, though the council decrees were rarely effective in resolving them and they were raised again and again, as we shall see. These also tended to be the same themes that were the subject of protest by later medieval dissidents and were still prominent in the Reformation, so the failure of the councils to put them right had huge consequences.

The Council of Bari

In 1098 a council was held at Bari in southern Italy. Some Greek bishops were invited, for this part of Italy had both its Byzantine and Roman Christian communities. Anselm, Archbishop of Canterbury, happened to be in Italy at the time seeking support from Pope Urban

II (1088–99) in his dispute with the English king. Aware of his fame as a theologian, the pope asked Anselm to explain to the Greeks why they were wrong on the theological points which had caused the division of 1054. Significant among these was the Western addition of the *filioque* clause to the Nicene Creed, implying that the Holy Spirit proceeds from both the Father and the Son. The Greeks maintained that this was unacceptable both because it changed what had been agreed by an ecumenical council and because it imputed 'two beginnings' (*duo principia*) to the Trinity. There was also disagreement about the rights and wrongs of the use of leavened or unleavened bread in the Eucharist.[10] Anselm asked for a few days to compose his thoughts and then made the attempt, reflecting further and writing considered treatises on these matters a few years later.

The Greeks were not persuaded by Anselm's arguments, and we shall see the discussion continue.[11] The resulting bad blood between Greek and Latin Christians was vividly described in a decree (4) of the Fourth Lateran Council of 1215. This maintains that as a consequence of the schism the Greeks detest the Latins. They have even been rebaptising those baptised by the Latins, which was the ultimate proof that they did not consider the Roman Christians to be Christians at all. The council 'ordered' the Greeks to 'conform themselves like obedient sons to the holy Roman church, their mother, so that there may be one flock and one shepherd'. This ecumenical recommendation begged the question as to which Church was right in its views, a theme that would recur. It also, more practically, tried to make provision (9) for mutual tolerance of 'difference of rites within the same faith', for 'in many places peoples of different languages live within the same city or diocese, having one faith but different rites and customs'. This raised the question of where the boundary lay between 'faith' and such matters as small liturgical variations.

The Investiture Contest and the First Lateran Council

The first medieval council in the West which saw itself as a 'general council' was held in 1123. It met in St John Lateran, the cathedral in which the seat (*cathedra*) for the Bishop of Rome had stood since the Emperor Constantine ordered it to be built in 324. This was to be the first of a series of four medieval 'Lateran Councils', whose rulings give a lively impression of the problems facing the twelfth- and early thirteen-century Church in the West.[12]

Fig. 22: Investiture: a king illegally hands a new bishop the pastoral staff of his office, which only the Church had authority to do

The most urgent matter for the First Lateran Council to address was political as well as ecclesiastical. It was the Church's responsibility to consecrate a new bishop, but the local ruler as landowner had to grant the use of the lands that went with the diocese. Emperors and kings had been exploiting that fact. Royal persons who were mere laymen had been intruding on the Church's role, 'investing' the candidate with the bishop's pastoral staff and putting the bishop's ring on his fingers. It was the dispute about who had authority to 'invest' which had given rise to the power struggle known as the 'Investiture Contest'. It involved a classic 'two swords' dispute and memorable stand-offs such as the humiliating episode at Canossa in 1077. Pope Gregory VII had excommunicated the Emperor Henry IV in 1076, the implications of which Henry could not afford to ignore. If a ruler was excommunicated his people were free to rebel against him, for some said that they too suffered the spiritual consequences of being cut off from the hope of salvation. So the emperor journeyed from Germany in snowy January to meet the pope at Canossa and ask for the excommunication to be lifted. The pope made him wait, and when he eventually came to meet him mounted on a horse, the emperor was forced to kiss his foot in its stirrup. This was a symbolic act of vassalage and amounted to conceding that of the two powers, spiritual and secular, it was the secular power that was the lesser.

A concordat was signed at Worms in 1122 between Henry V, now emperor, and Callistus II, who was then pope. The agreement was that lay rulers would be confined to the 'temporalities' or secular aspects of the making of bishops, and leave the 'spiritualities' to the Church authorities. The First Lateran Council formalised the position (8) by threatening sanctions against any lay ruler who interfered in ecclesiastical and sacramental matters. Lay persons, it underlines, 'however religious they may be, have no power to dispose of any ecclesiastical business [...] Let the bishop have the care of all ecclesiastical matters, and let him manage them as in the sight of God.' The First Lateran Council was called immediately afterwards, bringing together 300 bishops and twice as many leading abbots to approve and ratify the concordat.

The Second and Third Lateran Councils: the problem of unworthy priests

The First Lateran Council was followed by a second one in 1139. The immediate trigger was the need to resolve a papal schism, one of many during the Middle Ages. Pope Innocent II (1130–43) had spent eight years embattled with a rival claimant. He wanted it agreed that the 'acts' of the antipope Anacletus II should be disregarded.

The council took the opportunity to respond to mounting popular outrage about the 'unworthiness' of some of the clergy. It had been accepted from early in the history of the Church that if a sacramental act was properly performed by a validly ordained minister it 'worked' (*ex opere operato),* for the grace of God would act. However, clerical misbehaviour greatly offended the laity. How could they accept that their own eternal future depended on the ministry of such patently sinful individuals?

Late in the eleventh century the ecclesiastical authorities had taken issue with simony, named after Simon the sorcerer who tried to 'buy' powers from the apostles (Acts 8.9–24). This practice had

Fig. 23: Painting by Hans Collaert the Elder, *c.*1560: clerical fun and games. An amorous nun with an abbot and a monk, pictured in a later age but showing the sort of behaviour the medieval councils constantly criticised

become increasingly common as noble families tried to buy clerical 'livings' for their relations. Priests who held parishes that produced generous incomes (based on the one-tenth tax or tithe) might be ready to sell. There had also been serious attempts to enforce clerical celibacy. These abuses were linked, since a priest keeping a mistress (*fornicaria*) and having children might well be desirous of 'buying' a 'living' for a son destined to become a clergyman in his turn.

The anti-establishment dissidents whose voices were now being heard were protesting about clerical corruption, greed and incompetence. They argued that it could not be possible to get to heaven by depending on these bad examples to act as mediators just because they were ordained ministers of the sacraments. Such scandals proved hard for councils to eradicate, though one after another they tried.

Sexual sins were always a preoccupation. It was recognised[13] that the earlier attempts from the late eleventh century to impose clerical celibacy had had mixed results. Lateran II 'absolutely' forbade not only priests but also deacons or even subdeacons to live with concubines and wives, or even to live in the same house with women unless they were close relatives such as a mother, sister or paternal or maternal aunt 'about whom no suspicion could justly arise'. Anyone above the level of a subdeacon found cohabiting with a woman should be deprived of his benefice.

Ministers of God 'ought to be in fact and in name temples of God, vessels of the Lord and sanctuaries of the holy Spirit' and cohabiting with women even in marriage is a route to 'impurity' (Lateran II, 6–7). The laity should respond by refusing to hear the Masses of priests they know to be living in sin. The miscreants (including 'married' monks) should be separated from their partners, for no such marriage is a marriage at all under ecclesiastical law. Then they should do a heavy penance. The same sanction should apply to nuns if they try to marry (Lateran II, 7–8; Lateran III, 11; Lateran IV, 14).

The councils reproved homosexual activity as an 'unnatural vice', for the laity as well as the clergy. Priests are to 'be expelled from the clergy or confined in monasteries to do penance'; laymen 'are to incur excommunication and be completely separated from the society of the faithful' (Lateran III, 11).

Clerical bad behaviour took many forms beyond sexual sins. Lateran IV (15) called on clergy to 'abstain from gluttony and drunkenness' and refrain from taking part in drinking games designed to get everyone competitively drunk. Lateran IV (17) reproved 'carousing priests who spend the morning getting over their hangovers'. Clergy should not take part in hunting either, or 'presume to have dogs or birds for fowling' because that is not an appropriate use of their time. Lateran IV (16) turns to the way the clergy dress and behave, for they are not lay people and should not dress or conduct themselves as though they were. They should not 'watch mimes, entertainers and actors' and should stay out of taverns except when they are travelling and need a meal. They should not gamble or watch gamblers playing. In appearance, they should look like the clergy they are, with a tonsured haircut and plain clothing, 'neither too short nor too long'. They should certainly not try to keep up with fashion: 'Let them not indulge in red or green cloths, long sleeves or shoes with embroidery or pointed toes, or in bridles, saddles, breast-plates and spurs that are gilded or have other superfluous ornamentation.'

These clerical excesses can perhaps be partly explained by the fact that clergy often came from families where brothers and sisters kept up with fashion and enjoyed gaming, hunting and all the pastimes of their social class. Family links are hinted at in the way Lateran IV (19) seeks to stop clergy using churches to store family furniture and that of other people, which made churches look like domestic residences. The local church was in any case a village amenity and Lateran IV (20) stresses that Chrism and the consecrated Host must be kept under lock and key and not left around to be stolen by people who want to use them for magic.

Financial fraud was pervasive too. The Second Lateran Council (1) ordered that 'if anyone has been ordained simoniacally, he is to forfeit entirely the office which he illicitly usurped'. Canon 2 turns to the associated ill-gotten gains 'where the execrable passion of avarice has been the motive'. The guilty person is to lose what he 'wrongly acquired', and the buyer, seller and intermediary were to be 'stigmatised with the mark of infamy'. This evidently failed to solve the problem, for Lateran III (8) made another attempt to stop benefices being promised before they were vacant. Nor was it acceptable to leave benefices vacant for long periods so that the grantor could keep the revenues for himself.

The problem was still on the agenda of the Fourth Lateran Council (63), with the behaviour compared to the 'sellers of doves in the temple' which Jesus had condemned (Mathew 21.12). It was also no justification to claim that it was 'long-established custom'. Such practices were explicitly banned, together (64) with similar corruption uncovered in religious houses, even the houses of nuns: 'The disease of simony has infected many nuns to such an extent that they admit scarcely any as sisters without a payment, wishing to cover this vice with the pretext of poverty.' Anyone caught doing this 'shall be expelled from her convent without hope of reinstatement, and be cast into a house of stricter observance to do perpetual penance'. The council recognised that there were many nuns admitted to convents in this way before the enactment of this decree so special arrangements were to be made for them, moving them elsewhere or as a last resort allowing them to remain, in that case admitting them anew by special dispensation. The same pattern was also evident in the admissions of monks and other religious, and similar remedies were required.

A protection against 'wandering' clerics, sometimes falsely claiming to be ordained, was emphasised in Lateran III (5), which required that no one should be ordained unless he has a 'title', usually a parish, from which an income can be drawn. If that is not possible the bishop should support him until he can give him a role in some church which has wages attached. An exception would be made for someone with a private income or family wealth and here again there was room for simoniacal activity.

The practice of simony extended to the behaviour of bishops too (65). Sometimes when the vicar of a church died, a bishop refused to allow a new priest to be instituted until he had been paid. Bishops also tried to profiteer from the practice of elderly knights or clergy entering religious houses and dying there in the hope of being buried with the monks. Some bishops required a fee to permit this. When found out, the Fourth Lateran Council says, such bishops should pay as a fine twice the amount they have exacted. Parish priests also demanded fees for conducting funerals, marriages and other rites for their parishioners, a concern for the Fourth Lateran Council as it had been for the Second (II, 24). It specified that no fee was to be exacted for Chrism, holy oil and burials.

The fraudulent conduct involved in simony clearly extended to attempts to exact fees for carrying out priestly duties, Lateran III (7) observing that it is:

> utterly disgraceful that in certain churches trafficking is said to have a place, so that a charge is made for the enthroning of bishops, abbots or ecclesiastical persons, for the installation of priests in a church, for burials and funerals, for the blessing of weddings or for other sacraments, and that he who needs them cannot gain them unless he first makes an offering to the person who bestows them.

The eagerness for money was infecting the Church in other ways too, as the councils' decrees show. Lateran II (9) reproves those monks and regular canons who qualify as lawyers or physicians in order to make money. Several of the canons of the Third Lateran Council were concerned with the growth of undesirable money-making practices. Such practices were attracting criticism from groups of anti-establishment dissidents, outraged that the Church should apparently be countenancing such mammon-like activities. Jesus taught his disciples to trust local people to feed them when they preached but not to allow themselves to become burdensome. Canon 4 says that some of the senior clergy, particularly bishops, were making unreasonable exactions. There was evidence of church ornaments being sold to pay for a lavish meal that might entail the consumption in an hour of a quantity of food that would feed ordinary people for many days. The canon decreed that when an archbishop visited a diocese he should not arrive with an entourage requiring more than 40–50 horses; cardinals should not bring more than 20–25; bishops not more than 20–30; archdeacons 5–7; and deans no more than two. These clergy should not arrive with hunting dogs or birds and expect a banquet in their honour.

Clergy who have an income from ecclesiastical sources should not make money in secular professions, even if they are only in minor orders. Lateran III (12) prohibits clergy from acting as 'advocates in legal matters before a secular judge, unless they happen to be defending their own case or that of their church, or acting on behalf of the helpless who cannot conduct their own cases'. Nor should they take on the management of secular responsibilities such as running towns.

Yet more fraudulent clerical activities come to light in the decrees of Lateran IV. Where there are privileges excusing the payment of tithes, clergy had been assigning lands to the holders of the privileges to avoid the tithes (53).

Pluralism and absenteeism were problems because they interfered with the pastoral care of the people of a parish. Lateran III (13) mentions the greed that some clergy exhibited in trying to obtain several livings, even though they were scarcely able to do the duties of one of them properly. They cannot be present in all their livings so they are neglecting their people. There are cases (14) of clergy with six or more churches, an abuse made possible by wealthy laymen having the gift of the livings in question. The abuse is linked with (27) the practice of appointing to livings persons who were not fit to be priests at all. Bishops must ensure that those they ordain are properly trained and suitable for the ministry.

The problems did not go away. The Council of Florence made a number of decisions on clerical misbehaviour noted by the earlier medieval councils. Priestly misconduct continued to offend. Celibacy still proved difficult to enforce, many priests still living openly with 'concubines' and even if persuaded to send one away, might take another.[14]

Priests could become slapdash in various ways. They must perform their duties conscientiously and dress properly. No one who wanted to ask a favour from someone in secular power would appear before him in inappropriate clothing. 'A person who is about to make a request to a secular prince takes pains to compose himself and his words by decent dress, becoming gesture, regulated speech and close attention of mind.'[15] But priests were serving God wearing fancy and fashionable dress. They gossiped and joked in church even in what should have been solemn moments. The council set out in some detail what it considered proper clothing and deportment. Those who are to lead worship 'shall enter the church wearing an ankle-length gown and a clean surplice reaching below the middle of the shin-bone or a cloak, according to the different seasons and regions, and covering their heads not with a cowl but with an amice or a biretta'. Once they are in the choir, '[t]hey shall behave with such gravity as the place and the duty demand, not gossiping or talking among themselves or with others, nor reading letters or other writings'. It shall be made clear what are the 'duties of each canon or other benefice-holder as regards reading or singing at the individual hours during the week or a longer time'.[16]

Clergy discipline

It all added up to a need to take clergy discipline in hand. The Fourth Lateran Council (7–8) therefore addressed the reform of clergy 'morals'. This was to be undertaken by cathedral chapters in the case of cathedral canons and otherwise by the local bishop, in the interests of ensuring the proper care (*cura*) of souls. Bishops should follow a fair procedure as indicated in Scripture but they must expect to 'incur the hatred of many people and risk ambushes'. The accused should first be given a warning and encouraged to reform.

There should be no rushing to trial but if that became necessary, the person about whom the inquiry is being made ought to be present, unless he absents himself out of contumacy. He should be shown the accusations against him and allowed to defend himself. Normally he should be given the names of his accusers, because if anonymous accusations were allowed, people might be emboldened to bring false charges.

In this connection the council mentions the relatively novel fast-track 'notoriety' procedure, which was introduced in the late twelfth century. It was important that bishops be able to do this unpopular job without personal risk, but if a bishop became 'so notorious for his offences that an outcry goes up which can no longer be ignored without scandal or be tolerated without danger, then without the slightest hesitation let action be taken to inquire into and punish his offences, not out of hate but rather out of charity'. This provision was short-lived, as it opened the way to malicious accusations and merely required an accuser to spread sufficient gossip to meet the standard of 'notoriety' required.[17]

Papal monarchy and the failure of conciliarism

The Council of Constance (1414–18) was called by Pope John XXIII with the support of the German emperor and it promised to be a turbulent meeting. A canon of the late fourth-century Council of Toledo that had forbidden those present to gossip or make jokes or get into lengthy arguments was cited, and the council deplored the fact that the same sort of behaviour was still a problem: 'telling idle stories or jokes', 'tumult', 'contentious voices' being raised.

The fifteenth century would see a power struggle in the Church in Western Europe. Papal claims to monarchical power in the Church had been mounting, but bishops who were hostile to papal monarchy wanted to govern the Church collegially and enjoy a collective say in ecclesiastical affairs. This council opened in a period of heightened tension between popes and bishops, when the papacy was weakened by schism and was anxious to establish its validity and authenticity beyond doubt by claiming the highest possible authority, that of the Holy Spirit. It followed that 'everyone of whatever state or dignity, even papal, is bound to obey it in those matters which pertain to the faith and the eradication of the said schism'.[18]

In a session of April 1415, the council published a decree (*Haec sancta*) which asserted that councils were supreme over popes,[19] and so the power struggle between the papacy as an ecclesiastical 'monarchy' and the assembled bishops in a general council continued during the Council of Florence. It was still a live issue when the Fifth Lateran Council met from 1512 to 1517.

The insistence that councils should be held regularly, even frequently, proved another key element in the attempt to consolidate the role and status of the institution. The Council of Florence issued a decree on the 'frequent holding of general councils' in 1431,[20] and in 1433 it added the rider that provincial and diocesan councils should be frequent as well. A diocesan synod should be convened every year, normally after Easter, and last two or three days.[21] In every province a council should be held within two years of a general council and at least once every three years.

When a general council was in prospect it was decreed to be the provincial synod's task to elect representatives (even laity and women) to attend on behalf of the province and provide for the payment of their expenses. The role of these 'representatives' is to be taken seriously. In 1432 the Council of Florence promised safe conduct for those who attended.[22] They were to be allowed to make their comments freely, supporting their remarks 'with quotations from the sacred scriptures and the blessed doctors' if they wished, and also to make a reply to objections, even to 'argue about them' though 'in a charitable way', with reproach, abuse and taunting being completely forbidden. These 'representatives' were not, however, allowed to vote. Decision-making was still reserved for the assembled bishops.

There was evidently still cause to emphasise the need for good behaviour, with the matter mentioned more than once, and not only in connection with routine debate. There is mention of:

> that faction of agitators [...] votes and decisions [...] being extorted by various tricks [...] conspiracies, cabals, monopolies and cliques [...] vagabonds, quarrellers, fugitives, apostates, condemned criminals, escapees from prison [...] and other such human monsters, who brought with them every stain of corruption from those teachers of evil-doing.[23]

The core business, however, remained the legitimacy of a council and its claimed authority over the pope.[24]

ECUMENICAL AMBITIONS

Ecumenical dialogues

After the Second Vatican Council (1962–5), the late twentieth century saw a series of 'ecumenical dialogues' to try to restore the unity of the Church. Medieval Christianity had its own 'ecumenical' experiments. Attempts were made to tackle the problem of mending the schism of 1054 which divided Greek Christians from Western ones, after Anselm of Canterbury's proposals at the Council of Bari failed to persuade the Greeks.

Anselm of Havelberg talks to the Greeks

Another Anselm (*c.*1100–58), who became Bishop of Havelberg, tried again to heal the breach between East and West a generation later. He was drawn into diplomatic service on behalf of the imperial court and sent on a mission to Constantinople by way of Venice in 1136 by Emperor Lothar III, probably with papal backing. His task was to hold discussions with Nicetas, Archbishop of Nicomedia. He had with him three Greek-speaking translators to help overcome the language barrier: James of Venice, Burgundio of Pisa and Moses of Bergamo. There were two public debates, held a week apart, the first in the church of Hagia Eirene and the second in Hagia Sophia.[25]

The book with the Greek title *Antikeimenon* and the Latin title *Dialogi*,[26] in which Anselm records what happened, was written 14 years later. Anselm says he had been asked to write an account of these debates[27] and also claims that Pope Eugenius III had asked him to write the *Antikeimenon* because the pope needed to understand the position in order to know what to say to a delegation from Constantinople.

Anselm's account of the dialogues he had with the Greeks begins with a letter to Pope Eugenius III describing his many public and private discussions, in Latin and in Greek. He explains that he is now writing an account to collect together all these ideas, noting that the Latins often misunderstand what the Greeks mean because of the language difference. He has chosen the form of a dialogue to set out the contrary views in order to appeal to reason.[28] Anselm allows himself some humour in his imagery. Here is a wolf learning the alphabet. Here is someone milking a cow too enthusiastically so that the milk turns straight into butter. Here is a person blowing his nose so hard it makes it bleed.[29] Nonetheless, Anselm's approach has a serious objective: he wants to show how the Greeks and Latins are really part of the same Church; the question is how Christians have come to disagree. The one Church may be permitted diversity by divine grace but only in terms of rites, certainly not in relation to faith.[30]

In his 'book of opposing opinions', Anselm covers the main points of disagreement between the Latins and the Greeks, beginning with the procession of the Holy Spirit.[31] Anselm reports that citations were produced from Augustine and Jerome, the latter noted as *eruditus* in Greek as well as Latin and Hebrew.[32] But these were still Latin not Greek authorities. Nechites of Nicomedia had gently reminded everyone that that difference of language remained a great problem. The Greek word *proboleus* ('he who sends forth') is difficult for a Latin speaker to understand, Anselm admits.[33] Book III of the set goes on to consider the use of unleavened bread and the question of whether Roman Primacy took precedence over the claims of the Greek Patriarchates.[34]

Ultimately this effort to mend the schism failed, and there was no serious attempt to do so again for a century. For longer still, there was to be nothing by way of an attempt to discover a common faith, only discussions leading to the submission of other groups to the Roman Church.

The Council of Lyons and the Council of Florence try again

The Second Council of Lyons met in 1274 with a number of purposes. One was to tackle the still unsatisfactory state of the Middle East, where it claimed that 'the impious enemies of the Christian name, the blasphemous and faithless Saracens' were slaughtering Christian people. The 'Saracens' were taunting 'Where is the God of the Christians?' (Constitution II).

A second purpose of the Council of Lyons was to restore unity to the divided Church. The Byzantine emperor Michael VIII was one of the drivers of this ambition because he was eager for papal support to help him ward off Western imperial ambitions to invade his territory. The council saw unity in terms of submission to Rome: 'We also proposed to lead back the Greek peoples to the unity of the church; proudly striving to divide in some way the Lord's seamless tunic, they withdrew from devotion and obedience to the apostolic see.'

This was to be a major council and it was heavily attended not only by bishops but by academic observers from the universities acting as theological advisers and consultants, including leading mendicants who were themselves academics. Bonaventure (1221–74) the Franciscan was one of these mendicants. Thomas Aquinas was to attend on behalf of the Dominicans, but he died on the way. There was even a delegation of 'Tartars', observers from the invasion in progress into the Russian lands and Eastern Europe.

There was little progress towards unity in 1274, but the objective was now firmly on the agenda of the councils of Western Christendom. The council which put its shoulder decisively to the wheel ecumenically was the one which began to meet in Florence in the early fifteenth century, though it was forced to change its location more than once to avoid outbreaks of plague.[35]

The agreement with the Greeks was only the first of a series of 'ecumenical agreements' achieved during this council. The council regarded it as the second, counting the resolution of the discord with the Bohemians (the Hus affair) as having the highest priority. This wide-ranging ecumenical experiment was an ambitiously-conceived project, with the Bohemians grouped with the Greeks for the purposes of seeking unity.

But the task of reaching agreement with the Greeks was of a different order than had been the case with the Bohemians. Much pride was involved and much saving of face required even to arrange a place to meet. Constantinople was suggested but not in the end chosen. Representatives of the Greeks were to come to the council, the Western Church paying their travel and living expenses including those of the emperor and the 700-strong entourage he brought with him. The Westerners also undertook to pay for the defence of Constantinople if the Turks threatened it during the emperor's absence. Furthermore, the Western council was to fund a meeting in Constantinople where the Eastern 'prelates' could hold their own discussions.

The Greek bishops were to attend 'with full power and authority [...] confirmed by oath and suitable documents by both the secular authorities and the prelates'. It seems unlikely that the Latins understood the autocephaly of the Greek churches, which meant that any agreement of the council would need to be confirmed in the ecclesiastical territories of the Byzantine Church one by one. The discussion set out with good intentions, with a commitment that there should be no bad-tempered quarrelling, that discussion should be honest and straightforward (with no horse-trading) and that it should be charitable. But what was achieved foundered when it was taken back to Greece, as might have been foreseen.

The topics for discussion with the Greeks had themselves first to be agreed. Top of the list still was the question of the procession of the Holy Spirit. There could be no agreement about that if the Greeks detected any hint of the Westerners accepting 'two principles' (meaning two 'origins') in the Godhead, as they said was implied by speaking of the Holy Spirit as 'proceeding from the Father and the Son' in the Creed. A further point of continuing disagreement between East and West was whether to consecrate leavened or unleavened bread in the

Eucharist. This was resolved by Anselm of Canterbury's suggestion[36] that it be declared something that did not matter, a thing 'indifferent': 'Priests should confect the body of Christ [...] each priest according to the custom of his Western or Eastern church.'

The dispute about universal primacy had also still to be addressed, and the proposal here was that 'the patriarch of Constantinople should be second after the most holy Roman pontiff, third should be the patriarch of Alexandria, fourth the patriarch of Antioch, and fifth the patriarch of Jerusalem.'

From April 1438 the Greek bishops were present when the council met at Ferrara, and they moved with it to Florence where it continued to meet in January 1439. Agreement with the Greeks was recorded in 1434, employing a method that is familiar from much more recent ecumenical dialogue, that is, to accept that 'all were aiming at the same meaning in different words'.[37] The resulting agreement and its translation were to be regarded as 'legitimate, just and reasonable'. But in essence this was an agreement *by* the Greeks that the Latins were right, and when the Greek delegates eventually returned home they encountered a reluctance to accept what they had agreed. The schism had not been mended, but the council did not know that yet and proceeded optimistically to further declarations of unity on the same model.

Wider ecumenism

The council continued with its plan to bring stray sheep back to the Roman fold in the name of restoring the unity of the Church. In 1439 a Bull of Union with the Monophysite Armenians was issued, Armenian representatives having helpfully come to the council for the purpose of discussing matters.[38] As before, it was stressed that careful research and interchange had taken place. The questions between the Latins and the Armenians concerned both the procession of the Holy Spirit and the Council of Chalcedon (451), as well as some complex questions on the sacraments. The leader of the Armenian delegation declared himself willing to accept the Roman position, including paying more respect to the pope: 'Indeed we hold as reprobated and condemned whatever persons and things the Roman church reprobates and condemns.'

There followed in February 1442 a Bull of Union with the Copts, designed on the same principles that agreement really meant accepting

Rome's position.[39] A Bull of Union with the Syrian Monophysites (or 'Jacobites') was effected after their Patriarch sent Andrew, an Egyptian and monk of the monastery of Anthony of Egypt, to the council. He too agreed to accept 'the doctrine of the faith that the Roman church holds and preaches'.

In 1443, Pope Eugenius I convened yet another continuation of the Council of Florence, this time at the Lateran. It opened with an expression of satisfaction at the return to the fold of 'Greeks, Armenians, Jacobites [...] and other almost innumerable peoples, some of whom have been separated from the rite and the holy teaching of the Roman church for almost five hundred or even seven hundred years'.

The arrival of further envoys was now awaited, this time from Ethiopia, so that those led astray by the legend of Prester John,[40] imaginary ruler of the Nestorian Church, might also be restored to Roman obedience. In 1444 a Bull of Union with the Syrians was achieved too, broadly defined geographically speaking as including 'inhabitants of Mesopotamia between the Tigris and the Euphrates, whose thinking about the procession of the holy Spirit and some other articles had gone astray' and some 'beyond the bounds of the Euphrates' too. A session of August 1445 with their bishops resulted in a Bull of Union with the Chaldeans (East Syrian Monophysites) and the Arabic-speaking Maronites of Cyprus, once more on the principle that those who had gone astray had seen the error of their ways and were now restored to Rome.

So, on the face of it, this prolonged and ambitious council had mended a large number of schisms, including those which had begun with the Council of Chalcedon nearly a thousand years before, and brought all Christendom into union with Rome. But none of them would hold.

INTERFAITH DIFFICULTIES: CHRISTIANITY, ISLAM AND JUDAISM AT THE END OF THE MIDDLE AGES

Training missionaries

Ecumenical attempts to restore the unity of the Christian Church was one thing, missions to those of other faiths was quite another. But they did have something in common: just as Rome's idea of ecumenical agreement consisted of submission to Roman definitions and authority, so interfaith dialogue was directed towards the conversion of the other participant and not towards mutual tolerance. The Council of Vienne at the beginning of the fourteenth century had defined a mission as 'leading the erring into the way of truth and winning them for God with the help of his grace'.

But those to be evangelised might speak no European vernacular and no Latin. If a mission was to be all-embracing it would have to be polyglot, and missionary training would have to include the study of the necessary languages: '[The] holy church should be well supplied with catholic scholars acquainted with the languages most in use by unbelievers.'

A mission should also be practical. The 'missionary students' learning these languages must understand 'how to train unbelievers in the christian way of life, and to make them members of the christian body through instruction in the faith and reception of sacred baptism'.

The universities of Europe were to be enlisted in this enterprise. It was decreed that 'schools be established for the following languages wherever the Roman curia happens to reside and also at Paris, Oxford, Bologna and Salamanca'. 'In each of these places there should be catholic scholars with adequate knowledge of Hebrew, Arabic and Chaldaic', two experts for each language in each place. The teachers of these languages were not only to bring their students to a speaking knowledge of the new languages but also 'make faithful translations of books from these languages into Latin' for them to use. The salaries and expenses of the lecturers who were to teach in the Roman curia itself were to 'be provided by the apostolic see'. The king of France was to pay for those at Paris, and, more vaguely, those at Oxford, Bologna and Salamanca were to be funded by the prelates, monasteries, chapters, convents, exempt and non-exempt colleges, and rectors of churches, of England, Scotland, Ireland and Wales, and of Italy and of Spain, respectively.[41] The universities were less than cooperative. Salamanca appointed only one expert, but found it difficult to find anyone who could cover all three languages, so the post was not properly filled until a serious attempt was made to do so in the early sixteenth century.[42] Oxford did not appoint its first professor of Arabic until the seventeenth century.

Converting Jewish and Muslim 'unbelievers' to the Christian faith

There were recognised tensions in multi-faith communities. A decree of the Council of Vienne (25) takes issue with various practices in places where 'Saracens' live, 'sometimes apart, sometimes intermingled with Christians'. The call to prayer is heard loudly five times a day, even in places 'subject to Christian princes' and 'Saracen priests' and their people 'adore the infidel Mahomet' in their 'temples or mosques'. This, says the council, 'brings disrepute on our faith' and is a great stumbling-block to the faithful (*scandalum*). The council therefore forbids 'such practices henceforth in Christian lands [...] They are to remove this offence altogether from their territories and take care that their subjects remove it.'

The alternative to repression was conversion of the unbelievers. The Council of Florence's attempt to achieve a restored unity of the Church was also seen as an opportunity to ensure that Muslims were brought into the Christian Church: '[F]rom this union, once it is established, there is hope that very many from the abominable sect of Mahomet will be converted to the catholic faith.' Accordingly, this council too set out to achieve conversions of 'infidels' by encouraging missions.

This was not so easy to organise as the attempts at Christian unity. The latter involved persuading the leaders of divided churches to enter into discussions and to accept that Rome was right, an attempt at which the council in its various meeting places was surprisingly successful, at least on the face of it. In the case of the attempt to convert individual 'infidels', there were no such straightforward routes to success.

The proposed plan was to work by diocese, and in practice the objective was first and foremost to convert the Jews, for it was Jews who were to be found everywhere in medieval Christian Europe, not Muslims. Diocesan bishops were to select suitably qualified persons to preach several times a year in areas where the Jews 'and other infidels' live. Infidels of both sexes of suitable age ('years of discretion') shall be compelled to come and listen to these sermons, but the approach should at the same time be charitable and kindly. The constitution of the Council of Vienne, which had decreed that Hebrew, Arabic, Greek and Chaldean should be taught in some of the universities of Europe, was mentioned again in this new context.

It was not all to be done by kindness and sweet reason, however. Provision was made for sanctions. Those who refused to be converted were to be banned from business dealings with Christians. This, it was suggested, might be particularly successful in persuading the Jews who depended for their income on such business dealings. The council also decreed that Christians of whatever rank or status who in any way impeded the attendance of Jews at these sermons, or who forbade it, automatically incurred the stigma of being supporters of unbelief.

To strengthen the will of the Christian community to assist in this endeavour even further, the Council of Florence insisted that no Christians were to employ or have in their service Jews or other infidels. They might not engage them as doctors or notaries or agents, for any purpose. Christians must not socialise with Jews or attend their festivities or weddings or baths. Jews must not be allowed to hold public office or be granted degrees or to buy or accept as pawnbrokers objects of Christian significance such as crosses, chalices or books.

There was to be no keeping the head down and staying out of sight for the 'unbelievers'. Jews must dress in a way which marks them as Jews to the eye of the casual observer and they must live in what would now be called ghettos, separate from the local Christian communities. They must not open their shops on Sundays or engage in their normal work in any visible way.

Converts were to be instructed, not simply baptised, as evidence that they had agreed to be Christians. They must be seen to practise their new faith and to worship with Christians and must not continue to take part in the rituals of their former faith. Ideally they should marry 'born Christians' in order to ensure that they are not weakened in their resolve by continuing contact with other Jews. Jews who wish to be converted to Christianity will be allowed to keep their property unless it was acquired by usury or fraud. In some circumstances, the goods may remain in the custody of the Church which will put them to some pious use. Local bishops should protect the converts from 'detraction and invective' and provide them with financial support if necessary. But backsliders were to be dealt with severely.

Raymond Lull

Raymond Lull (*c.*1232–*c.*1315) was born in Mallorca to Catalonian parents, at a time when much of the Muslim population had been enslaved by the Christian Spanish conquerors of the Balearic Islands. Lull grew up to be a courtier and a royal tutor. He had a repeated vision which led him to see the conversion of Muslims to Christianity as a main part of his life's work, requiring educational institutions and a curriculum to be followed so that missionaries would be able to answer any argument a Muslim proposed. He retreated for some years to study and prepare himself. He was drawn to the Franciscans, but he could not enter the order as a friar because he was married with children. So he became a Franciscan 'tertiary', one of the lay people who sought a relationship with the friars in a 'Third Order'. Lull bought himself a Muslim slave to help him learn Arabic and understand the theology of Islam. Eventually he upset the slave by sneering at his faith and the slave attacked him and was imprisoned, where he hanged himself.[43]

Lull became a polymath with a number of particular interests beyond his 'mission'. He realised that the Arabs possessed philosophical knowledge not easily available to traditional Western scholarship, especially in the complex mathematical area which straddled astronomy and astrology. This was then a composite area of study in which astrology was precariously respectable. An astrologer, like an astronomer, might need to do calculations, but in his case so as to frame a horoscope rather than to plot the movement of the heavenly bodies scientifically in any modern sense.

Lull's intellectual curiosity took him down many alleyways, some of them questionable. Between 1271 and 1274 he published his *Ars Magna*, which employed an inventive system of diagrams and even paper mechanisms with rotating letters that could move until they spelt out a truth. His eccentricity verged on heresy and a series of popes condemned some of his books from 1376, yet he remained a widely respected and respectable figure.

Lull's combination of broad scholarly and missionary interests made him the chief begetter of the scheme launched by the Council of Vienne in 1311 to establish chairs in the universities of Europe in the languages missionaries might need. He travelled all over Europe meeting heads of state and other influential persons in the hope of setting up missionary colleges with their assistance. But Lull's hopes that a great mission to the Muslims would follow were to be disappointed.

Undeterred, Lull went on missionary journeys of his own, beginning with a mission to the Muslims in North Africa in 1285, only to be expelled from Tunis. As someone not easily discouraged, he returned there in about 1304 and tried to win the goodwill of the government by writing letters of appeal, but apparently with no more success. Lull had by now come to the conclusion that it was prayer alone, and certainly not invasions, that would bring about the conversion of Muslims to the Christian faith. He was enthusiastic about the conversion of the Jews too, organising public debates against leading rabbinic opponents from Barcelona and Salerno. His last missionary attempt was made when he was in his early eighties. In North Africa again in 1314 he was stoned by a Muslim mob, but was rescued by some Genoese merchants who took him back to his home in Mallorca where he died soon after.

Interfaith dialogues: some private enterprise

Not every high-profile figure thought that the attempt to bring non-Christians into the fold had a high priority. John Wyclif (*c.*1324–84) considered that the Christian clerics he was attacking were even worse adversaries of Christ than the Jews.[44] But individuals had long been busy publishing fictional 'dialogues' and probably holding real ones too. Jewish–Christian dialogues were perhaps the most common and had been in evidence for generations.[45] Among the twelfth-century examples was one by Peter Abelard (1079–1142) in which he presents fictional discussions involving Christian, Jew and 'philosopher'. This device enabled him to explore the implications of the fact that in a discussion with a Jew, a Christian missionary may cite the Old but not the New Testament and in a discussion with a pagan or philosopher he may use neither, only reason.[46] Gilbert Crispin, Abbot of Westminster (*c.*1055–1117) had made the same observation a little earlier in his separate 'dialogues' with a Jew and a 'Gentile'.[47]

For interfaith dialogues involving Muslims we have to look further east or to Spain. Samaw'al al-Maghribi, an older contemporary of the philosopher Maimonides (d. 1204), was converted from Judaism to Islam in 1163. He wrote a polemic 'Silencing the Jews', which included his autobiography. From this we learn that he had a good education in Baghdad in medicine and mathematics and also studied the Talmud and Jewish Law. He was probably destined for the life of an administrator at a Spanish court. He was proud of his command of rhetoric, which meant, as it did in late antiquity, studying history and illustrative stories to provide interest in his speeches. A courtier-civil servant was expected to be a cultured man and if he served a Muslim ruler he would master revisionist histories of the Arabs, rewritten to make them the heroes of many battles against Byzantines and Persians as well as Franks. Old Testament prophets were discussed alongside stories of the Prophet Mohammed and the way God worked miracles through him. Nothing quite comparable was available in the Judaic tradition and this fact seems to have contributed to al-Maghribi's decision to convert to Islam.

Al-Maghribi prepared a defence of the Qur'an because his fellow Jews found it crude in comparison with the Old Testament. The defence took a similar form to that used by Christians when challenged about the oddities and apparent contradictions in both Old and New Testaments. The counter-claim was that the text had many layers of meaning and its inwardness was supremely beautiful. Maimonides had warned Jews living under Muslim rule against studying history, for it was evidently proving dangerously seductive.

Byzantine–Muslim dialogue

Greek-speaking Christians were more likely to be in contact with Muslims living in geographical proximity than Christians in Western Europe outside the Iberian Peninsula. Nicetas Choniatas (1155–1217), a Greek civil servant, was the author of a history of the Byzantine Empire in the twelfth century. He had been educated in Constantinople with his elder brother Michael. In his 'Thesaurus of the Orthodox Faith' (*Thesaurus Orthodoxae Fidei*), Book XX, he describes the process to be used in converting a Muslim to Christianity. First, the convert must fast for two weeks; then he is urged to study the Gospels and the Creed. When his instruction is complete and he is ready for baptism, the presiding priest places his stole round him and he is surrounded by any other of the faithful who wish to be present. Standing before the baptismal font/pool (*piscina*), he is asked to renounce his previous faith:

> You who today leave the faith of the Saracens for the Christian faith, not forced or under any necessity, sincerely and with your mind and a pure heart, and for love of Christ and his faith, say, 'I renounce the whole religion of the Saracens. I anathematise Mohammed who, the Saracens honour as God's prophet and apostle'.

If the convert does not know Greek, an interpreter can assent for him, or his guardian can do so if he is a minor. There follows a long and detailed anathematisation of details of the Qur'an, particularly anything that 'perverts' the Old Testament in borrowing from it, such as the 'lies' told about Old Testament figures such as Noah, Abraham, Isaac, Jacob, Joseph, Moses, Aaron and others. The

Fig. 24: Byzantine emperor John Cantacuzenos (1347–54)

anathematisation also extends to descriptions of the afterlife in the Qur'an, the marriage laws of Muslims allowing divorce, and much else. Once all these beliefs have been abjured by the candidate, the baptism may take place.[48]

Joannes Cantacuzenos (*c.*1292–1383) was emperor of Byzantium from 1342 to 1355, when he retired to become a monk and write books. He wrote more than one 'apology for the Christian faith against the Mohammedan sect'.[49] He presented the case that Jesus Christ is the Son of God (*Apologia* 1), that he was made man, submitted to death by crucifixion, was buried and rose again, and that it was not God but man who suffered, and who will judge the world (*Apologia* 3). Then he described how the apostles taught all over the world, proving the truth of their faith by performing miracles (*Apologia* 3). By contrast, he says, Mohammed made many false claims (*Apologia* 4). Cantacuzenos presents a series of disputations in which the view of Muslims on various points was described in order for it to be rebutted, very much in the style of Western scholastic disputation. Can Mohammed be called a prophet? He explains that names gain their 'signification' from place, substance or as proper names (patronymics), or as job descriptions (*officium*), such as 'apostle', 'doctor' and perhaps for someone with the appropriate special gifts, 'prophet'. But how could anyone properly call a man a prophet if he makes no prophecies and simply adopts the title?[50]

In Manuel II Palaiologos (1350–1425) we meet yet another Byzantine emperor who was also a theologian and the author of interfaith dialogues. A letter to his old tutor Demetrios Cydone tells him that the king of Hungary has just arrived, in flight from the Turkish defeat of the French and Hungarian crusaders at Nicopolis on 15 September 1396. The letter stresses the importance of converting the Muslims from their error. They are God-haters who have been feasting on blood and massacres. If they are not punished, Islam will not be refuted.[51] Palaiologos was a skilled Latinist, and had started to translate Thomas Aquinas's *Contra Gentiles*, which he finished in 1354; then he started on the translation of Aquinas's *Summa Theologiae*. In the end he himself became a Roman Catholic.

Palaiologos's manual for the conversion of Muslims covers a number of familiar points and arguments. Muslims think the Christian Scriptures are corrupt; Christians have different ideas of paradise and judgement, pleasure and polygamy, and of the consequences of the fall of Adam, the story of Noah's Ark and other Old Testament events. The great question is whose are the true prophets? Moses is compared with Mohammed, who is alleged to have changed almost all the laws of Moses. There is a comparison between Mosaic and Islamic law, emphasising that Mohammed was not guided by the Holy Spirit. The laws Christ gave are what matter now. The Christian faith is set out as the truth, with a brief explanation of the doctrine of the Trinity.[52]

SPAIN RECAPTURED FOR CHRISTIANITY

The Reconquista

The Reconquista or 'reconquest' of the southern part of the Iberian Peninsula by the Christian kingdoms of northern Spain took far longer than the Islamic conquest of these lands had done in the eighth century. The first success was the capture of Toledo in 1085. Al-Andalus was taken in 1212, with the exception of Granada, which was not taken by the Christians until 1492, when Ferdinand of Aragon and his Queen Isabella of Castile recovered it.

The change of religious dominance put its stamp on southern Spain, with the medieval and baroque cathedrals dominating the city landscapes in styles which tend to reflect a later age than those of Northern Europe. But merely putting up a grand building does not change a culture. Centuries of competition and subtle mutual accommodation between Christians and Muslims, with the Jews a notable contributor, left Christian Spain with a heritage unique in medieval Europe. It is possible to glimpse some of these complexities.

Al-Khazraji, born in 1125 in Cordoba, was brought to Christian Toledo at the age of about 21, as a prisoner of war. The context was probably the revenge taken by Alfonso VII of Castile when the Muslim governor of Seville had mounted an attack on Cordoba in January 1146, a decade after its reconquest for the Christians by Fernando III in 1236. Al-Khazraji spent about two years in Toledo and became involved in religious discussions with a group of local Muslims conducted with the support of a Christian priest of apparent Visigothic descent.[53] He became the author of combative writings, although, as he complained, he was forced to live in a deeply disadvantaged way among his enemies, 'Satan's gang'. His *Hammer of crucifixes* may actually have been written after he was able to return to Muslim territory and become a teacher of Muslim *hadith* texts. It was claimed that he had dictated it to a slave because his eyesight was failing, but it seems unlikely that he would have had such a servant while he was himself in Christian captivity.

The Balearic Islands and the Christian slave trade

The stamp of this complex multicultural Spanish religious experience can be seen beyond the Iberian Peninsula itself. After some preliminary incursions in the ninth century, the Mediterranean islands of Minorca and Mallorca fell under Muslim rule in the tenth century. This made these islands 'Spanish' in the future, for they remained under the control of Christian Spain after the Reconquista. A first serious attempt by Christian Spain to recapture these strategically important islands was the successful invasion of Mallorca and Majorca in 1229 by the young monarch James I of Aragon. The conquering Christians set about actively purging the island of Arabic influences and imposing a new constitution. Again, impressive Christian edifices were built, but again, too, the inwardness of developments can be detected.

Pere Calafat, who died in Mallorca in 1267, was a Christian who had owned Muslim slaves and expected them to consent to be baptised as Christians. Under his will, his debts were to be paid, and he 'takes' 'for my soul', 600 royal sous of Valencia. The will detailed where he wanted to be buried and authorised payment of the Church and the rector provision made. A pound of wax or a wax image was to be provided for certain churches, and gifts 'for the table' given to local religious orders as well as sums for the poor, the hospitals and the ransoming of captives. Then were listed various gifts to relatives, including the customary return to a wife of the dowry she had brought him when they married: 'I praise, grant, and confirm to my lady and wife, her dowry, which she possesses over my goods, which gift is two hundred royal sous of Valencia.' The will granted freedom to his baptized slaves along with some money.[54]

It seemed politic at first because of the numbers involved to allow the Muslims still living in the newly Christian territory a fair amount of religious freedom and even protection. But some were regarded as prisoners of war. *Asir* (a prisoner of war) was the term used by Muslims for a Muslim who had been captured in a non-Islamic land. If one of these was sold into slavery, the West considered him to be bound by local laws, but Muslims believed the slaves retained all their original rights under their own law. This raised many practical questions. If married couples were separated, were they still married if divorced under different systems? If a Christian marriage was arranged by a master between two of his slaves, was it valid in Islamic law, especially if they returned to an Islamic land; and what was the status of any children they had?[55]

After a mass capture, Christian conquerors might hold onto more important captives who might be useful to them politically or in other practical ways, while the rest were sold into slavery.[56] This seems to have become quite common practice from the ninth century.

As was to be expected from the recent history of parts of Spain previously well governed by Islamic masters, captured Muslims included notaries, men of affairs and scholars, even 'discoverers', such as the resident of Granada, al-Wazzan al-Fasi (*c.*1494–*c.*1554), who explored Muslim Africa at the beginning of the sixteenth century and was captured by Christian Sicilian pirates on his return from Egypt in 1519. The pirates found his traveller's notes and realised that he might be valuable, so they made an arrangement to hand him over to the pope. Al-Wazzan al-Fasi was promptly baptised and took the name of 'John Leo the African'. In due course he published a book entitled *A Description of Africa*, and as Leo Africanus he taught Arabic at Bologna.[57]

Slaves put to work as copyists of the Arabic scientific and philosophical texts that were engaging interest from the thirteenth century took the opportunity to add notes to make it clear that they were doing this work as slaves, often adding a prayer that someone might 'redeem' the copyist. Some also made it clear that they were working for wealthy Jewish holders of substantial library collections who evidently wanted to add copies of further texts.[58] Some of these copyists had medical knowledge, including specialists in the treatment of particular diseases.[59]

Christian scholars also valued Muslim captives who understood Islamic theology. It was particularly valuable for 'missionaries' to equip themselves with such details in order to more effectively argue against them.[60]

Muslims were often forcibly baptised and given a new 'Christian' name before being sold on. The documents provided to the purchaser often made only a passing reference to their Muslim origin, or simply called them *pagani*, with no mention of their original names. Alternatively a new slave might be baptised by the master who bought him. The eleventh-century practice at Santa Man de Sobrado, a monastery in the province of La Corufia, was to baptise slaves when they arrived. If former Muslim slaves had children, they were baptised in infancy. Naturally some Muslim 'converts' tried to continue to observe their former faith. In Sicily in 1310 a law was passed requiring Muslims to hear the energetic preaching of the Gospel, and slave owners who attached little importance to the Christianisation of their slaves were at risk of facing sanctions and having their slaves freed if they did not comply with regulations.

Redemption

The system of 'redemption' – the freeing of captured Muslims – became quite elaborate. It soon became clear that there was money to be made out of 'redemptions' and it developed into a form of trade. Money was collected in mosques to buy back friends and relations from slavery,[61] while captives themselves might even be allowed to beg in the streets to raise money to buy their own freedom. A Muslim judge recorded a decision in 1303 which permitted two captives to do this in the Muslim areas of Valencia, at that time under the control of the Christian king of Aragon.[62] Or the captive might write home and ask his family to send him the money. A preacher from Murcia did this in verse in the thirteenth century.[63]

A 'redeemer' could usually expect compensation or reward, even if the person he redeemed ran away as soon as he was freed from slavery.[64] Jewish *alfaqueques* ('redeemers') were sometimes active in the 'redeeming trade', taking no sides. They brought Christian captives back to Christian lands as well as Muslim captives back to Muslim territories.[65] Christian captives in Muslim lands might look for help to religious orders or even guilds.[66] The Order of Our Lady of Mercy (La Merce) was founded in Barcelona in 1218 as a military order with the specific purpose of freeing Christian slaves. Its members, male and female, took a vow to die if necessary for someone who was at risk of losing his or her faith.[67] The Trinitarian Order was founded in 1198 by the Provençal Jean de Matha with a mission to rescue Christian slaves from Muslim captivity. Sometimes an exchange of Christian and Muslim captives might be arranged.[68]

Slaves might also be rescued in groups as well as individually. Among the more notable mass 'redemptions' was the one achieved by a Caliph of North African extraction, Abu Yaqub Yusuf (1135–84), who successfully conquered Al-Andalus in 1170 and held it, basing himself in Seville, until he was defeated and killed in battle by Alfonso I of Portugal in 1184. He was said to have saved the Muslim inhabitants of Seville from the 'trap' of unbelief into which baptism and Christianisation would lead them, and brought them back into the liberty of Islam.[69] There were also stories of miraculous rescues that bestowed a hero statues on those involved.[70] Some ambitious 'redeemers' cast their nets wide such as Ali the Saracen, from Granada, who in 1407 sought to 'redeem' Muslim prisoners held in Roussillon in the south of France.[71]

Renewed Christian hostility to the Jews

The Jews were driven out of Spain in 1492 (and required to leave behind their silver and gold) by a joint decree of Isabella of Castile and Ferdinand of Aragon.[72] This Spanish ejection of the Jewish people was one of a series of such expulsions in Western Europe in the later Middle Ages, including from England, France and parts of Germany. In Spain there had already existed a requirement that Jews should convert to Christianity, but many who appeared to do so only conformed to protect themselves and continued practising their Jewish faith in secret, while some made great efforts to reconvert the *conversi*. The civil authorities saw this as a threat and Ferdinand and Isabella asked Rome for an Inquisition in 1478. In 1487 they set up their own Spanish Inquisition and by 1492 the 'reconquest' of Spain from Islam was completed with the Christian monarchs' victory at the Battle of Granada.

A driving force behind the Christian Spanish monarchs' hostility to the Jews in particular may have been Isabella's new confessor, Francisco Jiménez de Cisneros. He had become a Franciscan only in middle age, abandoning earlier struggles to achieve his personal ambitions, and threw himself into his new life with the zeal of a convert, denying himself to an extreme degree. Cisneros also set about reforming the Franciscan Order in Spain and then other orders too, ending the permissiveness which allowed many friars to keep mistresses. Many hundreds responded indignantly by taking their wives into exile in North Africa and converting to Islam. It was the Archbishop of Toledo who suggested to Isabella that she should adopt Cisneros as her confessor. His influence may have been important in the decision to force the Jews as well as Muslims to convert. In 1499 he travelled with the Spanish Inquisition to Granada where the archbishop had been attempting to convert the Muslims by persuasion. There Cisneros set about burning Arabic manuscripts and enforcing mass conversions, a move that prompted rebellion.

The exiled Jews went to various places, south to the Mahgreb and elsewhere in North Africa, east to the Ottoman Empire (with the aid of rescue ships provided by the Sultan), and some only as far as Portugal, though that did not remain a refuge for them for long.

Patterns of conversion did not always take Jews towards Christianity. Sometimes they chose to become Muslim instead. Ridwan al-janawl came from Genoa but he had become a Muslim on a visit to North Africa late in the fifteenth century. His wife was Jewish but she too had converted to Islam. Al-janawl became famous as a holy man who could perform miracles and he also acted as a redeemer of slaves where he could.[73]

On occasion, there were heartening displays of multiculturalism. In 1440 the Infanta of Navarre travelled to Castile to marry her cousin, heir to the throne of Castile. A great party accompanied her and entertainments were arranged along the way. When they got to Briviesca the artisan guilds greeted them with banners, theatrical performances and dancing. Then came the Jews carrying the Torah and the Moors carrying the Qur'an, also dancing, with accompanying music. All three religions accompanied the party to the count's palace where a fine meal was served to the travellers.[74]

But there could also be indications that resentments might lie below the surface even when mutual tolerance was on display. In 1462, Miguel Lucas de Iranzo was elevated to the nobility by King Henrique IV, who had made him Constable of Castile in 1458. Iranzo was not welcomed by the established nobility and had to retreat to Jaen where he became the leader of the city. There he made the upper bourgeoisie into knights to earn their loyalty. He was very pious and arranged pageants and public performances for the city to mark the great liturgical feasts. People were expected to dress in their best clothes and there was a mixture of going to Matins and general fun and games. However, the lower classes resented him when he protected converted Jews.[75]

Christian persecution of Muslims

From the beginning of the sixteenth century, a period of active Christian persecution of Muslims began. Many who chose to 'convert' were accused of secretly remaining practising Jews or Muslims, and anyone refusing to drink alcohol or eat pork could be denounced as a crypto-refusenik. In 1499, Muslims in Granada were told to give up all their Arabic books to be burned. By 1567, Arabic was banned by law in Spain by Philip II, and Muslims were 'ethnically cleansed' by the Christian rulers or scattered to prevent their gathering as a force. This lost the Christian conquerors a great deal of revenue because the Muslims had been businessmen, craftsmen and scholars who were not easily replaced in the Spanish economy.

In the same period, the laws of Valencia decreed that if a Muslim man slept with a Christian woman both were to be burned alive. If a Christian man slept with a Muslim woman, he received no sanction but she would be punished under Islamic law for fornication or adultery, and would be flogged or stoned to death. Christian royal authorities usually commuted this to enslavement and sold the offender on to Christians who then pimped her as a prostitute. Mariem, one prostitute on trial, told her story of coming to Valencia with a man who promised to marry her. She was told she was to be sold to a nobleman, Don Altobello, but instead was put in a brothel. She was asked whether she wished to return to her husband or her mother, and she requested to be returned to her mother. Mariem was in due course handed over to the Muslim authorities who tried to find out whether or not she was a 'licensed' prostitute.[76]

In 1491, the usual Feast of Corpus Christi celebrations were held in Valencia, and Muslims as well as Christians came to watch. A Muslim who had had a plan to kill one of his enemies seized the chance when he saw him standing near the butcher's shop in the Muslim quarter, watching the procession as a float went by enacting a Bible story. His intended victim moved out of the sun with some friends and went to stand by a wall near the house of the apothecary. The would-be assassin approached his intended victim, pulled out his dagger from under his cloak and stabbed him.[77] In 1492, an 'expulsion of Jews' charter claimed that Jews want to steal faithful Christians from their faith so they must be expelled.[78]

We are also in the period of the late-medieval 'story' which presented Christian caricatures and attitudes. Thomas Malory (d. 1471) assembled in his *Le Morte d'Arthur* a collection of tales about King Arthur and the Round Table which had been maturing in the late medieval centuries. It proved popular enough to become one of the earliest books to be printed, by William Caxton in 1485. The Saracens feature in it with 'infidels' besieged in a castle,[79] slain in large numbers,[80] arriving to kill and lay waste, some 40,000 in number.[81]

6

FROM DISSENT TO REFORMATION

MONKS, NUNS AND FRIARS COULD BE TROUBLESOME

Geoffrey Chaucer's Monk is a 'manly man', fond of hunting, with enough personal wealth to keep the horses and dogs he needs to pursue his hobby. It is taken for granted that his choice of a monastery has depended on his family connections. He has the look of a successful man, well fed, well dressed, but he considers that the ascetic life of a monk is now out of date. He need not live like that. The Monk is only one of Chaucer's characters 'in the religious life' we meet on pilgrimage to Canterbury in *The Canterbury Tales*. Chaucer had the satirist's confidence that he knew what he was doing with these caricatures. His readers would recognise them and laugh knowingly.

The religious orders, monks and friars alike, began with the best of intentions, but they all had their difficulties in resisting secular temptations. The orders of friars, Franciscans, Dominicans and the others which began in imitation of such ideals, were mendicants, so by definition they were 'beggars'. They were free to leave their communities, and in fact they had to do so in order to carry out their mission of preaching. Some might be corrupted into seeking advancement, but others became the trusted 'confessors' of the great, and achieved political influence in high places.

The Fourth Lateran Council of 1215 sounded warnings about decay in contemporary monastic life, calling for 'greater religious observance in the monastic state, regarding clothing, poverty, silence, the eating of meat' and other good practice. The Council of Vienne (1311–12) approved and renewed all that had been decreed a hundred years earlier by the Fourth Lateran Council. Evidently these earlier attempts had not put everything right. It was the friars who now caused most disquiet, the council expressing concern about those mendicants who tried to transfer into non-mendicant traditional monastic orders, and sought office in those communities (13). It was eager to protect the standards of the Benedictines ('black monks'), so that (14) 'nothing unbecoming or corrupt find its way into that field of the Lord, namely the sacred order of the black monks, or anything grow into a ruinous crop, but rather that the flowers of honour and integrity may there produce much fruit'.

Activities of the religious orders, such as the running of hospices and leper houses, almshouses or hospitals, are also at risk of exploitation by the wealthy and secular-minded. They must be supervised and made to provide for the poor and sick and needy as they were founded to do.[1]

Part of the problem lay with the behaviour of the sons and daughters of wealthy families who had been given to the religious life by their families. They liked to be fashionable. Chaucer's overdressed and genteel Prioress is a satirical example. The Council of Vienne decreed that monks were to avoid all 'excess or irregularity with regard to clothes, food, drink, bedding and horses', and went into a good deal of detail about what should be permitted to monks and nuns. The 'quality of the cloth' of the 'upper garment next to their habit' should not 'exceed monastic moderation'. The garment itself should not be of fancy design; 'it should have broad sleeves extending to the hands, not sewn or buttoned in any way'. 'They should not wear silk in place of fur [...] None shall presume to wear an ornate belt, knife or spurs, or ride a horse with the saddle highly ornamented with nails or sumptuous in any other way, or with a decorative iron bridle.'

Monastic recruits from good families also liked to continue their favourite family pastimes. The decree says that they must 'abstain from hunting and fowling', even from watching such activities. They shall not keep hunting dogs or birds of prey or try to keep servants to look after these creatures on their behalf. The only exception is where the monastery has woods, game preserves or warrens, or has the right to hunt on property belonging to others, in which there might be rabbits or other wild animals, when dogs and birds may be kept for hunting, but even then not in the monastery itself and 'the monks themselves' must not 'appear at the hunt'. These scions of wealthy families show themselves reluctant to study. Each monastery should have a master competent to instruct recruits at least in the 'primary branches of knowledge', such as Latin, which they needed for worship and private prayer.

The Council of Vienne also addressed itself to problems with nuns (15). Convents should be visited annually by their 'ordinary' (presiding bishop), though it is acknowledged that some are 'subject to the apostolic see alone' and would have to be visited by the pope's personal 'deputy Visitor'. The Visitor should stop nuns from dressing fashionably, a practice to which, alas, they are as given as are some of the monks. They must not be allowed to 'wear silk, various furs or sandals' or 'wear their hair long in a horn-shaped style, nor make use of striped and multicoloured caps'. They should not attend dances or banquets or walk in the streets and towns 'by day or night'. They should be told – firmly – not to seek a life of luxury.

Even the Visitors, who were meant to be improving standards, could behave corruptly. The Council of Vienne (20) records with regret that it has been told that bishops visiting Cistercian houses have complained about the quality of the hospitality they have received. The food prescribed by the monastic Rule has not been good enough for them, it seems. They bring their own cooks and demand to be served meat. They bring their hunting dogs and falcons and hawks with them as well as large households. They want their horses shod and they demand money to pay for the service. They make other extortions too and if they do not get what they want they ransack the monastery church and seize the ornaments.

The success of this decree in eradicating such behaviour may be judged from Chaucer's satirical depictions later in the century in his *Canterbury Tales*. His Monk and Pardoner and Prioress are unedifying examples of their calling which he expected to prompt a knowing chuckle from his readers.

Confraternities: Beguines and Beghards

At the end of the twelfth century and the beginning of the thirteenth there arose experimental self-defined groups of lay people, both men and women, who felt called to some form of dedicated religious life but wanted to lead it in their own way, and not have to join an existing religious order.[2] These were 'confraternities', voluntary brotherhoods or sisterhoods. Forming them must have seemed natural enough when the model of the 'guild' of common interest and shared activity was everywhere to be seen in much of Western Europe. There were guilds of fishmongers, goldsmiths and scholars, so why not lay 'religious', making their own rules and deciding who to admit among them in the same way?

The Beguines were reputed to have been founded about 1240 in Marseille by Douceline of Digne (*c.*1215–74). Her brother was a Franciscan friar and she took 'vows' before him and founded her first community. A second community was soon established and Douceline became the focus of a cult. Pious women in the towns of the Low Countries formed themselves into similar lay communities dedicated to prayer and voluntary work for the local urban poor and the sick. Only small numbers tried this at first but from the thirteenth century onwards it became a popular choice. There were communities which welcomed the better-off applicant and other communities which welcomed the poor – or all comers. Many of the women brought property, which helped to support the venture, but those who had nothing to bring could work to support themselves within the community.

These were independently-minded women, who chose not to marry and thus could avoid the kind of life which was the only one available to laywomen, but they were not bound by vows so they could change their minds at any time. The communities made their own rules, often in the spirit of the Franciscan Tertiaries. There was an obvious danger that self-government would allow some to go astray into heresy or unconventional ways of life. It was soon being noticed that there were many mystics and spiritual oddities among the Beguines. Margaret Poreta was burned at the stake as a heretic in 1310. Others became beggars and were consequently condemned as 'vagrants', and vagrants were characters universally feared during the Middle Ages.

The Church began to take a firm line on this matter. In 1311 the pope accused the Beguines in general of heresy. The Council of Vienne (1311–12) produced decrees against them, though these were moderated by Pope John XXII a decade later, with the provision that the Beguines must reform themselves. The Council of Vienne (16) had identified the dangers of this way of life. These women known as Beguines, it pointed out, take no vow of obedience. They do not renounce their possessions or follow a rule. They are potentially out of control and wearing the dress of a Beguine is no guarantee of their orthodoxy of belief or their good behaviour. Some of them are actually heard preaching and engaging in theological arguments, putting forth heretical doctrines on the nature of God and on the Trinity. They can easily mislead the faithful. Exceptions may be made for 'faithful women, whether they promise chastity or not [...] living uprightly in their hospices, wishing to live a life of penance and serving the Lord of Hosts in a spirit of humility. This they may do, as the Lord inspires them.'

The Beguines prompted imitation by male counterparts, known as Beghards. They too made their own rules and ate at a common table, sharing their resources. Their recruits tended to be craftsmen such as dyers and weavers, for the Beghard movement had links with the craft guilds. Some communities also required their members to be members of a local guild. Popes condemned these too and bishops – especially in Germany – took action to suppress them. The Council of Vienne (28) seems to have agreed that Germany was the Beghard hotbed.

It would not be surprising to find popular heretical ideas among these gentle revolutionaries. The listed Beghard errors suggest an influence of Cathar beliefs and also hint at Waldensian claims to Christian independence from the ecclesiastical hierarchy and the sacraments – especially when directly inspired by the Holy Spirit. There are notions here redolent of Calvinism and even of the Anabaptists of the Reformation period. This was amateur lay theology but it belongs in a tradition, or a mixture of traditions, which flowed into Reformation thinking.

It is also likely that distorted reports of their beliefs were spread by rumour and hard to deny. These alleged errors include teaching that a person may achieve a perfection in this life which can never improve further, and that once someone is 'perfect' he need no longer fast or pray but can behave as he pleases, including giving way to the lusts of the flesh with impunity. The perfect are not subject to obedience to anyone or to the commandments of the Church, for the Spirit makes them free. The perfect should not show reverence to the consecrated Host at the Eucharist, for that would be to descend from the spiritual heights where they now dwell. (This non-reverent behaviour would be noticeable, for a faithful congregation normally rose to their feet when the Host was lifted up before them.)

Fig. 25: Etching by François Morellon de la Cave (b. 1696): a great procession of flagellants

Confraternities: the flagellants

The flagellants of the thirteenth and fourteenth centuries saw themselves as acting out a penitential pilgrimage. They had some links with the Beghards and Beguines. They walked in processions, carrying crosses, while they sang hymns and scourged themselves, possibly in an attempt to please God and improve the harvest. They seem to have appeared after an epidemic in Perugia in 1259, and then across northern Italy and Austria and Germany. They might organise processions when there was some natural disaster, such as the Black Death (1349), which suggested that God needed to be propitiated.

They apparently attracted some royal support, from Henry III in England and Catherine de Medici in France. But soon the Church authorities grew wary of them too. To draw popular support was always a threat to good order and there was no visible system of control of their activities. So their apparent spontaneity called for a check. A Bull of Pope Clement VI condemned them in 1349 and the papacy became increasingly convinced that they were as dangerous as the Beghards, with whom they had some overlap in membership.[3]

THE RISE OF AN ENQUIRING LAITY

Vernacular guidance for priests

In the later medieval centuries standards of priestly education continued to be modest. There was still no required ordination training. Only a tiny proportion took the higher degree in theology in the universities, which could take a man to his mid-forties to complete, and of those who did, few were likely to have become parish priests. It was said that a priest was likely to knock at the doors of theology like a child hungry for solid food.[4]

When he did so, he might be glad to be 'fed' in the vernacular. The *Mirror for Priests* (*Speculum sacerdotale*) is a fifteenth-century collection of sermons for the liturgical year, which includes expository material 'gathered out of diverse books made by old holy fathers'.[5] The *Mirror* is written in Middle English of the kind spoken in the London area at the time, so it was probably not directed at the more learned clergy. It is full of practical advice for the priest dealing with confessions, still probably the most regular requirement for anyone with parish responsibilities.

The section on penance and penitents describes the kinds of people who will come to confession and suggests how to deal with them. It is important, it is stressed, to consider the person's health and strength and ability to pay any fines when imposing penances.[6] Just as in earlier medieval centuries, much of the advice is concerned with allocating penances for sexual sins. For 'simple fornication' the penance might be fasting, but this is dependent on who the fornicator was. If he was a priest, he should also say the seven penitential psalms every day. If the fornication has been a 'habitual indulgence' then a longer penance is appropriate. If someone cannot fast (perhaps for medical reasons) he should at least be restricted to two meals a day, and must say the penitential psalms to make up for a limited obligation of fasting.[7] Another complication arises when a woman repents of adultery and cannot fast because her husband will suspect that she is doing penance and will ask why; so she should fast as unobtrusively as she can.[8] Fornication involving adultery is much more serious than 'simple fornication', as is sexual indulgence with a nun. Sodomy and incestuous fornication are also considered worse than fornication.[9]

Legal questions could arise too. All sorts of unexpected confessions may come the way of the parish priest. A knight comes, wanting separation from his wife after a long time, and when they already have a child. Only now does he claim consanguinity and try to say that the marriage is void. That is not justified. Clergy caught kissing girls or in an intoxicated state will need appropriate penances. The priest must be careful not to be too lenient or too harsh.[10]

And what if someone confesses to a killing? There are penalties for manslaughter, but what if a child is overlaid by a sleeping woman or dies suddenly (the modern 'infant death') without the mother having done anything to cause it? The priest must learn how to temper the penance as is appropriate to the offence.[11]

A literate bourgeoisie

Alongside an under-educated local clergy having trouble with its Latin was emerging a class of bourgeoisie who could read in their own language and were developing a taste for reading. Geoffrey Chaucer chose English for his rollicking *Canterbury Tales* and even for his technical treatise on the Astrolabe, a scientific instrument of measurement used by sailors, astronomers and astrologers. He says he wrote it for a boy called 'little Lewis' or Louis, but he pauses to explain his choice of language in broader terms. He says he has used English because the boy's Latin is still 'but small'. This route to easy reading he justifies with the explanation that much of Latin literature is itself a rendering from original works in other languages, such as Greek, Hebrew or Arabic. At the time, Middle English was gradually displacing the French of the Norman conquerors as the language of court and civil service, so he adds that the king of England is 'Lord of this language'.

Popular taste liked a good story; it warmed to talk of special and miraculous powers and it especially liked to hear of short cuts to success as might be offered by magic, especially if it came with a Christian overlay. The daring and unconventional woman poet Christine de Pisan (1364–*c.*1430) worked as court writer for several dukes. Widowed young, she had to earn money to keep her three children. She wrote in Middle French in a high moral tone made for acceptability even when the content was risqué. Her *The Epistle of Othea* became a popular work in French and was translated into English by Stephen Scrope (1397–1492), who had spent time as secretary to Sir John Falstalf in Normandy.[12] The book offered Christian allegories of secular and classical sources, using both Greek and Roman names for the gods. The god Saturn says that 'the good knight should be slow in judging another, that is to say, peise well the sentence before he give it,'[13] while Mercury advises that 'The knight of Jesus Christ should be arrayed with good preaching and words of teachings.'[14] Athene, goddess of wisdom, remarks that 'that which is noted for wisdom, should be joined with knighthood', referring to the early Christian author Origen. 'Origen says in the Homilies on Exodus that the hope of the good things to come is the solace of those who travail in this deedli life.'[15]

Giovanni Boccaccio (1313–75) wrote his *Decameron* using a literary convention also borrowed by Geoffrey Chaucer in writing his *Canterbury Tales.* He put a miscellaneous group of people together and left them to tell each other stories. Chaucer employed the device of making them all pilgrims on their way to the shrine of Thomas à Becket at Canterbury. Boccaccio put his group in a house outside Florence where they were shut in together to try to escape from the Black Death which was ravaging the city. They tell erotic and risqué stories as well as stories with lessons and morals. Bocaccio's original was written in Italian but by the mid-fifteenth century English versions were available.

A vernacular literature of virtues and vices continued to be popular in most parts of Western Europe. The *Somme le Roi* of Lorens d'Orleans, a thirteenth-century Dominican, was rendered into English in the thirteenth century as *The book of Vices and Virtues.*[16] Here, the Beast of Revelations with its seven heads (Revelation 13.1) becomes the seven vices. The text begins with Pride, which has its own seven branches, each with many twigs. Untruth, Pride's first branch, has twigs called 'ingratitude', 'madness', 'reneging' and so on.

This takes us into the broad question of what counted as 'edifying' writing for a popular Christian readership. Much of what might be deemed 'entertaining' literature seems to have been acceptable provided some sort of moral was drawn. The Dutchman William de Volder (1493–1568), whose name was rendered into Latin as Fullonius, was the author of several 'school' plays in Latin. He had been influenced by Luther and Melanchthon. A translation-paraphrase of his Latin verse into English survives, containing edifying lessons. 'How great a happiness [...] to a father to have his children by all things and in every condition obedient unto him, and for a father to have his children in all points or at all assays made to the beck or to be ruled with a wink.'[17]

The *Liber philosophorum*, a collection of 'moral sayings, wise saws', went on a long journey from the eleventh century. It was translated into Spanish in the twelfth century, then into French late in the fourteenth century, with a Middle English translation, *Dicts and Sayings of the Philosophers*, made from the French by the English nobleman Anthony Woodville (*c.*1440–83) on a sea-crossing to the pilgrimage site of Santiago de Compostela. *Dicts and Sayings* was popular enough to become the first dated book (1477) printed by William Caxton in England.[18]

Renderings from Latin (or occasionally from the Greek) into English could be fairly free. The etiquette of translation extended from the 'word for word' method (*de verbo ad verbum*) to the frank paraphrase. The *Bibliotheca Historica* of the Greek historian Diodorus Siculus was translated into English by John Skelton (*c.*1463–1529), Poet Laureate. Skelton's Preface calls his work an *interpretatio*, a word used both for translation and interpretation in its more modern sense. He also explains his own theory of poetry.[19]

Who might be reading these books or having them read to them? From the eleventh and twelfth centuries, a bourgeoisie was growing in flourishing towns in many parts of Western Europe, with entrepreneurial individuals, clever and confident, sometimes asking awkward questions as the Waldensians did. These were craftsmen and artisans and by derivation traders in their products. As craftsmen they organised themselves into corporations or guilds to strengthen their position in a society still based on land tenure.[20] Some of them, as we shall see, were attracted by the views of the groups of anti-establishment dissidents who pointed in disgust at the conspicuous wealth of higher clergy and asked whether an ecclesiastical system so manifestly corrupt could really be necessary to get people to heaven.

A further important division of the population of the faithful was between men and women. Female literacy was probably never high but there are glimpses of it here and there. *The Twelve Letters That Shall Save Merry England* begins with a woman 'working on a vestment' and embroidering 12 letters in a row.[21]

A wealthy woman in the later Middle Ages might own a *Book of Hours*, which became fashionable in the fifteenth century. These contained the words for the formal 'hours' of daily prayer – on the model of the 'hours' of monastic life but less rigid in form – texts and prayers. A well-born lady could browse such a book at her devotions, assisted by the often distractingly beautiful and highly detailed pictures.

Family life also offers insights into the complexities of lay education and the manners which went with class, and indicate patterns of moral expectation. 'How the good wife taught her daughter' is offered by one book of instruction, with a miscellany of Christian and social advice. Love God and the Church and go to church even if it is raining. You will benefit from your good behaviour. Give to the poor and try to help them. When you are in church, pray; don't chatter and squabble ('make thou no jangling') but be polite to those you meet there. Do not despise an offer of marriage but take advice. Do not let your lover lead you off into places 'where sin might be committed'. When you marry, love your husband above all earthly things. Answer him 'meekly' and he will be calmed: 'A fair word and a meek eases wrath.' Be 'fair' of speech, glad and mild in mood. Do not laugh too loudly. Be true in word and deed and of good conscience, and behave in such a way that no one can say you have acted shamefully. Do not walk too fast nodding your head and wriggling your shoulders. Do not talk too much, nor gad about the town or haunt taverns or get drunk. Do not go to public shows like a strumpet; stay at home. Modesty demands that if a man speaks to you, you greet him politely but then pass on. If you start a conversation he could lead you astray. Do not accept gifts from a man – it leads to ruin. Run your household with discipline and make the servants work. Keep the keys yourself and pay the servants' wages promptly. Be grateful for what you have and do not envy your neighbours. Work hard all week and worship on Sundays and holy days. Do not be extravagant with your husband's money. If your children misbehave, do not shout at them; beat them. If you have daughters, begin to collect goods for their weddings at once.[22]

The same source gives 'the wise man's advice to his son'. This is much shorter. Pray to God first thing each morning. Do not gossip. Work hard. Do not 'seek positions' because everyone will hate you even if you do your duty in them. Avoid drunkenness and gambling. Do not marry for money, as a meek wife who is poor will be the better wife. Do not shout at your wife or call her names – fair words will tame her better. Do not boast how rich you are – only fools do that. Be good and make amends for your sins.[23]

The poems in *The Babees Book* (*c.*1430) describe 'good' behaviour as open and frank, but self-disciplined, courteous and respectful of elders. Fitzstephen, who wrote A 'Life' *(Vita)* of Thomas à Becket, says nobles in England used to send their sons to the Chancellor's household to be trained in honourable living and learning until they were old enough to be knighted.[24] He had 'many' of these in the same age-group 'and their proper retinue and master and proper servants in the honour due'. Such high-born children had each 'an honest servant' to keep their rooms tidy and to dress them. It was the custom from at least the twelfth century to send such children to grow up in a great house of another noble family where they could be taught 'curtesie' and chivalric principles, make useful connections and learn to read and speak French and perhaps understand at least the Latin needed for legal and administrative purposes.[25]

A glance at the surviving literature of the English Middle Ages reveals its range, from the comic to the serious. One game was to mix Latin and English in a macaronic jumble. In a fourteenth-century poem, William de la Pole, 4th Earl and 1st Duke of Suffolk (1396–1450), is mocked by his nickname Jack Napis (the origin of 'Jackanapes') in a piece called *Placebo et Dirige*. The bishops speak in rotation. *Placebo* [I will please], begins the Bishop of Hereford in Latin; *dilexi* [I have loved] says the Bishop of Chester; *hew michi* [heu mihi, woe is me] says Salisbury, and so on.[26]

Self-appointed lay theologians

In this climate of growing lay literacy, a self-appointed theologian like Richard Rolle (1290/1300–1349) could pick up a number of quite advanced theological ideas and write about them. In an era when anyone could attach himself to a master for a fee, Rolle had studied for a time at Oxford.[27] In his 'The form of living', written to the recluse Margaret de Kyrkby, Rolle called himself companionably 'Richard the hermit'. He cautions her that it is not only worldly men and women living openly in gluttony or lechery or other 'open sins' in whom Satan takes an interest, but also those who 'seem in penance and in good life'. 'A thousand wiles he has in what manner he may deceive' such earnest and good-living souls. Some he tricks into error, some he convinces of the rightness of their opinions so that they listen to no one else.[28]

HERETICS OR DISSENTERS?

The dualists

In the medieval West, heresy came to be regarded as an ever-present danger. It represented the spiritual 'terrorism' of its day. A strip of medieval Western Europe running from southern France and northern Spain in the West, eastwards to the Lombard plain and beyond had become a hotbed of latter-day dualism from at least the late twelfth century too. The medieval dualists known as Albigensians, Cathars or Bogomils were not all of one view; there were fine theological distinctions within this system of belief as within Christianity itself. But dualists all believed in an evil Being as eternal enemy to the good God Christians worshipped, and a cosmology in which good and evil were forever at war.

There is some evidence of the way these latter-day dualists lived. The 'perfect' among them were those who received the *consolamentum*: a ritual which might take various forms but which set these 'elect' persons apart. The Cathars had 'bishops' who supervised the arrangements for single-sex communities of the '*perfecti*' to live a life in local houses – not specially-built monasteries – in which they ate no meat and little other food, because it was considered important not to embrace the evil material world. They prayed almost continuously, allowing themselves practically no sleep. Married couples would live separately, perhaps visiting one another's communities for a meal. Sometimes only husband or wife was 'perfect'. As in Augustine's time, those who did not want to make this extreme commitment could remain followers and perhaps receive the *consolamentum* when they were close to death.[29]

Heresies which sounded familiar were often addressed using the ready-made arguments to be found in early Christian texts. For example, these latter-day 'dualist' ideas seemed familiar to those who had read Augustine's writings against the Manichees. Alan of Lille quoted a good deal of Augustine in the section of his *Contra Haereticos* dealing with this heresy.

Attempts at reasoning these heretics back to orthodox Christianity by preaching were unsuccessful. Some were found to be attending church as well as meetings of their heretic groups. So a military solution was tried, an 'Albigensian Crusade' (1209–29). The Fourth Lateran Council of 1215 (3) promised these crusaders the same plenary indulgence (full remission of all outstanding penances due

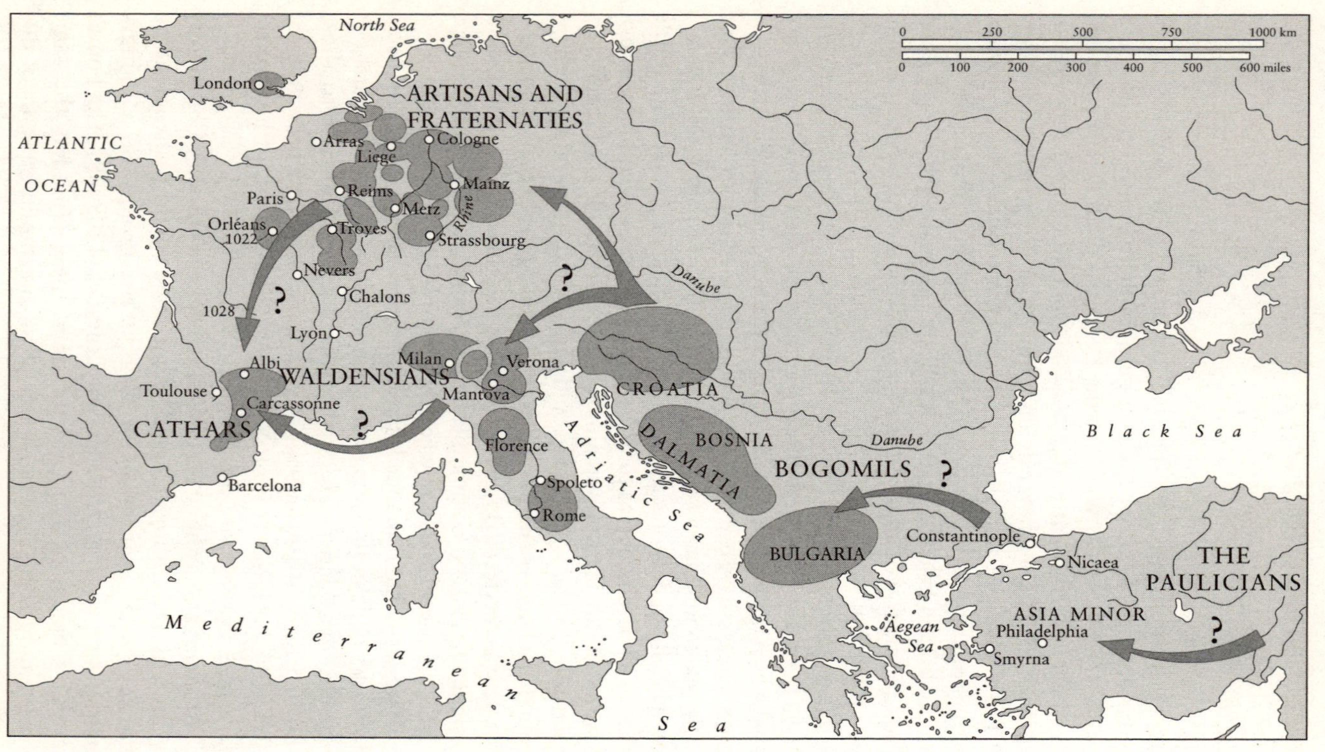

Map 5: Catharism: its spread throughout Europe

and instant admission to heaven) as crusaders to the Holy Land were granted at the Council of Clermont which launched the First Crusade. When the fighting ended, it was still not clear that the heresy had been eradicated, and an Inquisition was set up to seek out any who still called themselves Cathars.

A 'social protest' heresy: the dissenters

Heretics were also seen as presenting novel dangers to the true faith. The heresy of the Waldensians (or 'Poor Men of Lyons') and their successors began a trend in the Western Middle Ages that continued into the Reformation of the sixteenth century. These were articulate lay people, who, disgusted by the wealth and corruption of some of the clergy, argued that a Christian could be saved without the apparatus of the Church and its sacraments. They pointed to the very same abuses which a succession of councils had tried to cure, but such objections had a very different ring when they came from a disaffected laity.

The Waldensian challenge was not primarily to the secular order. The famous couplet challenging the assumption that a class system is

Fig. 26: Engraving by Bernard Picart (1673–1733): public penance of those condemned by the Spanish Inquisition

the will of God. 'When Adam delved and Eve span / Who was then the gentleman' has been attributed to the radical preacher John Ball about 1380, but it was the Church not the state which had most to fear from these anti-establishment heretics. There seems to have been a general lay acceptance of the hierarchical arrangement of society with its nobility and peasantry, as it gave increasing scope for the endeavours of an entrepreneurial bourgeoisie.

The followers of Waldes included intelligent members of a new bourgeoisie who sought to know more about what the Bible said. They consulted sympathetic local clergy who helped them and became quite skilled at answering back with relevant quotations when the Church tried to suppress them or convert them to more acceptable views. An articulate laity was itself something new and threatening in a Christian society where the Church through its clergy had almost a monopoly of literacy.

Some of the self-taught Waldensians engaged in unlicensed 'popular preaching'. In the thirteenth century, Caesarius of Heisterbach (*c.*1189–1240) calls them 'the Devil's servants', describing how some of those thrown out of Montpellier had turned up in Metz, accompanied by a scholar who helped them frame their rejoinders. They tried open-air preaching, without the required preaching licence from the local bishop, designed to ensure that the faith was taught only by those with adequate education and the correct opinions. The local clergy objected and quoted Romans 1.15 ('How shall they preach unless they are sent?'). The heretics promptly answered that they were sent by the Holy Spirit. The ecclesiastical authorities dared not get rid of them because powerful citizens who disliked the local bishop supported the Waldensians.

There is every likelihood that in some places local people were drawn into adopting confused combinations of Waldensian and Albigensian ideas, with some ordinary Christian beliefs mixed in. People minded to agree that the sacraments were not necessary for salvation nevertheless brought their babies to be baptised by their parish priests, just in case. Caesarius of Heisterbach records such muddled thinking, observing that the Cathars are like the Waldensians in that they say that prayer by the living cannot benefit the dead so the whole apparatus of the system of indulgences is rejected. They say that no one's soul benefits from going to church or praying in church; they repudiate baptism and the other sacraments as useless;

they deny transubstantiation. They are also sympathetic to the ideas of the late twelfth-century prophet Joachim of Fiore (*c.*1135–1202), which were condemned by the Fourth Lateran Council of 1215, involving talk of a Last World emperor and the end of the world and interpreting history in terms of the Ages of the Father, the Son and the Holy Ghost. The hotbeds of dualism overlapped geographically with areas where the Waldensians seem to have flourished. This tendency to command broad but confused allegiance made heresy all the more challenging to the ecclesiastical authorities.

Caesarius of Heisterbach has many colourful tales of heresy and heretics in his *Dialogue on Miracles*.[30] Moves were made to spy on them by clerics deputed to infiltrate themselves into the heretical gangs. Master William of Poitou had been a student at the brand new University of Paris. He formed a group of friends among his fellow-students, some clergy, some middle-aged theology students, a goldsmith who believed he was a prophet, a secretary or notary, all making common cause on a number of points which became familiar among later medieval dissidents: they were against the worship of images and praying to saints.

The goldsmith-prophet went to Master Rudolph of Nemours with some of these ideas and the master became suspicious. He asked whether any others thought in the same way and was told of the group of friends. Master Rudolph realised that he could not round up these heretics on his own, so he pretended the Holy Spirit had warned him and went to tell the story to the Abbot of St Victor in Paris, the Bishop of Paris and other leading authority figures. Then he attached himself to the heretics and pretended to be impressed and stayed with them 'under cover' for three months gathering evidence. Then the Bishop of Paris had the group arrested, tried for heresy and stripped of their clerical status, which was as far as the authority of the Church extended. Then, as soon as the king was back and secular authority could be invoked, they were burnt at the stake.

Caesarius reports a story in which emerged yet another aspect of heretical belief which threatened the Church's institutionalised system of spiritual control. He tells of a conversation with a knight who explains that his lands yield crops with which he feeds his family, giving the surplus as alms for the poor. He believes the almsgiving will benefit his soul after death, but because he is an Albigensian not an orthodox Christian he envisages that his soul will migrate to a new person according to how well he has lived his life. So if he has been good, his soul will enter the infant body of a future king, and if not, it will find itself in the infant body of a future beggar.

Cataloguing the heresies

Heresy may have a tendency to confuse but it also has a tendency to fissiparousness. It breeds new forms, as heretics quarrel among themselves on various points and set up new offshoots. Praepositinus of Cremona, writing in the late twelfth or early thirteenth century, made an attempt to catalogue the heresies he had heard about.[31] Some were fringe groups not easily classifiable with the dualists or the anti-establishment heretics. The Passagini fell loosely into the category of the 'vagrants' (*vagantes*), who represented a threat to true faith and good order in the Church, as had been recognised from the early Christian centuries. These were unlicensed preachers and believers who stayed outside the institutional structures of the Church, often claiming to be inspired by the Holy Spirit and not to need the support of the sacraments. Some of the Passagini said they were Sabbatarians, who held that the Old Testament Law must be observed to the letter, including circumcision, Sabbath observance, the Hebrew Passover and Jewish dietary laws. No one who kept the Law exactly could go to hell, they believed. Baptism was considered unnecessary because an infant child was not yet a sinner. At the Eucharist, they argued, the priest did not produce the body and blood of Christ. It was thought they believed that Christ was a mere creature.

Later in the thirteenth century the Dominican Thomas Aquinas attempted a *Summa*, a comprehensive handbook of erroneous beliefs with the appropriate responses to each one. His 'Handbook against the unbelievers' (*Summa contra gentiles*) arranged wrong opinions under headings determined by points of theological dispute. When a Dominican preacher faced a heretic he would be able to find and use the appropriate counter-arguments to demonstrate to the heretic where he was wrong.[32]

Then there were the oddballs, characters who may simply have been psychologically disturbed. A female heresiarch called Guglielma, of a noble family, appeared in Milan in the 1270s. She won many followers and high honour. She claimed that a second redemption of the world would be carried out by a woman, who would rise from the dead and ascend into heaven. The Inquisition decided after her death that she had been a heretic and her bones were burned; her successor, Manfreda, and a male and female disciple were burned too.[33]

Concerns about heresy in Eastern Christendom

In the East the pattern of concern and the classification of heresies was different. Orthodoxy considered that theological truth had been defined once and for all in the period of the early ecumenical councils. Nicetas Choniates (*c.*1155–1255/6), a Greek civil servant, put together a 'Thesaurus of the orthodox faith' (*Thesaurus Orthodoxae Fidei*) which provides a useful clue to contemporary awareness of heresies in twelfth-century Byzantium. He runs through the notable heresies of earlier centuries, referring to what theologians have said about them, a list generally known to scholars of the West too but putting emphasis on different points.

For example, Nicetas notes the *Aphtartodocetarum haeresi*s, the belief that the body of Christ was purely some sort of phantasm or appearance. Adherents of this view could not accept that Christ could have had a real human body that was subject to change or corruption. Then there were those who said that Christ must have had two wills, divine and human, and the Armenians, with their particular refinement of the non-Chalcedonian Monophysite position.[34] Open for discussion in the East but less so in the West were the beliefs abandoned by those who have converted from Islam, for many teachings of Islam were unacceptable.[35] For example, he anathematises the 'false belief' of Muslims concerning paradise.[36]

The classification and countering of heresies was evidently a practical matter as well as a theoretical one for Nicetas Choniates. For example, he describes the process of converting a Muslim. First he fasts for two weeks and then is urged to study the Gospels and the Creed. The presiding priest places his stole round him and he is surrounded by any other of the faithful who wish to take part, and in front of the baptismal font or pool (*piscina*) he is addressed as follows: 'You who today leave the faith of the Saracens for the Christian faith, not forced or under any necessity, sincerely and with your mind and a pure heart, and for love of Christ and his faith, say, "I renounce the whole religion of the Saracens. I anathematize Mohammed, who the Saracens honours as God's prophet and apostle."' If he does not know Greek, an interpreter can assent for him, or his guardian if he is a minor. There follows a long and detailed anathematization of various details of the Qur'an. Then comes the baptism.[37]

The cataloguing of erroneous and false beliefs in Eastern Christendom was not restricted to Christians. Muslims were busy in this area too. Ibn Hazm (d. 1064), writing on contradictions in the four Gospels, made lists of conflicting passages, concluding that '[this shows that] the [Christian] community is altogether vile'.[38]

REPRESSING DISSENT

Inquisition

Those of other faiths were called 'unbelievers', but so were heretics, defined as Christians who had departed from the true faith. Gregory IX set up the Inquisition as a papal tribunal in about 1232, to seek out and try such persons in Western Europe. This represented a strong and condemnatory approach rather than a mission to convert those in error back to the right way of thinking.

It was not long before the Inquisition was accused of corrupt practices. The Council of Vienne noted that Inquisitors, appointed by the apostolic see to suppress heresy, were exceeding their powers and bullying the innocent, sometimes for 'temporal advantage'(26). Inquisitors were being allowed to act 'independently' of bishops and 'summon, arrest or hold for sake-keeping, even securing those arrested hand and foot if it seems necessary'. They may make reasonable enquiries, but they may not act without the local bishop, or he without them, to imprison suspects or use torture or do anything which 'seems more like punishment than custody'.

Provision was to be made for situations where the local bishop and the Inquisitor quarrel and cannot work together. Guards should have keys to 'each room of the prison', one each for the bishop's man and the Inquisitor's guard. Such guards, on appointment, must take an oath on the holy Gospels. They must swear to treat those imprisoned on charges of heresy with due care; there must be no private conversations with the prisoners; and the food provided for the prisoners must be distributed properly, as must food offered 'by relatives, friends or other trustworthy persons' in order to ensure that there is no fraud. Notaries acting as secretaries to the Inquisition shall take a similar oath and there must be conscientious refraining from 'imputing maliciously or deceitfully such a disgraceful crime to an innocent person'. The same council (27) decreed that no one may be an Inquisitor before the age of 40. There must, on pain of excommunication, be no attempt to use the powers of the office to extort money or take bribes even in order to give the money to the Church. Notaries and officials of the Inquisition have a duty to make public any such 'extortions' they become aware of.

The 'eradication of heresies': the Council of Constance

The Council of Constance put the eradication of heresy on its agenda. The main concern at that time was the teaching of John Wyclif, himself dead but his followers still active and influential; John Hus (1372–1415) and Jerome of Prague (1379–1416), currently active in Bohemia.[39]

John Wyclif we have already briefly met. He was an Oxford academic who held several livings in the course of his career. He was selected in 1374 for a diplomatic commission sent to Bruges to discuss papal taxation and England's disputed obligations to Rome. He does not seem to have been much of a success in this capacity, but it helped to crystallise his opinion that the property of the Church should come under civil authority. He was well received as a popular preacher in London, but made an enemy of powerful people as a consequence. Wyclif began to develop contentious theories about 'dominion', the truth of the Bible, the papacy, the religious orders and transubstantiation, until he became altogether too dangerous a figure and was forced to leave Oxford and retreat to his parish at Lutterworth, where he died. The Council of Constance considered him still dangerous even in death. He had too many enthusiastic disciples and heirs.

The conspicuous wealth and self-aggrandisement of the higher clergy was a matter on which the Church councils, one after another, clearly shared a concern with the dissenters. Yet the Church was far from consistent, for example on the division within the Franciscans between those who thought poverty essential to the spirit of their founder, and those who were willing to accommodate a certain amount of wealth in order to ensure that the order survived. Now, among the condemned teachings of John Wyclif, were to be found the claims that 'it is against sacred scripture for ecclesiastics to have possessions' and that 'it is against Christ's command to enrich the clergy'. That, Wyclif argued, meant that rich clergy were *ipso facto* heretics, as were laymen who abetted them; the emperor and secular lords have endowed the Church with wealth at the instigation of Satan. Members of religious orders are similarly tainted, Wyclif had claimed, and his animus against such 'sects', as he called them, was particularly vivid. These dissenting condemnations could be extreme, claiming that the founders of religious orders sinned and acted at the behest of the Devil, and that their members were not Christians at all but belonged to Satan. Anyone who gives them alms is automatically excommunicated. Such sweeping condemnations of religious orders and their founders, members and behaviour (such as friars begging not working for their livings) were rejected by the council.

Wyclif had also campaigned against the making of excessive claims for the powers of priests, most particularly where they involved private Masses, for people were paying to have special prayers said for individuals. Dissenters wrongly claimed, insisted the council, that 'special prayers applied by prelates or religious to a particular person avail him or her no more than general prayers, if other things are equal'. The council thought otherwise.

In Wyclif's mind, this anti-establishment feeling extended to condemnation of corrupt secular officers too. The council accused him of saying that 'nobody is a civil lord or a prelate or a bishop while he is in mortal sin'; 'people can correct sinful lords at their discretion'; 'tithes are purely alms, and parishioners can withhold them at will on account of their prelates' sins'.

The Council of Constance set about condemning the now dead John Wyclif by listing 45 of his unacceptable opinions, which were still very much alive. He could not be executed – but he and his writings could be denounced.

The council's condemnation of a second figure, the Bohemian radical John Hus, was an attack on a living reformer and his ideas. He was called before the council in person to answer for his views. The council's sentence against him linked his ideas with those of Wyclif: 'John Wyclif, of cursed memory, by his deadly teaching, like a poisonous root, has brought forth many noxious sons', Hus among them. It was certainly true that copies of Wyclif's writings were to be found at the University of Prague, though Wyclif's books had been burned by the Archbishop of Prague in 1410. Hus had helped to create a hotbed of dissent in the University of Prague, and had, it was alleged, been publicly resisting in the very schools of the same city the condemnations of Wyclif's ideas made more than once by the authorities in the university.

The council's method of dealing with this dangerous development was the routine one of publishing a list of banned opinions. These opinions, it says, are to be found in Hus's writings, especially in his book on the Church (*De ecclesia*),[40] so that book is banned, including any translations. Indeed the book was to be burned in the city of Constance, publicly and solemnly.

Careful study of Hus's opinions, said the council, had been undertaken by academic experts to justify this extreme sanction. His great offence has been to appeal directly to Christ for authority, 'by-passing' the Church's intermediaries. Hus's ecclesiology (proto-Calvinist to the modern eye) relied on certain principles that would have been attractive to many reformers of the next century. He held – much as Augustine had done – that membership of the one holy Church is only for the predestined; that these cannot lose their predestined status due to any sin of their own, for God's choice cannot fail; that the damned are also predestined and can never become members of the Church or be saved.

That St Peter was never the Church's head just because he could be counted as the first Bishop of Rome, and therefore the pope is not now its head as his successor, was an idea that was going to be embraced by many later reformers who sought to separate themselves from the Church of Rome. Hus went further, claiming, in a Wycliffite spirit, that a pope who is a wicked man is therefore not even a member of the Church; that the papacy is a creation or emanation of the Empire and there is no divinely appointed duty of obedience to the pope; and that unworthy priests such as a pope like this are condemned because they pollute their own priestly actions.

Hus's views threatened to undermine ecclesiastical control in other ways too. He demanded that the ordinary faithful should be allowed to received both the bread and the wine ('both kinds' of the consecrated 'elements') at the Eucharist. It had been customary for some centuries in the West for the laity to receive only the bread. Session 13 of the council, on 13–15 June 1415, countered his claim and gave authority to the practice, with a decree that any priest who gave the laity communion in both kinds would be excommunicated.

Hus had moreover been challenging the rule that a preacher must have a licence to preach from the local bishop. He claimed that any priest knowing his Bible and filled with the desire to instruct people in the faith had not only a right but a positive duty to preach, even if he had been excommunicated. This, if permitted, was seen as having dangerous potential for a popular demagogue to mislead the faithful.

Hus's deposition was to be read out openly and publicly. Condemned, he was to be handed over to the secular authorities for execution, since the Church could not itself carry out the death penalty.

Jerome of Prague, one of the city's academics, was also condemned as a follower of Wyclif. He recanted once before the council but 'returned to his vomit' by thinking again and asking for an opportunity to address the council on the very points he had forsworn. The council condemned him as a heretic who had relapsed into heresy and as an excommunicated and anathematised person.

A topic which would become more prominent in the ensuing century, when it began to disturb Martin Luther, got a mention at Constance: 'It is ridiculous to believe in the indulgences of popes and bishops.' This claim came in a cluster of ecclesiological condemnations of the papacy. They say that it is not necessary for salvation to believe in the primacy of the Church of Rome; that Silvester and Constantine[41] erred; that the Church of Rome is 'Satan's synagogue'; that the pope is not the vicar of Christ and the practice of election by the cardinals was the Devil's invention; that decretals are apocryphal and lead the faithful astray.

More troublemakers

Not all dissenting leaders and their followers got a personal mention at the Council of Constance, even those who were famous academics. The views of the ecclesiastical hierarchy were equivocal when it came to the universities. The University of Oxford had itself condemned and outlawed Wyclif in the end. The academic Wyclif's own disgruntled criticism of universities is included among the council's condemnations of Wycliffite heresy, for the 'heretics' say that 'Universities, places of study, colleges, degrees and academic exercises in these institutions were introduced by a vain pagan spirit and benefit the church as little as does the devil.'

Dissent in the fifteenth century was to spread mainly through movements expressing popular discontent, rather than through intellectual leadership. Such popular movements began alongside the more sophisticated arguments of Wyclif, Hus, Jerome of Prague and their like. Wyclif's contemporary John Ball (*c.*1338–81) had been a renegade priest in Kent. He used to wait for the people to come out of church after Mass and then preach stirring ideas, disrespectful of both secular and ecclesiastical authority. Ball told his listeners that we are all equally descendants of Adam and Eve; that slavery was not in God's plan; and insisted that honest workmen ought to be paid fairly for their labour. England would never flourish until there was neither lord nor master, he said – everyone must be equal. There must no longer be a class of the wealthy and privileged, better housed, better dressed and better fed through no merit of their own.

The people heard these sermons with such enthusiasm that the Archbishop of Canterbury had Ball arrested as a dangerous demagogue and threat to good order, and imprisoned him for three months. The moment he was released he returned to his sermonising and speech-making. Ball's ideas caught on and a national campaign began, with a call for all supporters to come to London to mount a protest. He died in the ensuing Peasants' Revolt of 1381, but in parts of England resentment was brewing and people continued to claim they were being oppressed.

John Ball's reputation even spread to France. The chronicler Froissart describes the way he preached and compared him to the French revolutionary, Jacques Bons-hommes.[42] Froissart explains the custom in England, France and elsewhere under which the nobility have powers and privilege over the 'common' people, keeping them in bondage.

Piers Plowman, another fourteenth-century indicator of trouble to come, is a 'vision' story which tells its own tale of criticism of the clergy in its detailed pictures of contemporary life, with morals drawn for the reader. Its probable West Midlands author, known as 'William Langland', is likely to have been born in the 1330s and to have died in the 1380s. He may have been a cleric or a layman, but he chose to write in English. Langland does not seem to have been a ringleader of an active revolt, but he was anticlerical in his sympathies and a sharp critic of corruption in the Church. He spoke out against the encouragement of pilgrimage and other money-making ventures prevalent in the Church, possibly because he belonged to the community of clergy without livings or benefices who tended to be radical and resentful of a system that did not work for them. Vagabond clergy could earn an insecure living by acting as temporary secretaries to patrons, and Langland might have been one of those.

The friars, with their mission of urban preaching, also on occasion became accidental and sometimes deliberate popularisers of ideas and practices which could lead to sedition. They wrote a variety of books, some addressed to the laity, some political, satirical and even seditious.[43] This encouraged the use of the vernacular, and lay preachers, seeing the friars preaching in the open air, began to imitate them. Norman French might have its place as the language of public administration, but Middle English was the common language.

The perceived threat from these varied challenges tended to embattle authority, not only in the Church but also in the state.[44] A 'Mirror of princes' literature[45] emerged, concerned with the exercise of divine power on earth through human agents and with the relationship between secular power and divine authority. Satire against secular and ecclesiastical authorities could be extreme.[46] 'Political tracts' questioned whether kings needed to be rich to discharge the role God has given them.[47] The rule of law was needed to maintain royal authority,[48] '[b]ut people doubt whether kings should punish sins, and it seems not because of their jurisdictions, for worldly and spiritual are always separate'. The clergy, who punish people's sin claiming Christ's authority, should 'live cleanly' and not have impressive houses and positions in the secular state. They should not be an expense to people that they dwell among.[49]

Lollardy

The transition from Wyclif's campaigning to the 'Lollardy' which followed on its heels in England is hard to trace. Though he was demonised by ecclesiastical officialdom to the point where his books were burnt, the copies carried off to Prague by sympathisers ensured that they were not wholly lost. And the ideas themselves, many of which were shared with leaders of popular discontent since the time of the Waldensians, had by now a natural appeal to ordinary lay people.

Archbishop Courtenay expressed concern in 1382 that preachers were spreading Wyclif's ideas not only in churches but in all sorts of places.[50] Preaching in a town, as with Wyclif's London sermons, could rouse mob feeling without necessarily teaching much theology.[51] Wyclif's ideas seem to have caught on early in Leicester, where William Swinderby (fl. 1382–92) was preaching.[52] Swinderby was one of Wyclif's keenest supporters and in the decade following his death one of the most prominent. Little is known about his education, but he made a name for himself as a preacher and he had lived as a hermit with the partial approval and partial disapproval of the Augustinians. He proved difficult to silence once he began actively to preach Wycliffite ideas. Several attempts were made to get Swinderby condemned for heresy, but he would just reappear somewhere else and carry on. His real threat was his popularity. Swinderby was accused of preaching 'to please the people' (*ob favorem popularem*) so that 'the common crowd enjoyed coming to hear him' (*vulgus commune solet gaudenter audire*).[53]

He was discovered preaching along the Welsh border about 1390, when an attempt was made to condemn him on the basis of a list of articles of alleged heretical belief that he was said to be teaching. In 1391 he was condemned as a heretic, but escaped from the attempt to imprison him and then tried unsuccessfully to appeal to the king and Parliament. Swinderby was last heard of about 1392, in Wales, where he was being hunted in an effort to recapture him.

The way the authorities tried to deal with him set a pattern. The articles of heretical belief became a more or less standard list, matching quite closely the sort of thing Wyclif had been exploring in his writings, but also reflecting stock dissenting opinions that had been circulating since the twelfth century or earlier. A good deal of it boiled down to anti-clericalism, particularly the condemnation of clerical wealth. Transubstantiation was unpopular because it imputed immense power to priests, while the doctrine that priests had power to absolve sinners was disliked for the same reason. There were frequent claims that the right to preach should not be restricted to clerics licensed by bishops.

'Lay theologians' and self-appointed clerics appear

Did all this amount to the formation of a *Secta Wyclif*?[54] No body of personal followers bearing his name seems to have formed or survived. Perhaps there were simply too many rival demagogues. Swinderby was not alone in spreading the word about Wyclif's ideas, or to be more precise, ideas quite generally held to which he had given expression. Wyclif's works were 'indexed' for reference, including his published sermons.[55] William Ramsbury, who claimed to have been ordained by a friend, went around preaching in inns as well as churches and celebrating a 'Mass' in Dorset, Berkshire and Wiltshire in the 1380s.[56] He, like other laymen (and laywomen) of Lollard sympathies, seized upon the idea that they too could 'do' theology, just as well as priests.

Books, pamphlets and broadsheets seem to have been important in the early dissemination of 'Lollard' ideas and of course committing these opinions to the written word helped to create an agenda for the movement.[57]

'Wandering scholars' from the universities seem to have been attracted to dissident groups. Bristol and Northampton became early 'Lollard' centres, partly no doubt because refugees from Oxford preached in these places. In 1393, the names of 'wandering preachers' (*vagantes presbiteros*) were called for on episcopal authority,[58] for priests and academic clerics who were not necessarily priests sometimes assisted these lay efforts. In one case it was said that the *receptrix lollardorum* was Anna Palmer, an anchorite at St Peter's Church who had been entertaining Lollards.[59] This sort of development suggested a dangerous blurring of the defining lines of ordination.

Episcopal enquiries into the presence of what were coming to be called 'Lollards' were affected by the historical boundaries of dioceses and their by now untidy mapping onto the centres of populations. For example, the west of London lay in the corners of four dioceses.[60] For that reason, clusters of heretics were never going to be discovered easily by searches within dioceses. Family members sometimes 'told on' one another to the authorities as a result of family squabbles, but it is also likely that families influenced one another and formed Lollard households.[61]

The sophistication to be found among the 'dissenting' laity is impressive. Business letters of a family who included staplers, wool gatherers, grocers and merchants, trading as exporters in Calais and Bruges, exemplify the pattern of European trade and the growing refinement of the urban and merchant laity.[62] Lollards met in house groups and studied the Scriptures in the English translation associated with Wyclif though not his own work. They built a body of 'Lollard' opinion on the standard topics of contemporary dissent which were also being consolidated in other parts of Europe.[63]

With widening lay interest, justification for the use of the vernacular to 'do theology' naturally grew, even if it was first defended in Latin.

The *Tractatus de regibus* is by Wyclif or a follower. It is hostile to bishops holding important positions in government and mentions the persecution of Lollard preachers which began in earnest as early as 1382.[64] Its (Latin) sentiment is that 'wisdom lies not in language but in underlying truth, for it is the same wisdom in Latin as in Greek or Hebrew, and truth should be openly known to all kinds of people, truth moves many men to speak opinions in English that they have gathered in Latin; and for this reason are men counted as heretics'.[65]

Reasons are given why explaining things in English – or any vernacular – is a good thing. For example, it will help to 'make this thing better known', 'so that kings may hearby see that they should not be idle but rule by God's law to win the bliss of heaven', 'for kings should not be tyrants of their people, but rule them by reason that falls to their state', 'for thus should God's law be better known and defended'.[66] 'It has been often written before that kings should be respected above other people' (1 Peter 2.17), but Christians are urged to 'show proper respect to everyone, love the family of believers, fear God, honor the emperor'.[67] Then comes a discussion of the appropriateness of the choice of the English word 'worship' for a monarch (translated above as 'respect').[68] The word does not of course mean the sort of 'worship' owed to God. It concerns treating the ruler as 'worthy', that is honouring him; kings should be 'worshipped' in this sense more than priests in worldly matters, though where worship of God is concerned, priests should surpass kings.[69]

The heresy trials begin

When the Church tackled the problem systematically, it did so by trying people for heresy. Those who were condemned were, where appropriate, handed over to the secular authorities for execution. In 1448 'a heretic was burned at Tower Hill'. He was named John Cardmaker of Coventry.[70] He held many false opinions and two in particular.[71] One was not accepting transubstantiation, the other the belief that an infant born of a Christian married couple did not need baptism.[72]

These were not papal inquisitions but heresy trials instituted by local bishops. Heresy trials in Norfolk are recorded in some detail from the first half of the fifteenth century. The records provide names and personal details. For example, Margery was the wife of William

Baxter, wright, of Martham, East Norfolk. Depositions made against her included those of Johanna, who was the wife of William Clyfland. The allegations were detailed and help to give a picture of the domestic character of theological discussions. Joanna described a conversation when she and Margery were sitting together in a room, in the presence of various persons, who were also named.[73] She described what was discussed and the unsatisfactory views of the accused.

This was, however, a guided process. The inquisitors asked leading questions, searching for evidence on key points of error. The record notes the same 'heretical' ideas again and again. Typical examples of views considered heretical included claiming that confirmation by a bishop was unnecessary, that the child did not need it and that the Holy Spirit simply acted through grace when the child was old enough to understand the faith. Confession to a priest was unnecessary, for only God could forgive sins. Transubstantiation was another area where heretical error was searched for, a heretic usually referring to it as false doctrine. A heretic could also be expected to say that images should be outlawed because reverence for images was idolatrous; that pilgrimages should be outlawed, because they just made the monks and clergy rich; that fasting was not necessary, because God did not institute it.

An important general indicator much used to test for heresy was to ask the accused to swear an oath before a judge. The Council of Constance (43) condemned those who said that oaths taken to confirm civil commerce and contracts between people were unlawful. This reluctance to swear arose from Jesus' instruction to his disciples that their yes should be a simple yes and their no, no (Matthew 5.37), reinforced by the Epistle of James (5.12), where James urges Christians not to swear by anything or take any oath.

The trials of the heretics continue

Heresy trials were still taking place at the beginning of the sixteenth century. The standardised questions were designed to test whether the attitude of those on trial to each of the sacraments was sound and that they held no unacceptable opinions about veneration of images, praying to the saints, reservation of the sacrament or the use of holy water. In Kent, as recorded in the Register of Warham, Archbishop of Canterbury (*c.*1450–1532, Archbishop from 1503), three final questions were listed, designed to elicit a statement that the accused did not now hold any heretical opinions, would make a truthful confession and owned no books containing heretical opinions.[74]

In the case of the heresy trials in Kent, it is possible to glimpse the sorts of people who came under suspicion because their trades and ages are noted: cordwainers, cutlers, shoemakers, weavers, fletchers, tailors, servants, glovers, with ages ranging from 21 to 74.

It is hard now to grasp the full terror of the scene that confronted accused artisans and other ordinary men and women, on trial for their lives, when they were brought up before the Chancellor and professors of theology and a Doctor of both civil and canon law (*utriusque iuris doctor*).[75] Some individuals no doubt responded with truculence, some with trembling. Robert Harrison, aged 60, had the charges read to him and had to say whether he agreed or not with the opinion put to him in each. On one charge, 'as he said, he did not know how else it was possible to be saved'.[76]

Named witnesses would testify that the accused had expressed opinions 'against the Catholic faith and the sacraments of the Church'. These depositions are given in the record, and the style of the testimonies often appears circumstantial and therefore the more convincing. Yet these were friends and neighbours who could be intimidated into testifying by the threat that if they did not do so then they would reveal themselves to be heretics and so face trial.[77] If the evidence is about a private conversation, it was one man's or woman's word against another's. Christopher Grebill, tailor, aged 22, described how he and Harrison, the accused, were walking together on the Eve of the Assumption the previous year when Harrison said that going on pilgrimage was not profitable to a man's soul but a waste of time. He also said that indulgences and pardons were useless and it was also pointless to offer money or candles to images in the church. Grebill was asked if anyone else was present and he said no. He added that the two of them had discussed all these matters quite often.[78] In this case there was confirmation from another source. William Ryche, a glover, aged 40, who said that he had had a talk with Harrison at Tenterden on St Mark's Day at the fair, and heard him say that the consecrated bread was just bread, something he claimed to have heard Harrison say many times.

Ryche also accused John Ive and William Olbert of expressing similar sentiments. William Olbert, aged 64, confirmed he had been present with the others a year earlier on the Feast of the translation of St Thomas at John Ive's house where they had all discussed the Eucharist and agreed that the consecrated bread was just bread ('oonly materiall bred'). Agnes Ive, a widow, aged 60, said she and Elizabeth White had asked William Olbert to go with them to Harrison's house and they all did. There she heard Harrison speak of pilgrimages 'as she now remembreth and thynketh'. And she conjectured that he would have gone on to talk about the sacraments except that someone came in and interrupted them. Although this seems to suggest that all of the group had participated in risky conversations, the judges excommunicated only Olbert.

William Carder of Tenterden seems to have been combative when charged.[79] His response to the charges included, 'You are full of questions. Believe what you like. I will believe as a Christian man should do.' But Christopher Grebill's father John, aged 60, testifed that 20 years previously, William Carder used to read the Gospels and try to teach him his beliefs. This last winter the two of them used to meet secretly and discuss these views and agree about them. He said Carder had made it plain that Carder's father and mother were of the same 'secte'. No one else was present except 'he supposith' Christopher Grebill. Grebill indeed confirmed he had been present and his father said he was there last winter. Witness Stephen Castellen, aged 22, a cutler, said Carder given him his opinion about the doctrine of transubstantiation three years earlier: that the consecrated Host was 'only bread' and not the body of Christ. Witness William Riche, aged 40, a glover, had often discussed theology with Carder over a period of eight years, with no one else present, and had agreed on opinions as he now confirmed. Carder was excommunicated too.

Family members were persuaded to testify against one another. In the case of Agnes Grebill, John's wife, aged 60,[80] her husband and two sons, including John the younger, aged 21, were willing to do so. Harrison, Agnes and Carder were 'relinquished to the secular arm' for punishment.[81] But they and some others forswore their wrong opinions and the excommunications were lifted.

Recanters could make especially enthusiastic witnesses against their former friends. John Browne said he had abjured his errors before the Archbishop of Canterbury, Cardinal Morton, at Maidstone 12 years earlier and 'he bore [carried] a faggot for his penance'. This was a public humiliation to be endured as a token of genuine repentance.

Browne claimed to have learned these errors from John Riche, who he thinks was burned at Halden in the diocese of Canterbury.[82]

The trial of John Browne of Ashford, cutler, relied on the deposition of Joan Harwode who said that about Christmas six or seven years earlier, Browne came to her husband's house and 'then and there in an evening sitting by the fire in the hall', they talked about the sacrament of the altar. The three of them together concluded, affirmed, held and believed that the Host was 'oonly brede'.[83] On another occasion, she said that she and her husband went to Browne's house and sitting together by the fire eating and drinking they had 'communication' against worshipping of the images of saints and going on pilgrimage. Browne's wife, Elizabeth, joined in and agreed that going on pilgrimage was nothing else but to spend money wastefully and they all agreed that the saints were in heaven so their images should not be worshipped on earth.[84] William Baker on Lady Day 12 months earlier had been in a garden at Charte (whose garden it was exactly he could not tell), when he and John Browne had communication together about purgatory. According to Baker, Browne had said there was no such place.[85]

The trials could be very lengthy, such as that of Edward Walker, which lasted from 8 May to 3 October.[86] Assorted and somewhat random punishments were imposed, including for one heretic, 'treating his wife well'.[87] Some were sentenced to be imprisoned in a religious house, perhaps for life. Being handed over to the secular arm could mean burning; one sentence consisted of watching the burning of William Carder, an awful warning against continuing with heretical attitudes.

Did such popular dissidence give rise to the Reformation?

Conclusion

RENAISSANCE AND EXPANSION

A history of medieval Christianity must have an end, though events ran on. In the sixteenth century, Western Europe embarked on 'renaissance', Reformation and Counter-Reformation and expansion into the New World of the Americas. The Reformation of the sixteenth century was going to create a range of 'Churches', fragmenting the comparative unity over which the Bishop of Rome had presided for so long. Meanwhile, Christianity in Eastern Europe and the Middle East entered into new political relationships with the conquering Ottomans. The Roman Empire which had survived so long in Byzantium ended at last in 1453 and Christian energies were going to be needed to protect tradition rather than to challenge it. The lands which lay on the border between Eastern and Western European Christendom were left under threat. The westward advance of the Ottomans was finally rebuffed only in 1683 in a battle for control of Vienna.

CHRISTIANITY IN WESTERN EUROPE AT THE END OF THE MIDDLE AGES

About 1500, a Wycliffite poet, imitating Piers Plowman, offered a sketch of the life of the poor, and a picture of the animosity between friars and secular clergy and the forlorn state of the laity faced with their neglect. The poet says he knows his *paternoste*r and his *ave Maria* but not yet his Creed. So he has asked around for guidance. First he consulted the friars, who said it was their secret. Each kind of friar criticised the others as unsound, money-grabbing, unsafe with women. The Dominicans, he notices, had a particularly extravagant convent. The friars all wanted gifts and would pardon him, for a payment, without his learning the Creed. Then he met a ploughman, badly dressed, with mud up to his ankles, with his wife and three children. He says he is Piers the Plowman. He has a lot more to say about the friars. Then he teaches the enquirer the Creed (properly) and moves on to try to explain the doctrine of transubstantiation about which there is a lot of argument. It is apparent that the friars do not understand it either. It is the meek who receive the Holy Spirit.[1]

The great themes of the reformers' theology in the sixteenth century overlapped a good deal with the concerns of the medieval dissidents of Western Europe, but they included important new ideas. The central question did not change, however: individuals still sought a reassurance that they would be 'saved' from an eternity in hell. But the ecclesiastical and sacramental apparatus involved had become overcomplicated and there was widespread disillusionment over the levels of corruption perceived.

Of all this overwhelming apparatus of the 'salvation system' of the medieval Western Church which Martin Luther (1483–1546) wanted to get rid of, 'indulgences' seemed to him the worst and certainly the least defensible in theological terms. It offended him to see the Church making money out of 'selling' time off purgatory, with dubious pardoners peddling remission of penitential 'sentences'. But behind this stood the underlying penitential system on which this practice rested. Luther's doctrine of 'justification by faith' cut through the whole edifice by claiming that all that was needed was faith in Christ (*sola fides*), and all the Christian needed to read about faith was contained in the Bible (*sola Scriptura*).

John Calvin went further still, claiming that no one could get to heaven by effort, because God had already chosen those he would admit. Augustine of Hippo would have agreed on that point, but not with Calvin's further opinion, that God had also chosen who was to be damned, as distinct from allowing the non-elect to fall into the consequences of original sin universal to humanity, and go to hell by default.

The task of clearing other parts of the crowded theological decks of the late Middle Ages remained. The Mass had come to be seen as an additional sacrifice, not merely a commemoration of the one decisive sacrifice to atone for the sins of the whole world which Christ had made on the Cross. The emergence of the doctrine of transubstantiation in the eleventh and twelfth centuries had reinforced this idea, with its insistence that the consecrated bread and wine actually became the body and blood of Christ, so that he died again in each Mass. That 'sacrifice' could be made only by a priest, and some priests would do it privately for money, 'applying' it to the benefit of named individuals.

Hatred of the religious orders, especially the friars, so vivid in Wyclif, did not diminish in the sixteenth century, but the focus of reforming pressure changed. The new idea was to close down ('dissolve') religious houses. Numerous monks and nuns left their religious houses and married, casting aside their vows of celibacy.

A 'renaissance' in Western Europe closely accompanied the Reformation. Scholars such as Erasmus (1466–1536), John Colet (1457–1519) and Luther's friend and ally Melanchthon (1497–1560) – some of whom were also leading reformers – learned Greek and read the classics of Greece and Rome with fresh eyes. Some mastered Hebrew too, though Erasmus found he could not manage both. These scholars went back *ad fontes*, to the 'sources' of the Bible text in the Greek and Hebrew versions, and criticised inaccuracies in Jerome's Vulgate Latin translation. That presented an automatic challenge to the authority of the Church, which insisted that the Vulgate *was* the Scripture. To admit that it contained mistakes would be to undermine the Western Church's teaching of a thousand years, and cast aside a whole exegetical tradition of close analysis of the Latin words and phrases.

Too much was at stake for any of this to be regarded as merely the arrival of interesting new ideas and knowledge. Concepts of citizenship that had been natural to Augustine of Hippo, but had had limited relevance since the end of the ancient world, reappeared for discussion. The maintenance of good order, rule by just and merciful kings, with an accepted hierarchy in which everyone had a place and function, had seemed settled in a Christian *politeia* for a thousand years, but while that had accommodated an immense range of local variants, it had rarely – except in Italy, where cities persisted – been 'civic'. The late medieval city in Italy brought the image of Jerusalem down to earth as a place for living in and not merely for worship in church buildings. There was building for beauty, with gemstones and marble, colour and brilliance, light. The ideal city should be set in beautiful countryside with flowing rivers and fertile lands and forests, and landscape began to acquire its own aesthetic. 'Citizenship' was being rethought and with it the Christian's place in the universe and his relationship with his God.

CHRISTIANITY IN EASTERN EUROPE AND THE END OF THE MIDDLE AGES

In Eastern Europe there was to be no counterpart of the Protestant Reformation. When Luther approached Byzantium for support for his own reforming challenges, he found the only common ground he had with the Christians there was a mutual hatred of the papacy.

The Greek Churches were busy with other challenges. The Byzantines had found themselves facing Ottoman invasions from the thirteenth century. This Turkish tribe had taken over Anatolia and then begun to move westwards into Europe. The Ottomans had reached Bulgaria by 1366 and brought it under their control, and in 1389 they defeated Serbia at a battle at Kosovo. A crusade was called by the West in an attempt to push the invasion back, but it failed – defeated at the Battle of Nicopolis in 1396. Approach by sea remained just possible while Constantinople was surrounded by the invaders, and the Venetians kept trade going until the Ottomans finally took the city in 1453. They also captured the Arab lands of the Middle East and brought Islamic rule to a vast territory in which Christianity had first established itself.

The conquest of Constantinople represented a symbolic victory of great importance, and the Ottomans set about making their mark. Mehmed II (1432–81) declared himself the protector of the Christian Church and behaved as a Byzantine emperor in choosing the next Patriarch. Nevertheless, the conquest formally made the region Muslim. Hagia Sophia was turned into a mosque and became a main centre of worship for Sunni Islam. At the same time, administrative arrangements were changed to suit Ottoman and Islamic norms and expectations, and the language of the court was now to be Turkish.

As in Reformation and 'renaissance' Western Europe, but for different reasons, radical rethinking of the principles of secular as well as spiritual authority was to take place. There was no counterpart in Islam to the Christian distinction between the jurisdiction of a king (temporal) and that of a pope or bishop (spiritual). The Sultan was a religious as well as a secular leader. He was Imam as well as monarch to his people. Despite the corruptions of Byzantine rule for so many centuries, that line had never been crossed. In one respect, the Ottoman conquest was merciful. Christian communities, including Greek Orthodox and Armenians as well as Jews, were allowed to run their own schools and courts and to worship in their own way. About 1502 the Moors in Spain turned to the Ottoman Sultan for protection of the practise of their religion.[2]

For more than a century after 1453 these Islamic conquerors ruled parts of south-east Europe and the Balkans and tried to press further west. The politics of the Balkans has remained profoundly affected by the difficulties of multi-faith living in communities of mixed Christians, both Orthodox and Roman Catholic, and Muslims.

CHRISTENDOM EXPANDS ACROSS THE WORLD AT THE END OF THE MIDDLE AGES

Christendom was not only facing upheaval. It was also expanding geographically. From the end of the fifteenth century, 'discoveries' were being made by Christian explorers, looking for a way to reach the Far East by sea.

In this quest, and applying the possibility that the earth was round, 'discoverers' sailed to the west across the Atlantic. Christopher Columbus (1450/1–1506), an Italian adventurer backed by the Spanish monarchy, made a first attempt in 1492 and found not China (his ultimate objective) but a new continent. Christianity arrived in South America with the conquest and settlement of the new lands. The Roman Catholic Church brought not only a new faith but a new language, so that Spanish still dominates the countries of South America, with the exception of Brazil.

In what is now Brazil, the Portuguese had the rights of colonisation under the terms of the Treaty of Tordesillas (1494), which had drawn a metaphorical dividing line north to south across the Atlantic, with the Portuguese granted dominion over land to the east of it and the Spanish granted dominion over land to the west. Brazil, it turned out, stuck out into the Portuguese half. The Protestants of Northern Europe arrived in North America in the later sixteenth and early seventeenth centuries and left their own stamp of Christian belief and language there.

An alternative route to the East by sea was to sail round the Cape of Good Hope and into the Indian Ocean, circumnavigating the continent of Africa. For most of the Middle Ages it had not been realised that Africa extended a long way south of the Sahara. Maps of the period show an abbreviated continent. In time, Portuguese explorers discovered its true extent, eventually sailing into the Indian Ocean and onwards to India itself.

By that route the Portuguese landed at Calicut in 1498, in a ship captained by Vasco da Gama. It brought trade and only secondarily the Christian religion, though the explorers had sailed with a commission from the pope. The local people were Hindus and they lived in fear of the Mongols then invading northern India from Afghanistan. The Mongols included Muslims, and the Portuguese, coming from the Iberian Peninsula, regarded Muslims as their natural enemies too.[3] Pedro Alvarez Cabral brought six ships full of missionaries to Calcutta, an episode that ended in violence, but they sailed on and encountered the existing Christians of India further south.

These were the 'Thomas' Christians, descendants of the Syrian community of Mar Thoma, numbering perhaps 100,000 along the Malabar coast. They recognised the Nestorian patriarch in Persia at the time, currently Shimon V (1472–1502). He sent them two Syrian-Persian bishops and his successor provided them with a metropolitan and two more bishops. If the Portuguese had hoped to find the local Christians in charge of trade and politics, they were disappointed; the Muslims and Hindus had control.

The newcomer Christians were also ignorant of the implications of the differences in practice and belief arising from the fact that these Indian Christians were Nestorians. Nonetheless, the contrasts in custom and practice were obvious enough: for example, Thomas Christian priests could marry; their churches were empty of images; and they worshipped not in Latin but in Syriac. The newcomers thought, naively, that they had only to enlighten the natives to change these points of practice. Nestorian beliefs presented a more profound divergence, but nevertheless, Roman Christianity was soon established in Portuguese India, with native-born priests being ordained and a Catholic bishopric (1539) made a suffragan see of Funchal in the Atlantic.[4]

The Jesuits arrived 40 years later, led by Francis Xavier, co-founder of this missionary order with Ignatius Loyola. Xavier found perhaps a hundred Catholic priests already in Goa, but his goal was to bring the faith to rural India. He discovered many already baptised as Christians in the fishing villages, but largely untaught about the faith. It seems likely that these people had consented to baptism in order to gain the protection of the Portuguese in the face of Muslim attacks on their vessels and their trade. Asked what they believed, they replied they had not been able to understand what they had been told in Portuguese.[5] Xavier concluded that the Portuguese authorities had set a poor example as Christians, guilty as he believed them to be of corruption.

Xavier did not restrict his efforts to India, believing he had a mission to the whole of Asia, including Japan (1549–52); he would eventually die off the Chinese coast. Once he had left the area of Portuguese influence in India, divisions began to emerge between the Thomas Christians and the Roman Christians, while a schism also emerged in the Nestorian patriarchate in Persian Kurdistan.[6]

IS THERE A MODERN 'CHRISTIAN EUROPE'?

In late April 2014, Rowan Williams, the former Archbishop of Canterbury, spoke to the press about whether Britain was still a 'Christian society'. In the Middle Ages there would have been only one answer to that question. The Christian tradition, including all its 'popular' variants and distortions, saturated the societies of Europe except where the interface with Islam and the presence of the Jews threw up alternatives and challenges. Christian assumptions shaped society as well as people's thinking, from the highly educated to the simplest soul whose theological ideas are not hard to recapture, but who understood the rules for living a good Christian life.

'Are you a Christian?' The ordinary person in most of Europe throughout the Middle Ages would have answered, 'Yes of course.' It was what society expected. Anyone answering 'No' would have stood out uncomfortably in the local community. Every child (except the children of Jews and Muslims) would be baptised in infancy. This did not mean that people were necessarily any better able to explain exactly what they believed or to rehearse the history of their faith than the modern young European adult with perhaps little more than a smattering of 'multicultural religious studies' recollections from school.

From the fall of the Roman Empire, for a thousand years until the Reformation began, the Christian faith in Western Europe became the subject of endless argument and speculation among theologians. It has been less easy to pin down in this book what being a Christian meant to the majority of illiterate people, who did not have the education to write or even read books, and to those who were functionally literate but who could not engage with the intricacies of Latin debates. Nonetheless, there exists a vast literature of 'popular' religion, whether the lives of saints, the writings of people – including laywomen – some of whom had mystical experiences, sermons full of stories designed to appeal to an audience, and texts such as those of the Cistercian Caesarius of Heisterbach which contain lively stories for popular edification. What was written and spoken for the instruction of ordinary people has a good deal to tell us about the way they were encouraged to answer the questions that every generation asks.

A society suffused with an actively and consciously Christian view of the way the world works came into being with the Middle Ages. The period ended with a radical reshaping of the medieval assumptions about what this meant for believers. Centuries of adjustment followed, with passionate partisanship and changing educational expectations, to produce a modern population generally less well informed about Christianity in the areas of its medieval triumph. Fewer sleepers today are likely to wake to worries about their uncompleted penances, though there may well be a lingering sense of guilt about something done or not done. But the depth and extent of Christian penetration of medieval Europe shaped a continent and its hinterlands. It left a legacy of immense importance to a civilisation which has had, in its turn, an enormous impact upon the world at large.

Further Reading

Abelard, Peter, *Historia Calamitatum*, ed. J. Monfrin (Paris, 1967).

——— *Collationes*, ed. and tr. John Marenbon and Giovanni Orlandi (Oxford, 2000).

Abucaras, Theodoros, *Opusculum*, 35 PG 97.1587–92.

Abulafia, Anna Sapir, *Christians and Jews in Dispute: Disputational Literature and the Rise of Anti-Judaism in the West (c.1000–1150)* (New York, 2011).

——— *Jewish–Christian Relations 1000–1300* (Harlow, 2011).

Adamson, Peter, *Al-Kindi* (Oxford, 2007).

Aelfric's Lives of Saints, 2 vols, ed. Walter W. Skeat, EETS 76 and 82 (1881 and 1885).

Alan of Lille, *Liber Poenitentialis*, 2 vols, Prologue, ed. J. Longère, *Analecta Medievalia Namurcensia* 17 (Louvain, 1965).

Alfonsi, Petrus, *Disciplina clericalis*, ed. A. Hilka and W. Söderhjelm (Helsinki, 1911).

——— *Dialogue against the Jews*, tr. I. Resnick (Washington, 2006).

Ambrose, *Letters*, ed. Mary Melchior Beyenka (Washington,1954).

Ammianus Marcellinus, *History*, ed. J. C. Rolfe (Cambridge, MA, 2014).

Anonymi Versus de Querimonia Cleri, Anglo-Latin Satirical Poets, ed. T. Wright, Rolls Series (Cambridge, 2012, reprint), II, pp. 213–18.

Anselm of Canterbury, *Opera Omnia*, ed. F. S. Schmitt (Rome/Edinburgh, 1965), Vol. II.

Anselm of Havelberg, *Dialogi*, PL 188. 1139ff.

Anskar, *Epistolae Variorum*, 16, ed. E. Perels, Monumenta Germaniae Historica, Epistolae.

Apostolic Constitutions, tr. A. Roberts et al., Ante-Nicene Fathers (Grand Rapids, MI,1999–2005).

Apuleius, *The Golden Ass*, tr. W. Adlington and S. Gaselee (Cambridge, MA, 1915).

Arendzen, I., *Theodori Abu Kurra De cultu imaginum libellus e codice arabico* (Bonn, 1897).

Augustine, *De Catechizandis rudibus*, ed. J.-B. Bauer, CCSL 46 (Turnhout, 1939).

——— *Confessions*, tr. H. Chadwick (Oxford, 1992).

——— *De Doctrina Christiana*, ed. and tr. R. P. H.Green (Oxford, 1995).

——— *City of God*, tr. H. Bettenson, intro. G. R. Evans, Penguin Classics, new edn (London, 2003).

——— *De Civitate Dei*, tr. E. R. Dods (Edinburgh, 2009).

——— *Contra Donatistas*, ed. M. Petschenig, CCSL (Turnhout, 2010).

Augustine on Faith and Works, tr. Gregory Lombardo, Ancient Christian Texts (New York, 1988).

Avicenna, *De congelatione et conglutinatione lapidum, being sections of the Kitāb al-shifâ* (Paris, 1927).

Bacha, C., *Les oeuvres arabes de Théodore Aboucara* (Beyrout, 1904).

——— *Un traité des oeuvres arabe de Théodore Abou-Kurra* (Tripoli (Syria) and Rome, 1905).

Barber, Malcolm, *The Trial of the Templars*, 2nd edn (Cambridge, 2006).

— *The Crusader States* (New Haven, CT, 2012).

Barnard, L. W., *The Graeco-Roman and Oriental Background of the Iconoclastic Controversy* (Leiden, 1974).

Baumgarten, Elisheva, 'Daily commodities and Jewish religious identity', in John Doran, Charlotte Methuen and Alexandra Walsham (eds), *Religion and the Household*, Studies in Church History 50 (2014), pp. 97–121.

Beckingham, Charles, *Prester John, the Mongols and the Ten Lost Tribes* (Aldershot, 1996).

Bede, *Ecclesiastical History of the English People*, ed. R. A. B. Mynors and B. Colgrave (Oxford, 1969).

Belo, Catarina, *Chance and Determinism in Avicenna and Averroes* (Leiden, 2007).

Benedict, *Rule*, tr. T. Kardong (Collegeville, MN, 1996).

John Benet's Chronicle, ed. G. L. Harriss, RHS, Camden 4th Series, 9 (London, 1972), p. 194.

Bernard of Clairvaux, *Opera Omnia*, ed. J. Leclerc., C. H. Talbot and H. Rochais (Rome, 1968), Vol. III.

Bibliotheca Historica of Diodorus Siculus, tr. John Skelton, ed. F. M. Salter and H. L. R. Edwards, EETS 233 (1956).

Bishko, Charles Julian, 'Peter the Venerable's journey to Spain', *Studia Anselmiana* 40 (1956).

Blund, John, *Tractatus de Anima*, ed. D. A. Callus and R. W. Hunt (London, 1970).

Boethius, *Consolatio Philosophiae*, ed. E. K. Rand, H. F. Stewart and S. J. Tester (Cambridge, MA, 2004).

——— *De Hebdomadibus, Theological Tractates*, ed. E. K. Rand, H. F. Stewart and S. J. Tester (Cambridge, MA, 2004).

Bolton, Brenda, *The Medieval Reformation* (London, 1983).

Bongars, *Gesta Dei per Francos*, 1, pp. 382ff., in Oliver J. Thatcher and Edgar Holmes McNeal (eds), *A Source Book for Medieval History: Selected Documents Illustrating the History of Europe in the Middle Age* (New York, 1905), pp. 513–17.

Boniface, *Letters*, http://www.fordham.edu/halsall/basis/boniface-letters.asp (accessed 17 March 2016).

Bonner, C., *The Homily on the Passion by Melito, Bishop of Sardis* (London, 1940).

Book of Common Prayer

The Book of Vices and Virtues, ed. W. Nelson Francis, EETS 217 (1942).

Brown, Peter, *Cult of the Saints* (Chicago, 1981).

——— *The Rise of Christendom*, 2nd edn (Oxford, 2003), p. 60.

Brown, P. R. L., *The Cult of the Saints: Its Rise and Function in Latin Christianity* (London, 1981).

Buridan, John, *Quaestiones super libris quattuor de caelo et mundo*, tr. M. Marshall Clagett, *The Science of Mechanics in the Middle Ages* (Madison, 1059).

Burke, Peter, 'Strengths and Weaknesses in the History of Mentalities', in *Varieties of Cultural History* (Cambridge: Polity Press, 1997), pp. 162–82; revised from original publication in *History of European Ideas* 7 (1986), pp. 439–51.

Burnett, Charles, 'The works of Petrus Alfonsi: questions of authenticity', *Medium Aevum* 66 (1997): 42–79.

Burnett, Charles (ed.), *Ibn Baklarash's Book of Simples: Medical Remedies between Three Faiths in Twelfth Century Spain* (Oxford, 2008).

Caesarii Heisterbacensis monachi ordinis Cisterciensis Dialogus Miraculroum, 2 vols, ed. J. Strange (Paris, 1851).

Caesarius of Heisterbach, *Dialogue on Miracles*, https://legacy.fordham.edu/halsall/source/caesarius-heresies.html (accessed 17 March 2017).

——— *Dialogus Miraculorum*, *De* contritione, 2 vols, XXII, ed. J. Strange (Cologne, 1851).

Cassian, *Collationes*, ii.13, in Jacques de Vitry, *Exempla*, ed. T. F. Crane (London, 1890), no. LXXXI.

——— *Conferences*, tr. Owen Chadwick and C. Luibhéid (New York, 1985).

——— *Institutions*, tr. Boniface Ramsey (New York, 2000).

Cato, *De re rustica*, ed. H. B. Ash (Cambridge, MA, 1935).

Chadwick, Henry, *Priscillian of Avila* (Oxford, 1976).

Chartularium Universitatis Parisiensis, ed. H. Denifle and A. Chatelain (Paris, 1905), I.

Clement, *First Epistle to the Corinthians*, ed. A. Hingenfeld (Leipzig, 1876).

Cline, Rangar, *Ancient Angels: Conceptualising Angeloi in the Roman Empire* (Leiden, 2011).

Cobb, Paul M., 'Virtual sacrality: making Muslim Syria sacred before the Crusades', *Medieval Encounters* 8 (2002): 35–55.

Cohn, Norma. *The Pursuit of the Millennium: Revolutionary Millenarians and Mystical Anarchists of the Middle Ages* (Oxford, 1970), Ch. 7.

The Comedy of Acolastus, tr. from Fullonius by John Palsgrave, ed. P. L. Carver, EETS 212 (1937).

Comnena, Anna, *Alexiad*, tr. E. R. A. Sewter (London, 2003).

Constable, G. (ed.), *The Letters of Peter the Venerable* (Cambridge, MA, 1967).

Constable, Olivia Remie, *Medieval Iberia* (Philadelphia, 1997).

Contra Mahometem orationes quatuor, from Basle 1543 edition, PG 154. 583–692.

Contra Sectam Mahometicam pro Christianae religione apologia, PG 154. 371–582.

Corbari, Eliana, *Vernacular Theology: Dominican Sermons and Audience in Late Medieval Italy* (Berlin, 2013).
Crispin, Gilbert, *Works*, ed. A. Abulafia and G. R. Evans (London, 1986).
Crook, John, *English Medieval Shrines* (Woodbridge, 2011).
Cumont, F., *The Mysteries of Mithra* (London, 1903).
——— *Afterlife in Roman Paganism* (Yale, 1922).
——— *Oriental Religions in Roman Paganism* (New York, 1956).
Cyril of Jerusalem, *Catechetical Lectures*, ed. F. L. Cross (London, 1951).
Dalarun, Jacques, *Robert of Arbrissel*, tr. Bruce L. Venarde (Paris, 1986; Washington, 2006).
D'Alverny, Marie-Thérèse, 'Motives and Circumstances, Methods and Techniques of Translation from Arabic to Latin', Colloquium on the Transmission and Reception of Knowledge, Dumbarton Oaks, 5–7 May 1977 (Washington, 1977).
d'Alverny, M. T., *Deux traductions latines du Coran au moyen âge*, in *Archives d'histoire doctrinale et littéraire du moyen âge* 22–23 (1947–8).
——— *La connaissance de l'Islam dans l'Occident médiéval*, ed. C. Burnett (Abingdon, 1994), I, in M. T. d'Alverny, *Deux traductions latines du Coran au moyen âge*, in *Archives d'histoire doctrinale et littéraire du moyen âge* 22–23 (1947–8): 69–131, 70.
——— 'Pierre le Vénérable et la légende de Mahomet', AHDLMA, 16 (1948): 161–70.
——— *Avicenne en occident* (Paris, 1993).
——— *La connaissance de l'Islam dans l'Occident médiéval*, ed. C. Burnett (Abingdon, 1994), III.
D'Avray, David, *The Preaching of the Friars: Sermons Diffused from Paris before 1300* (Oxford, 1985).
——— *Medieval Marriage Sermons: Mass Communication in a Culture without Print* (Oxford, 2001).
Decrees of the Ecumenical Councils, ed. Norman P. Tanner (Washington, DC, 1990).
The Dicts and Sayings of the Philosophers, ed. Curt F. Bühler, EETS 211 (1941).
Didache, tr. J. B. Lightfoot (Grand Rapids, MI, 1956).
Dio Cassius, *Historia Romana,* ed. E. Cary and H. B. Foster, Loeb Classical Library (Cambridge, MA, 2014), vols 17, 32, 37, 53, 66, 82–3.
Duffy, Eamon, *Saints and Sinners: A History of the Popes* (Yale, 2002).
Engelmann, Ursmar, *Der heilige Pirmin und sein Missionsbüchlein* (Konstanz, 1958).
Eusebius of Caesarea, *Historia Ecclesiastica*, tr. P. Schaff and H. Wace, Nicene and Post Nicene Fathers (Buffalo, 1890), Vol. 1.
——— *Praeparatio Evangelica*, tr. E. H. Gifford (London, 1903).
Euthymios Monachos, *Disputation on the Faith with a Saracen,* PG 131.19–33.
Evans, G. R., *Law and Theology in the Middle Ages* (London, 2002).
——— *History of Western Monasticism* (London, 2016).
Finucane, R., *Miracles and Pilgrims: Popular Beliefs in Medieval England* (London, 1977).
Flavius Josephus, *The Wars of the Jews*, ed. W. Whiston (London, 1928).
——— *Against Apion*, tr. and comment John M. G. Barclay (Leiden, 2013).

Foot, Sarah, 'Households of St. Edmund', in John Doran, Charlotte Methuen and Alexandra Walsham (eds), *Religion and the Household*, Studies in Church History 50 (2014), pp. 47–59.

Frend, W. H. C., *The Rise of the Monophysite Movement* (Cambridge,1972).

Fulcher of Chartres, *Gesta Francorum Jerusalem Expugnantium*, in Frederick Duncan and August C. Krey (eds), *Parallel Source Problems in Medieval History* (New York, 1912), pp. 109–15.

Furnivall, F. J. (ed.), *Political, Religious and Love Poems*, EETS 15 (1866), p. 1.

——— *Education in Early England (The 'Babees Book')*, EETS 32 (1868).

Genet, J-P. (ed.), *Four English Political Tracts of the Later Middle Ages*, Camden 4th series, 18 (London, 1977).

Gennadius of Marseilles, *De viris illustribus,* ed. E. C. Richardson (Leipzig, 1896); also includes Jerome, *De viris illustribus*.

Geoffrey de Villehardouin, *Memoirs* or *Chronicle of The Fourth Crusade and The Conquest of Constantinople*, tr. Frank T. Marzials (London, 1908).

Gerber, Jane S., 'The world of Samuel Halevi: Testimony from the El Transity Synagogue of Toledo', in Jonathan Ray (ed.), *The Jew in Medieval Iberia* (Boston, 2012).

Gesta Francorum et aliorum Hierosolimitanorum, ed. and tr. Rosalind Hill (Oxford, 1967).

Gregory the Great, *Dialogues*, ed. O. J. Zimmerman (Washington, 1959).

Gregory of Tours, *History of the Franks,* tr. E. Brehaut (New York, 1969).

Grosseteste, Robert, *On the Six Days of Creation*, tr. C. F. J. Martin (Oxford, 1996).

Grunebaum, G. E. von, 'Byzantine iconoclasm and the influence of the Islamic environment', *History of Religions* 2 (1962): 1–10.

Guibert de Nogent, *Historia quae dicitur Gesta Dei per Francos,* Recueil des historiens des croisades, Historiens occidentaux (Farnborough, 1967).

——— *Historia quae dicitur Gesta Dei per Francos* (Paris, 1967).

——— *De Vita Sua*, tr. J. F. Benton (Toronto, 1984).

Guillaume de Deguileville, *Pilgrimage of the Lyfe of the Manhode*, ed. A. Henry, EETS (Oxford, 1885–8).

Hamilton, Bernard, 'Perfectionism and pragmatism: Cathar attitudes to the household', in John Doran, Charlotte Methuen and Alexandra Walsham (eds), *Religion and the Household*, Studies in Church History 50 (2014), pp. 86–96.

Hanham, Alison (ed.), *The Cely letters (1472–1488)*, EETS 273 (1975).

Hauréau, B., *Notices et Extraits de quelques manuscrits latins de la Bibliothéque nationale*, 6 vols (Paris, 1890–3).

Hebrew Chronicles of the First Crusade, ed. Eva Haverkamp, MGH (Hanover, 2005).

Hermannus quondam Judaeus Opusculum de Conversione Sua, ed. Gerlinde Niemeyer, MGH (Wiemar, 1963).

Horace, *Odes*, ed. H. E. Gould (London, 1952).

How Religious Men Should Keep Certain Articles, *The English Works of Wyclif*, ed. F. D. Matthew, EETS 74 (1880), pp. 219ff.

How Satan and his Children ..., *The English Works of Wyclif*, ed. F. D. Matthew, EETS 74 (1880), pp. 209ff.

Hudson, Anne, *The Premature Reformation* (Oxford,1988).

Irenaeus, *Five Books Against Heresies*, tr. John Keble (Oxford, 1972).

Irvine, Susan (ed.), *Old English Homilies from MS Bodley 343*, EETS 303 (1993).

Isidore, *Etymologies*, ed. W. M. Lindsay (Oxford, 1911).

Jacques de Vitry, *Exempla*, ed. T. F. Crane (London, 1890).

Jerome, *De viris illustribus*, CCSL (Turnhout, 2010).

John de Joinville, *Chronicles of the Crusades*, ed. J. A. Giles (London, 1865).

John of Hildesheim, *The Three Kings of Cologne*, ed. C. Horstmann, EETS 85 (London, 1886).

John of Salisbury, *Policraticus*, ed. C. C. J. Webb (London, 1932).

——— *Metalogicon*, ed. J. B. Hall and K. S. B. Keats-Rohan, CCCM 98 (Turnhout, 1991).

'King Alfred and the Latin Manuscripts of Gregory's Regula Pastoralis', *Quidditas* 6 (1985): 1–13.

Koningsveld, P. S. van, 'Muslim slaves and captives in Western Europe during the late middle ages', *Islam and Christian–Muslim Relations*, 18 April 2007, http://www.tandfonline.com/loi/cicm20 (accessed 17 March 2016).

Krey, August. C., *The First Crusade: The Accounts of Eyewitnesses and Participants* (Princeton, NJ, 1921), pp. 23–40, 42–3.

Lactantius, *On the Deaths of the Persecutors*, *Works*, Ante-Nicene Christian Fathers (1999–2005).

Laing, Gordon J., *Survivals of Roman Religion* (New York, 1931).

The lay folks' catechisme, ed. F. Simmons and H. E. Nolloth, EETS (1901).

Lees, Jay T., *Anselm of Havelberg: Deeds into Words in the Twelfth Century* (Leiden, 1998), pp. 40–7.

Le Goff, Jacques, *The Birth of Purgatory*, tr. Arthur Goldhammer (Aldershot, 1984).

Levy, Ian Christopher, 'Useful foils: lessons learned from Jews in John Wyclif's call for Church reform', *Medieval Encounters* 4 (2001): 125–45.

Libellus de diversis ordinibus, ed. G. Constable (Oxford, 1972).

The Life of Saladin, ed. Sir Hamilton Gibb (Oxford, 1973).

Life of St. Hugh of Lincoln, ed. Decima L. Douie and D. H. Farmer, Vol. II (Oxford, 1985).

Lindberg, David C. and Michael H. Shank (eds), *The Cambridge History of Science*, Vol. 2: *Medieval Science* (Cambridge, 2013).

Lo Nero, Carolina, 'Christiana Dignitas: new Christian criteria for citizenship in the late Roman Empire', *Medieval Encounters* 7 (2001): 146–60.

Lucian of Samosata, *De morte Peregrini*, in *Works*, 8 vols, ed. with English tr. A. M. Harmon, K. Kilburn and M. D. Macleod (Cambridge, MA, 1961–79).

Malory, Thomas, *Le Morte d'Arthur*, http://www.gutenberg.org/files/1251/1251–h/1251–h.htm#link2HCH0002 (accessed 17 March 2016).

Manuel II Palaiologos, *Dialoge mit einem 'Perser'*, ed. E. Trapp (Vienna, 1966).

——— *Letters*, ed. George T. Dennis (Dumbarton Oaks, 1977).

Martin of Braga, *De correctione rusticorum*, CCSL (Turnhout, 2010).

Martine di Braga, *Contro le superstizioni*, ed. M. Naldini (Florence, 1991).

McGinnis, Jon, *Avicenna* (Oxford, 2010).

McHardy, A. K., *The Church in London 1375–1392*, London Record Society 13 (London, 1977).

Minio-Paluello, L., 'Iacobus Veneticus Grecus: canonist and translator of Aristotle', *Traditio* 8 (1952): 265–304.

——— *The Latin Aristotle* (Amsterdam, 1972).

Moffett, Samuel Hugh, *A History of Christianity in Asia*, 2 vols (New York, 2005).

Monnot, G., 'Les citations coraniques dans le "Dialogus" de Pierre Alphonse', *Cahiers de Fanjeaux* 18 (1983): 261–77.

Monroe, James T., *Islam and the Arabs in Spanish Scholarship* (Leiden, 1970).

Moore, R. I., *The Birth of Popular Heresy* (Toronto, 1995).

Morris, R. (ed.), *Old English Homilies of the Twelfth Century*, Second Series, EETS 53 (1873).

——— *The Blickling Homilies*, EETS 58 and 73 (1880).

MS BL Arundel 206, fol. 46 rb, in hac duplici missione tota vita apostolorum et apostolicorum virorum significatur, que fuit in duobus, scilicet predicatione et utilitate proximorum; item in contemplatione et exercitio virtutum.

Munro, Dana C., 'Urban and the Crusaders', *Translations and Reprints from the Original Sources of European History*, Vol 1 (Philadelphia, 1895), pp. 5–8.

Nicetas of Byzantium, *Confutatio libri Mohamedis*, PG 105.669–806.

Noble, Thomas F. X., *Images, Iconoclasm and the Carolingians* (Philadelphia, 2009).

Origen, *Contra Celsum*, tr. H. Chadwick (Cambridge, 1953).

Owst, G. R., *Preaching in Medieval England* (Cambridge, 1926).

——— *Literature and Pulpit in Medieval England* (Oxford, 1961).

Palmer, James T., 'Rimbert's *Vita Anskarii* and Scandinavian Mission in the Ninth Century', *Journal of Ecclesiastical History* 55 (2004).

Pelikan, J., *The Christian Tradition: A History of the Development of Doctrine*, Vol. 2: *The Spirit of Eastern Christendom (600–1700)* (Chicago, 1974).

Peter the Chanter, *Liber casuum conscientiae, Summa de sacramentis et animae consiliis*, ed. J-A. Dugauquier, Analecta medievalia Namurcensia 4 (1954), Vol. III.

Petrus Cantor, *Summa de sacramentis et animae consiliis*, ed. J. A. Dugauquier (Louvain, 1954).

Phelan, Owen M., 'Catechising the wild: the continuity and innovation of missionary catechesis under the Carolingians', *Journal of Ecclesiastical History* 61 (2010): 455–74.

Pierce the Ploughmans Crede, ed. W. Skeat, EETS 31 (1877).

Pirenne, H., *Medieval Cities* (Princeton, NJ, 1952).

Pisan, Christine de, *The Epistle of Othea*, tr. Stephen Scrope, ed. Curt F. Bühler, EETS 264 (1970).

Plutarch, *De Iside et Osiride*, ed. J. Gwynne Griffiths (Cardiff, 1970).

Poschmann, Bernhard, *Penance and the Anointing of the Sick*, tr. F. Coutney (London, 1964).

Powell, Sue, 'The Transmission and Circulation of The Lay Folks' Catechism', in A. J. Minnis (ed.), *Late-Medieval Religious Texts and their Transmission* (Cambridge, 1994), pp. 67–84.

Praepositinus of Cremona, *Summa contra haereticos*, ed. Joseph N. Garvin and James A. Corbett (South Bend, IN, 1958).

Procopius, *The Vandalic Wars, On the Wars*, ed. H. B. Dewing (Cambridge, MA, 1908).

Ratramnus, *Epistola de Cynocephalis ad Rimbertum Presbyterum Scripta*, Patrologia Latina 121.

Ray, Jonathan (ed.), *The Jew in Medieval Iberia* (Boston, 2012).

Reeves, Marjorie, *The Influence of Prophecy in the Later Middle Ages* (Oxford, 1969).

Robert of Flamborough, *Liber Poenitentialis. A Critical Edition with Introduction and Notes*, ed. J. J. Francis Firth, Studies and Texts 18 (1971).

Robert the Monk: *Historia Hierosolymitana*, in RHC, Occ III.

Rolle, Richard, *Ego dormio*, *Prose and Verse*, ed. S. J. Ogilvie-Thomson, EETS 293 (1988).

——— 'The form of living', *Prose and Verse*, ed. S. J. Ogilvie-Thomson, EETS 293 (1988).

Rubenson, Samuel, 'Translating the tradition: some remarks on the Arabization of the patristic heritage in Egypt', *Medieval Encounters* 2 (1996): 4–14.

Rubin, Miri, *Corpus Christi: The Eucharist in Late Medieval Culture* (Cambridge, 1991).

Scragg, D. G. (ed.), *The Vercelli Homilies*, EETS 300 (1992).

Secretum secretorum; nine English versions, ed. M. A. Manzalaoui, EETS 276 (1977).

Septimus, B., 'Petrus Alfonsi on the cult at Mecca', *Speculum* 56 (1981): 517–33.

Silverstein, Theodore, *Visio Sancti Pauli*, Studies and Documents IV (London, 1935), pp. 87–9.

Smith, Julia M. H., 'Material Christianity in the early medieval household', in John Doran, Charlotte Methuen and Alexandra Walsham (eds), *Religion and the Household*, Studies in Church History 50 (2014), pp. 23–46

Speculum sacerdotale, ed. Edward H. Weatherly, EETS 200 (1936).

Spicer, Andrew, *Defining the Holy: Sacred Space in Medieval and Early Modern Europe* (Aldershot, 2005).

Spinka, Matthew, *John Hus' Concept of the Church* (Princeton, NJ, 1966).

Spring, Eileen, *Law, Land and Family* (Chapel Hill, NC, 1993).

Statius, *Thebaid,* ed. D.Shackleton Bailey (Cambridge, MA, 2014).

Steneck, N., *Science and Creation in the Middle Ages: Henry of Langenstein (d. 1397) on Genesis* (Notre Dame 1976).

Stern, Selma, *The Court Jew: A Contribution to the History of Absolutism in Europe* (Philadelphia, 1950).

Sweet, H. (ed.), *King Alfred's West-Saxon Version of Gregory's Pastoral Care*, EETS 45 (1871).

Tacitus, *Germania*, ed. H. Volkman and W. Reeb (Leipzig, 1930).

Tanner, Norman, *Kent Heresy Proceedings 1511–12*, Kent Records 26 (1997).

——— *Decrees of the Ecumenical Councils*, ed. Norman Tanner (London, 1990), 2 vols.

——— (ed.), *Heresy Trials in the Diocese of Norwich 1428–1431*, Camden 4th Series, 20 (London, 1977).

Tertullian, *De Baptismo,* ed. E. Evans (London, 1964).

——— *Apologia*, ed. T. Glover (London, 2003).

Theophanes, *Chronographia*, ed. C. de Boor (Leipzig, 1883–5).
Thomas of Monmouth, *The Life and Miracles of William of Norwich*, ed. M. R. James and James Jessop (Cambridge, 1897).
Thompson, K., *The Monks of Tiron* (Cambridge, 2014).
Tillyard, E. M. W., *Elizabethan World Picture* (London, 1963).
Tractatus de diversis materiis praedicabilibus, in *Anecdotes Historiques, Légendes et Apolologues tirés du recueil inédit d'Etienne de Bourbon, dominicain du xiiie siècle, publés pour la Société de l'Histoire de France, par A. Lecoy de la Marche* (Paris, 1877).
Tractatus de Purgatorio Sancti Patricii, ed. Robert Easting, EETS 298 (1991).
Urban II, *Letter of Instruction*, December 1095,
Varner, William, *Ancient Jewish–Christian Dialogues: Athanasius and Zacchaeus, Simon and Theophilus, Timothy and Aquila: Introductions, Texts, and Translations* (Lampeter, 2004).
Vetus Latina (Freiburg, 1949).
Wallach, Luitpold, 'Nicaea and the "Synodica" of Hadrian I (je 2448): a diplomatic study', *Traditio* 22 (1966): 103–25.
Walzer, Richard, 'New light on the Arabic translations of Aristotle', *Oriens* 6 (1953): 91–142.
Williams, Rowan, *Arius: Heresy and Tradition* (London, 1987).
Willibrord, *Life of Boniface*, ed. C. H. Talbot (London, 1981).
Wright, Thomas (ed.), *Anglo-Latin Satirical Poets and Epigrammatists of the Twelfth Century*, 2 vols, Rolls Series 57 (London 1872).
Yates, F., *Giordano Bruno and the Hermetic Tradition* (London, 1964).

Notes

ABBREVIATIONS

CCSL
Corpus Christianorum Series Latina

CL
Cyril of Jerusalem, *Catechetical Lectures*, ed. F. L. Cross (London, 1951).

CR
Augustine, *De Catechizandis rudibus*, ed. J.-B. Bauer, CCSL 46 (Turnhout, 1939).

Csi
Bernard of Clairvaux, *De consideratione*, *Opera Omnia*, ed. J. Leclerc., C. H. Talbot and H. Rochais (Rome, 1968), Vol. III.

EETS
Early English Text Society

MGH
Monumenta Germaniae Historica

PG
Patrologia Graeca

PL
Patrologia Latina

Translations of extracts from the decrees of Councils are taken from *Decrees of the Ecumenical Councils*, ed. Norman P. Tanner (London, 1990), 2 vols.

INTRODUCTION: THE BEAUTIFUL VISION

1 E. V. Hitchcock, P. E. Hallet and A. W. Reed (eds), *The Lyf of Syr Thomas More*, EETS 222 (London, 1950), Dedicatory Epistle, p. 304, authorship not certain.

CHAPTER 1: LAUNCHING THE FIRST THOUSAND YEARS OF CHRISTENDOM

1 F. Cumont, *Oriental Religions in Roman Paganism* (New York, 1956), pp. 20–2.
2 Ibid., pp. 56–7.
3 Gordon J. Laing, *Survivals of Roman Religion* (New York, 1931), pp. 141ff.
4 Initiates might recognise one another by signs such as handshakes (*syndexioi*).
5 Lucian of Samosata, *De morte Peregrini*, 11–13.
6 Ibid., 13.
7 Justin Martyr, *Dialogue with Trypho*, 8–14.
8 See p. 141.
9 Simon Schama, *The Story of the Jews* (London, 2014), pp. 88ff., on the Roman period and the revolts.
10 Flavius Josephus, *The Wars of the Jews or History of the Destruction of Jerusalem*, VII. i.1.
11 The original Temple tax (Exodus 30.13) had been as described in Matthew 17.24–27, when the tax-collectors tried to test Jesus. The Romans wanted to prevent the export of gold and silver by way of the payments so they replaced it after AD 70 with a new tax, called the *fiscus Judaicus*. This may have been imposed indiscriminately on Christians as well as Jews until 96, when the Emperor Nerva distinguished between the two and only the Jews were required to pay.
12 Helen Rhee, *Early Christian Literature: Christ and Culture in the Second and Third Centuries* (London, 2005).
13 Eusebius, *Historia Ecclesiastica*, 4.2.1–5.
14 Dio Cassius, *Roman History*, 69.12–14.
15 He used the Greek Septuagint translation in his study of the Old Testament.
16 In his *Hypothetica*. This is now lost but parts of it survive in the book of introduction to the Gospel (*Praeparatio Evangelica*) of the historian Eusebius of Caesarea (260/5–339/40) and cf. Eusebius of Caesarea, *Praeparatio Evangelica*, viii, 5, 11.
17 John's Gospel mentions the distinction between 'flesh' and 'spirit'; Jewish law, it is suggested, was constraining and burdensome while the Gospel offers a new freedom in the Spirit (6.63). The idea appears again in 2 Corinthians 3.6, with its distinction of the 'letter' from the 'Spirit': 'for the letter kills, but the Spirit gives life'.
18 Paul's missionary journeys (whose dates and sequence and locations have not been finally determined) seem to have taken him from Antioch in Syria to Antioch in Galatia, and to Ephesus, Philippi and Corinth about AD 52, where he wrote both his letters to the Thessalonians (Acts 18.5). In about

AD 56, Paul probably wrote 1 Corinthians at Ephesus (Acts 19.22). Romans has been dated to AD 57 (Acts 20.2–3), with Galatians and 2 Corinthians written from Macedonia.

19 Julia M. H. Smith, 'Material Christianity in the early medieval household', in John Doran, Charlotte Methuen and Alexandra Walsham (eds), *Religion and the Household*, Studies in Church History 50 (Martlesham, 2014), pp. 23–46; Sarah Foot, 'Households of St. Edmund', in John Doran, Charlotte Methuen and Alexandra Walsham (eds), *Religion and the Household*, Studies in Church History 50 (Martlesham, 2014), pp. 47–59.

20 *ceruice tinguet; te nihil attinet*
temptare multa caede bidentium
paruos coronantem marino
rore deos fragilique myrto.
Horace, *Odes* III.23.15.

21 Augustine, *Confessions*, VI, 2.

22 Laing, *Survivals*, pp. 13–14.

23 Ibid., pp. 11–13.

24 Apuleius, *The Golden Ass*, Book III, 19–23.

25 Ibid., III, 24–9.

26 For the background to this idea, which lingered through the Middle Ages and beyond, see F. Yates, *Giordano Bruno and the Hermetic Tradition* (London, 1964).

27 Apuleius, *The Golden Ass*, Book IV, 32–3.

28 Ibid., Book VI, 32–4.

29 *Civ.*, VIII, 12–13.

30 Ibid., VIII, 14.

31 Ibid., VIII, 15.

32 Tertullian, *De Baptismo*, 15.

33 *Apostolic Constitutions*, VIII, 12.

34 CR 16.25.

35 Ibid., 16.24.

36 Ibid., 17.26–7.

37 Ibid., 18.2.9ff.

38 Ibid., 19.31ff.

39 See p. 187.

40 Ambrose, Letter XX.

41 Tertullian, *Apologia*, vii.

42 Ibid., *Praescriptio adversus Haereses*, xiv.

CHAPTER 2: NEW FAITHS FOR EUROPE

1 The reign of the Emperor Julian the Apostate, emperor from 361 to 363 only briefly interrupted this Christian imperial dominance.

2 Eusebius of Caesarea, 'Life' of *Constantine*, *Historia Ecclesiastica*, tr. P. Schaff and H. Wace, Nicene and Post Nicene Fathers (Buffalo, 1890), 1.28.

3 Lactantius, *On the Deaths of the Persecutors*, 44, *Works*, Ante-Nicene Christian Fathers, Vol. II (1995–2002), p. 203.

4 At the peace of Augsburg in 1555.
5 See p. 37.
6 Martine di Braga, *Contro le superstizioni*, ed. M. Naldini (Florence, 1991), 3.1.
7 Rowan Williams, *Arius: Heresy and Tradition* (London, 1987).
8 Ammianus Marcellinus, *History*, III–IV, ed. J. C. Rolfe (Harvard, 2014).
9 Eusebius, *Historia Ecclesiastica*, V.i–iv.
10 Gregory of Tours, *History of the Franks*, tr. E. Brehaut (New York, 1969).
11 Gennadius of Marseilles, *De Viris Illustribus,* ed. E. C. Richardson (Leipzig, 1896); also includes Jerome, *De Viris Illustribus*.
12 Irenaeus, *Five Books Against Heresies*, tr. John Keble (Oxford, 1972).
13 Henry Chadwick, *Priscillian of Avila* (Oxford, 1976).
14 Olivia Remie Constable, *Medieval Iberia* (Philadelphia, 1997), pp. 5–11.
15 Ibid., pp. 15–16.
16 Ibid., p. 17.
17 Ibid., p. 18.
18 Ibid., p. 16.
19 Ibid., p. 17.
20 Ibid., p. 19.
21 Ibid., p. 21.
22 Ibid., p. 23.
23 Procopius, *The Vandalic Wars*, III.2.25–26.
24 Bede, *Ecclesiastical History of the English People*, ed. R. A. B. Mynors and B. Colgrave (Oxford, 1969), i.
25 Ibid., ii.9.
26 Ibid., ii.12.
27 Ibid., ii.13.
28 Ibid., ii.10–11.
29 Ibid., ii.1.
30 Willibrord, *Life of Boniface*, ed. C. H. Talbot (London, 1981).
31 Ratramnus, *Epistola de Cynocephalis ad Rimbertum Presbyterum Scripta*, Patrologia Latina 121:1153–6.
32 Ibid.
33 Augustine, *City of God*, tr. H. Bettenson, intro. G. R. Evans, Penguin Classics, new edn (London, 2003), XVI.8.
34 Anskar, *Epistolae Variorum*, 16, ed. E. Perels, Monumenta Germaniae Historica, Epistolae, vi.163, and see James T. Palmer, 'Rimbert's *Vita Anskarii* and Scandinavian Mission in the Ninth Century', *Journal of Ecclesiastical History* 55 (2004).
35 Cassian, *Institutions*, tr. Boniface Ramsey (New York, 2000).
36 Cassian, *Conferences*, tr. Owen Chadwick (New York, 1985).
37 Benedict, *Rule*, tr. T. Kardong (Collegeville, MN, 1996).
38 Gregory the Great, *Dialogues*, ed. O. J. Zimmerman (Washington, 1959), I.3.
39 Martin of Braga, *De correctione rusticorum*, CCSL (Turnhout, 2010), 8–9.
40 Owen M. Phelan, 'Catechising the Wild: The Continuity and Innovation of Missionary Catechesis under the Carolingians', *Journal of Ecclesiastical History* 61 (2010): 455–74.

41 Boniface, *Letters*, Letter 11.723–4, http://www.fordham.edu/halsall/basis/boniface-letters.asp (accessed 17 March 2016).
42 Ursmar Engelmann, *Der heilige Pirmin und sein Missionsbüchlein* (Konstanz, 1958).
43 Ibid., para.1, p. 24.
44 Ibid., para. 2, p. 24.
45 Ibid., paras 3–7, pp. 25–30.
46 Ibid., paras 7–11, pp. 30–40.
47 Ibid., para. 12, p. 40.
48 Ibid., para. 13, p. 44.
49 The emergence of what was to become the traditional seven mortal sins was already well on its way. Before the end of the sixth century, Gregory the Great had offered a list made up of lust, gluttony, avarice, sloth, anger, envy and pride.
50 *Dicta Pirmini*, para. 27, p. 76.
51 J. Pelikan, *The Christian Tradition: A History of the Development of Doctrine*, Vol. 2: *The Spirit of Eastern Christendom (600–1700)* (Chicago, 1974).
52 A term favoured by John Henry Newman, and see Apostolic Constitution, *Fidei Depositum*, 11 October 1992. On the Vulgate, see p. 92.
53 Samuel Hugh Moffett, *Christianity in Asia* (New York, 2005), explores the further reach of Christian encounters in Asia.
54 W. H. C. Frend, *The Rise of the Monophysite Movement* (Cambridge, 1972), pp. 308–10.
55 Ibid., p. 312.
56 Ibid., pp. 296–7.
57 Ibid., p. 320.
58 Ibid., pp. 296–7.
59 Ibid., p. 304.
60 Ibid., p. 320.
61 Ibid., p. 323.
62 Ibid., pp. 335–7.
63 Ibid., p. 342.
64 G. E. von Grunebaum, 'Byzantine iconoclasm and the influence of the Islamic environment', *History of Religions* 2 (1962): 1–10, 9.
65 Ibid., p. 6.
66 PG 105.777.
67 L. W. Barnard, *The Graeco-Roman and Oriental Background of the Iconoclastic Controversy* (Leiden, 1974), p. 15.
68 Ibid., p. 14.
69 Ibid., p. 13.
70 Ibid., p. 18.
71 Ibid., pp. 16–17.
72 Theophanes, *Chronographia*, ed. C. de Boor (Leipzig, 1883–5), I.405.
73 Thomas F. X. Noble, *Images, Ionoclasm and the Carolingians* (Philadelphia, 2009), pp. 159–61, p. 159.
74 Luitpold Wallach, 'Nicaea and the "Synodica" of Hadrian I (je 2448): a diplomatic study', *Traditio* 22 (1966): 103–25, 104–8ff.

75 Ibid., p. 110.
76 Ibid., p. 111.
77 Embracing peoples now in Ukraine, Russia and Belarus.
78 Eusebius, *Historia Ecclesiastica*, 6.34, 6.36.3, 6.39.
79 Peter Brown, *The Rise of Christendom*, 2nd edn (Oxford, 2003), p. 60.
80 Constable, *Medieval Iberia*, p. 17.
81 Ibid., p. 21.
82 Ibid., p. 23.
83 Carolina Lo Nero, 'Christiana Dignitas: new Christian criteria for citizenship in the late Roman Empire', *Medieval Encounters* 7 (2001): 146–60.
84 Barnard, *The Graeco-Roman and Oriental Background of the Iconoclastic Controversy*, p. 36.
85 Ibid., p. 37.
86 Theophanes, PG 109.357B.
87 Barnard, *The Graeco-Roman and Oriental Background of the Iconoclastic Controversy*, pp. 33ff.
88 William Varner, *Ancient Jewish–Christian Dialogues: Athanasius and Zacchaeus, Simon and Theophilus, Timothy and Aquila: Introductions, Texts, and Translations* (Lampeter, 2004), pp. 23ff.
89 Ibid., p. 85.
90 Ibid.
91 Paul M. Cobb, 'Virtual sacrality: making Muslim Syria sacred before the Crusades', *Medieval Encounters* 8 (2002): 35–55.
92 http://www.birmingham.ac.uk/facilities/cadbury/quran-manuscript/index.aspx (accessed 17 March 2016).
93 Constable, *Medieval Iberia*, pp. 48–9.
94 PG 105.669–842.
95 PG 105.706.
96 PG 105.714.
97 PG 105.709–11
98 Nicetas of Byzantium, *Confutatio libri Mohamedis*, PG 105.669–806.
99 PG 105.727.
100 PG 105.714.
101 PG 104.1386.
102 Its date is not agreed. It may be as late as the thirteenth century.
103 PG 104.1381–444.
104 Frend, *The Rise of the Monophysite Movement*, pp. 352–3.
105 PG 130.1331ff.
106 Euthymius of Athos, *Panoplia dogmatica*, PG 130.1331ff.
107 Of the kind listed by Gennadius and Jerome in his *De viris illustribus*, ed. E. Richardson, CCSL (Turnhout, 2010).
108 Constable, *Medieval Iberia*, p. 31.
109 Ibid., pp. 37–8.
110 Ibid., p. 41.
111 PL 83.1017–58.
112 Constable, *Medieval Iberia*, p. 41.
113 P. S. van Koningsveld, 'Muslim slaves and captives in Western Europe

during the late middle ages', *Islam and Christian–Muslim Relations*, 18 April 2007, http://www.tandfonline.com/loi/cicm20 (accessed 17 March 2017).

114 Constable, *Medieval Iberia*, pp. 51–2.
115 Jonathan Ray (ed.), *The Jew in Medieval Iberia* (Boston, 2012), p. 7.

CHAPTER 3: CHRISTIANITY AFTER THE MILLENNIUM

1 Peter the Chanter, *Liber casuum conscientiae, Summa de sacramentis et animae consiliis,* ed. J-A. Dugauquier, Analecta medievalia Namurcensia 4 (1954), Vol. III, p. 313.
2 Ibid.
3 Luke 22.19.
4 Miri Rubin, *Corpus Christi: The Eucharist in Late Medieval Culture* (Cambridge, 1991), p. 83.
5 See p. 177.
6 See p. 85.
7 See p. 109.
8 It may have been helpful that the inveterate writer of anecdotal history, James of Vitry, was suffragan bishop of Liège from 1216; Rubin, *Corpus Christi*, pp. 174, 185.
9 See p. 78.
10 Rubin, *Corpus Christi*, p. 213.
11 The date of Pentecost in a given year was determined by the date of Easter, which was always a 'moveable feast'.
12 Rubin, *Corpus Christi*, p. 211.
13 Ibid., p. 215.
14 Ibid., p. 213.
15 Bernhard Poschmann, *Penance and the Anointing of the Sick*, tr. F. Coutney (London, 1964).
16 Peter the Chanter, *Summa de sacramentis et animae consiliis*, Vol. 1, pp. 39–40.
17 Ibid., p. 34.
18 Robert of Flamborough, *Liber Poenitentialis. A Critical Edition with Introduction and Notes*, ed. J. J. Francis Firth, Studies and Texts 18 (1971).
19 Jacques Le Goff, *The Birth of Purgatory,* tr. Arthur Goldhammer (Aldershot, 1984).
20 See p. 187.
21 David D'Avray, *Medieval Marriage Sermons: Mass Communication in a Culture without Print* (Oxford, 2001).
22 Ibid.
23 Peter the Chanter, *Summa de sacramentis et animae consiliis*, Vol. 1, p. 19.
24 Ibid., Vol. III, p. 315.
25 Ibid., Vol. III, p. 317.
26 See G. R. Evans, *History of Western Monasticism* (London, 2016).

27 Guibert of Nogent, *De Vita Sua*, tr. J. F. Benton (Toronto, 1984).
28 R. I. Moore, *The Birth of Popular Heresy* (Toronto, 1995).
29 Jacques Dalarun, *Robert of Arbrissel*, tr. Bruce L. Venarde (Paris, 1986; Washington, 2006), p. xvii.
30 See p. 84.
31 K. Thompson, *The Monks of Tiron* (Cambridge, 2014).
32 Dalarun, *Robert of Arbrissel*, pp. 31–3.
33 *Libellus de diversis ordinibus*, ed. G. Constable (Oxford, 1972).
34 Bernard of Clairvaux, *Opera Omnia*, ed. J. Leclerc., C. H. Talbot and H. Rochais (Rome, 1968), Vol. III.
35 Lateran III, Canon 9.
36 Ibid.
37 Ibid.
38 Malcolm Barber, *The Trial of the Templars*, 2nd edn (Cambridge, 2006).
39 'King Alfred and the Latin Manuscripts of Gregory's Regula Pastoralis', *Quidditas* 6 (1985): 1–13.
40 H. Sweet (ed.), *King Alfred's West-Saxon version of Gregory's Pastoral Care*, EETS 45 (1871).
41 Guibert de Nogent, *De Vita Sua,* Book 1.17.
42 John of Salisbury, *Policraticus*, ed. C. C. J. Webb (London, 1932), II.28.
43 *The lay folks' catechisme*, ed. F. Simmons and H. E. Nolloth, EETS (1901), and Sue Powell, 'The Transmission and Circulation of The Lay Folks' Catechism', in A. J. Minnis (ed.), *Late-Medieval Religious Texts and their Transmission* (Cambridge, 1994), pp. 67–84.
44 D. G. Scragg (ed.), *The Vercelli Homilies*, EETS 300 (1992).
45 R. Morris (ed.), *The Blickling Homilies*, EETS 58 (1880), p. 73.
46 Ibid., *Old English Homilies of the Twelfth Century*, Second Series, EETS 53 (1873), p. 7.
47 Susan Irvine (ed.), *Old English Homilies from MS Bodley 343,* EETS 303 (1993).
48 Morris, *Old English Homilies of the Twelfth Century*, pp. 125–9.
49 Ibid.
50 Eliana Corbari, *Vernacular Theology: Dominican Sermons and Audience in Late Medieval Italy* (Berlin, 2013).
51 David D'Avray, *The Preaching of the Friars: Sermons Diffused from Paris before 1300* (Oxford, 1985), pp. 43–6 and *MS BL Arundel 206, fol. 46 rb, in hac duplici missione tota vita apostolorum et apostolicorum virorum significatur, que fuit in duobus, scilicet predicatione et utilitate proximorum; item in contemplatione et exercitio virtutum.*
52 G. R. Owst, *Literature and Pulpit in Medieval England* (Oxford, 1961), pp. 4–5.
53 D'Avray, *The Preaching of the Friars*, p. 51.
54 Ibid.
55 Ibid.
56 B. Hauréau, *Notices et Extraits de quelques manuscrits latins de la Bibliothéque nationale,* 6 vols (Paris, 1890–3).
57 *Tractatus de diversis materiis praedicabilibus.* The tales used in this pamphlet are from *Anecdotes Historiques, Légendes et Apolologues tirés du recueil*

inédit d'Etienne de Bourbon, dominicain du xiiie siècle, publés pour la Société de l'Histoire de France, par A. Lecoy de la Marche (Paris, 1877).

58 *Caesarii Heisterbacensis monachi ordinis Cisterciensis Dialogus Miraculroum*, 2 vols, ed. J. Strange (Paris, 1851).

59 Jacques de Vitry, *Exempla*, ed. T. F. Crane (London, 1890). Crane provides notes which identify where the stories otherwise survive.

60 Cassian, *Collationes* ii.13, found in Jacques de Vitry, *Exempla*, no. LXXXI.

61 Jacques de Vitry, *Exempla*, no. LXXXVII, p. 39.

62 Ibid., no. II.

63 Ibid., no. CXCVII.

64 Ibid., no. CCXLI.

65 Ibid., no. LXXX.

66 Ibid., no. CXCVIII.

67 Ibid., no. CCCIII.

68 Ibid., no. CCXLIX.

69 Ibid., no. CCXC.

70 Ibid., no. CCLXXXII, pp. 117ff.

71 Owst, *Literature and Pulpit in Medieval England*, pp. 2–3.

72 MS Harl. 2272 f.9, *c.*1343, and see G. R. Owst, *Preaching in Medieval England* (Cambridge, 1926), p. 1.

73 See p. 228.

74 D'Avray, *The Preaching of the Friars*, p. 29.

75 Ibid.

76 See p. 177.

77 D'Avray, *The Preaching of the Friars*, p. 34.

78 Ibid., pp. 37–8.

79 Ibid., p. 38.

80 See p. 188.

81 Marjorie Reeves, *The Influence of Prophecy in the Later Middle Ages* (Oxford, 1969), p. 248.

82 P. R. L. Brown, *The Cult of the Saints: Its Rise and Function in Latin Christianity* (London, 1981).

83 Ibid., pp. 69ff.

84 EH iii.11, pp. 246–9.

85 *Life of St. Hugh of Lincoln*, ed. Decima L. Douie and D. H. Farmer (Oxford, 1985), Vol. II, pp. 217–20.

86 Ibid., pp. 31–2.

87 John Crook, *English Medieval Shrines* (Woodbridge, 2011), p. 118.

88 Caesarius of Heisterbach, *Dialogus Miraculorum, De contritione,* XXII, 2 vols, ed. J. Strange (Cologne, 1851).

89 David C. Lindberg and Michael H. Shank (eds), *The Cambridge History of Science*, Vol. 2: *Medieval Science* (Cambridge, 2013), p. 613.

90 *Aelfric's Lives of Saints*, 2 vols, ed. Walter W. Skeat, Vol. 1, EETS 76 and 82 (1881 and 1885), pp. 91–117.

91 R. Finucane, *Miracles and Pilgrims: Popular Beliefs in Medieval England* (London, 1977).

92 *Tractatus de Purgatorio Sancti Patricii*, ed. Robert Easting, EETS 298 (1991).

93 See p. 4.
94 Caesarius of Heisterbach, *Dialogus Miraculorum*, Vol. I, p. 91.
95 Ibid., Vol. I, pp. 276–7.
96 Ibid., Vol. I, p. 279.
97 Ibid.
98 Ibid.
99 Ibid.
100 Ibid.

CHAPTER 4: CHRISTIANS, JEWS AND MUSLIMS

1 Olivia Remie Constable, *Medieval Iberia* (Pennsylvania, 1997), p. 147.
2 Ibid.
3 Anna, Sapir Abulafia, *Christians and Jews in Dispute: Disputational Literature and the Rise of Anti-Judaism in the West (c.1000–1150)* (New York, 2011).
4 See pp. 35, 58, 111, 119.
5 Jonathan Ray (ed.), *The Jew in Medieval Iberia* (Boston, 2012), and Selma Stern, *The Court Jew: A Contribution to the History of Absolutism in Europe* (Philadelphia, 1950).
6 Ray, *The Jew in Medieval Iberia*, p. 5.
7 Charles Burnett (ed.), *Ibn Baklarash's Book of Simples: Medical Remedies between Three Faiths in Twelfth Century Spain* (Oxford, 2008).
8 Ray, *The Jew in Medieval Iberia*, pp. 102–37.
9 Anna Sapir Abulafia, *Jewish–Christian Relations 1000–1300* (Harlow, 2011).
10 Ray, *The Jew in Medieval Iberia*, p. 6.
11 Abulafia, *Jewish–Christian Relations 1000–1300*, p. 122.
12 Jane S. Gerber, 'The world of Samuel Halevi: Testimony from the El Transito Synagogue of Toledo', in Jonathan Ray (ed.), *The Jew in Medieval Iberia* (Boston, 2012), pp. 33–59.
13 Ray, *The Jew in Medieval Iberia*, p. 33; Samuel Rubenson, 'Translating the tradition: some remarks on the Arabization of the patristic heritage in Egypt', *Medieval Encounters* 2 (1996): 4–14.
14 Peter Adamson, *Al-Kindi* (Oxford, 2007), p. 511.
15 Ibid., p. 6.
16 Avicenna, *De congelatione et conglutinatione lapidum, being sections of the Kitāb al-shifâ* (Paris, 1927).
17 Marie-Thérèse D'Alverny, 'Motives and Circumstances, Methods and Techniques of Translation from Arabic to Latin', Colloquium on the Transmission and Reception of Knowledge, Dumbarton Oaks, 5–7 May 1977 (Washington, 1977).
18 M. T. d'Alverny, *La connaissance de l'Islam dans l'Occident médiéval*, ed. C. Burnett (Abingdon, 1994), in M. T. d'Alverny, *Deux traductions latines du Coran au moyen âge*, in *Archives d'histoire doctrinale et littéraire du moyen âge* 22–23 (1947–8).
19 Constable, *Medieval Iberia*, pp. 137–42.

20 PL 210.422–30.
21 Charles Julian Bishko, 'Peter the Venerable's journey to Spain', *Studia Anselmiana* 40 (1956).
22 M. T. d'Alverny, *La connaissance de l'Islam dans l'Occident médiéval*, III; M. T. d'Alverny, 'Pierre le Vénérable et la légende de Mahomet', AHDLMA 16 (1948): 161–70.
23 G. Constable (ed.), *The Letters of Peter the Venerable*, 2 vols (Cambridge, MA, 1967), Letter 111, Vol. I, pp. 274–99, especially pp. 294–5; and see Vol. II, pp. 275–84 where the parallel texts are printed.
24 M. T. d'Alverny, *La connaissance de l'Islam dans l'Occident médiéval*, I; M. T. d'Alverny, *Deux traductions latines du Coran au moyen âge*, in *Archives d'histoire doctrinale et littéraire du moyen âge* 22–23 (1947–8), pp. 69–131, p. 70.
25 Constable, *The Letters of Peter the Venerable*, Vol. II, pp. 331–43.
26 Thomas of Monmouth, *The Life and Miracles of William of Norwich*, ed. M. R. James and James Jessop (Cambridge, 1897).
27 Constable, *Medieval Iberia*, pp. 199–200.
28 Caesarius of Heisterbach, *Dialogus Miraculorum*, *De contritione,* XXII, 2 vols, ed. J. Strange (Cologne, 1851), Vol. I, pp. 92–3.
29 Ibid., XIV, Vol. I, p. 185.
30 See pp. 14, 45.
31 See p. 192.
32 Guillaume de Deguileville, *Pilgrimage of the Lyfe of the Manhode*, ed. A. Henry, EETS (Oxford, 1885–8).
33 John of Hildesheim, *The Three Kings of Cologne*, ed. C. Horstmann, EETS 85 (London, 1886).
34 See p. 50.
35 Guibert de Nogent, *Historia quae dicitur Gesta Dei per Francos* (Paris, 1967).
36 I and II Maccabees.
37 Guibert de Nogent, *Historia quae dicitur Gesta Dei per Francos.*
38 Robert the Monk, *Historia Hierosolymitana* (Paris, 1967).
39 August C. Krey, *The First Crusade: The Accounts of Eyewitnesses and Participants* (Princeton, NJ, 1921), pp. 33–6.
40 Ibid., pp. 42–3.
41 Fulcher of Chartres, *Gesta Francorum Jerusalem Expugnantium*, in Frederick Duncan and August C. Krey (eds), *Parallel Source Problems in Medieval History* (New York, 1912); Bongars, *Gesta Dei per Francos*, 1, pp. 382ff., in Oliver J. Thatcher and Edgar Holmes McNeal (eds), *A Source Book for Medieval History: Selected Documents Illustrating the History of Europe in the Middle Age* (New York, 1905), pp. 513–17.
42 *Gesta Francorum*, in A. C. Krey, *The First Crusade: The Accounts of Eyewitnesses and Participants* (Princeton, NJ, 1921), pp. 28–30.
43 Anna Comnena, *Alexiad*, tr. E. R. A. Sewter (London, 2003).
44 *Hebrew Chronicles of the First Crusade*, ed. Eva Haverkamp, MGH (Hanover, 2005).
45 Ibid.
46 Ibid.

47 Ibid.
48 Malcolm Barber, *The Crusader States* (New Haven, CT, 2012).
49 Constable, *The Letters of Peter the Venerable*, Vol. I, p. 330, Letter 130 to King Louis of France.
50 Ibid., Vol. I, p. 328, Letter 130 to King Louis of France.
51 Csi.
52 *The Life of Saladin*, ed. Sir Hamilton Gibb (Oxford, 1973), p. 21.
53 Ibid., p. 1.
54 Ibid., pp. 1–3.
55 Geoffrey de Villehardouin, *Memoirs* or *Chronicle of The Fourth Crusade and The Conquest of Constantinople*, tr. Frank T. Marzials (London, 1908).
56 John de Joinville, *Chronicles of the Crusades*, ed. J. A. Giles (London, 1865).

CHAPTER 5: SOME HARD TALKING

1 *Chartularium Universitatis Parisiensis*, ed. H. Denifle and A. Chatelain (Paris, 1905), I, pp. 78–9.
2 See p. 73.
3 http://www.birmingham.ac.uk/Documents/college-artslaw/ptr/theology/research/CMR1900/Petrus-Alfonsi.pdf (accessed 17 March 2016).
4 Petrus Alfonsi, *Dialogue against the Jews*, tr. I. Resnick (Washington, 2006); Charles Burnett, 'The works of Petrus Alfonsi: questions of authenticity', *Medium Aevum* 66 (1997): 42–79; B. Septimus, 'Petrus Alfonsi on the cult at Mecca', *Speculum* 56 (1981): 517–33.
5 John of Salisbury, *Metalogicon*, ed. J. B. Hall and K. S. B. Keats-Rohan, CCCM 98 (Turnhout, 1991).
6 The original manuscripts of the collection were burned in World War II, but a facsimile survives.
7 L. Minio-Paluello, *The Latin Aristotle* (Amsterdam, 1972).
8 Ibid., 'Iacobus Veneticus Grecus: canonist and translator of Aristotle', *Traditio* 8 (1952): 265–304.
9 *Chartularium Universitatis Parisiensis*, I, p. 70.
10 Anselm of Canterbury, *Opera Omnia*, ed. F. S. Schmitt (Rome/Edinburgh, 1965), Vol. II.
11 See p. 154.
12 A Fifth Lateran Council was held at the beginning of the sixteenth century. All references to and quotations from the council are taken from *Decrees of the Ecumenical Councils*, ed. Norman P. Tanner (Washington, DC, 1990).
13 Lateran IV (10).
14 Council of Florence, Session 20.
15 Ibid., Session 21.
16 Ibid.
17 G. R. Evans, *Law and Theology in the Middle Ages* (London, 2002).
18 Council of Constance, Session 3, 26 March 1415.
19 Ibid., Session 5, 6 April 1415.

20 Ibid., Session 1, 14 December 1431.
21 Ibid., Session 15, 26 November 1433.
22 Ibid., Session, 20 June 1432.
23 Ibid., Session 7, 4 September, 1439.
24 Ibid., Session 23, 26 March 1436.
25 Jay T. Lees, *Anselm of Havelberg: Deeds into Words in the Twelfth Century* (Leiden, 1998), pp. 40–7.
26 Anselm of Havelberg, *Dialogi*, PL 188.1139.
27 PL 180.1159–60, Lees, *Anselm of Havelberg*, pp. 224–81.
28 PL 188.1141.
29 PL 188.1184.
30 PL 188.1143–4.
31 PL 188.1159ff.
32 PL 188.1165ff.
33 PL 188.1179.
34 PL 188.1184.
35 Council of Florence, Session 8, 18 December 1432.
36 In his 'Letters on the Sacraments'.
37 Council of Florence, Session 6, 6 July 1439.
38 Bull of union with the Armenians, Council of Florence, Session 8, 22 November 1439.
39 Bull of union with the Copts, Council of Florence, Session 11, 4 February 1442.
40 Charles Beckingham, *Prester John, the Mongols and the Ten Lost Tribes* (Aldershot, 1996).
41 Council of Vienne, 24.
42 James T. Monroe, *Islam and the Arabs in Spanish Scholarship* (Leiden, 1970).
43 P. S. van Koningsveld, 'Muslim slaves and captives in Western Europe during the late Middle Ages', *Islam and Christian–Muslim Relations*, 18 April 2007, http://www.tandfonline.com/loi/cicm20 (accessed 17 March 2016).
44 But see Ian Christopher Levy, 'Useful foils: lessons learned from Jews in John Wyclif's call for Church reform', *Medieval Encounters* 4 (2001): 125–45.
45 See p. 163.
46 Peter Abelard, *Collationes*, ed. and tr. John Marenbon and Giovanni Orlandi (Oxford, 2000).
47 Gilbert Crispin, *Works*, ed. A. Abulafia and G. R. Evans (London, 1986).
48 PG 140.123–48.
49 *Contra Sectam Mahometicam pro Christianae religione apologia*, PG 154.371–582.
50 *Contra Mahometem orationes quatuor*, from Basle 1543 edition, PG 154.583–692.
51 Manuel II Palaeologos, Letter 31, in *Letters*, ed. George T. Dennis (Dumbarton Oaks, 1977), pp. 81–4.
52 Manuel II Palaiologos, *Dialoge mit einem 'Perser'*, ed. E. Trapp (Vienna, 1966).

53 Van Koningsveld, 'Muslim slaves and captives in Western Europe during the late Middle Ages'.
54 Olivia Remie Constable, *Medieval Iberia* (Philadelphia, 1997), pp. 246–9.
55 Van Koningsveld, 'Muslim slaves and captives in Western Europe during the late Middle Ages'.
56 Ibid.
57 Ibid.
58 Ibid.
59 Ibid.
60 Ibid.
61 Ibid.
62 Ibid.
63 Ibid.
64 Ibid.
65 Ibid.
66 Ibid.
67 Ibid.
68 Ibid.
69 Ibid.
70 Ibid.
71 Ibid.
72 Jonathan Ray (ed.), *The Jew in Medieval Iberia* (Boston, 2012), pp. 33–59.
73 Van Koningsveld, 'Muslim slaves and captives in Western Europe during the late Middle Ages'.
74 Constable, *Medieval Iberia*, pp. 317–19.
75 Ibid., pp. 320–2.
76 Ibid., pp. 341ff.
77 Ibid., pp. 338ff.
78 Ibid., pp. 352ff.
79 Thomas Malory, *Le Morte d'Arthur*, V, ii, http://www.gutenberg.org/files/1251/1251–h/1251–h.htm#link2HCH0002 (accessed 17 March 2016).
80 Ibid., V, xi.
81 Ibid., V, xviii.

CHAPTER 6: FROM DISSENT TO REFORMATION

1 Council of Vienne (17).
2 Brenda Bolton, *The Medieval Reformation* (London, 1983).
3 Norma Cohn, *The Pursuit of the Millennium: Revolutionary Millenarians and Mystical Anarchists of the Middle Ages* (Oxford, 1970), Ch. 7.
4 Miri Rubin, *Corpus Christi: The Eucharist in Late Medieval Culture* (Cambridge, 1991), p. 86.
5 *Speculum sacerdotale*, ed. Edward H. Weatherly, EETS 200 (1936).
6 Ibid., Ch. 22ff., p. 74.
7 Ibid., Ch. 23, p. 75.
8 Ibid., Ch. 23, p. 77.

9 Ibid., Ch. 23, p. 78.
10 Ibid., Ch. 23, pp. 82–9.
11 Ibid., Ch. 23, pp. 79–80.
12 Christine de Pisan, *The Epistle of Othea*, tr. Stephen Scrope, ed. Curt F. Bühler, EETS 264 (1970).
13 Ibid., p. 19.
14 Ibid., p. 23.
15 Ibid., p. 25.
16 *The Book of Vices and Virtues*, ed. W. Nelson Francis, EETS 217 (1942).
17 *The Comedy of Acolastus*, tr. from Fullonius, by John Palsgrave, ed. P. L. Carver, EETS 212 (1937).
18 *The Dicts and Sayings of the Philosophers*, ed. Curt F. Bühler, EETS 211 (1941), p. xxxvii. Six writers were known to have been interested in this collection in the third quarter of the fifteenth century. Stephen Scrope tr. dated 1450; he and William of Worcester were attendants of Sir John Falstolf. Worcester revised the translation.
19 *Bibliotheca Historica of Diodorus Siculus*, tr. John Skelton, ed. F. M. Salter and H. L. R. Edwards, EETS 233 (1956).
20 See H. Pirenne, *Medieval Cities* (Princeton, NJ, 1952).
21 F. J. Furnivall (ed.), *Political, Religious and Love Poems*, EETS 15 (1866), p. 1.
22 Ibid., *Education in Early England (The 'Babees Book')*, EETS 32 (1868), pp. 36–47.
23 Ibid., pp. 48–59.
24 Henry Fitzstephen, *Vita* of Becket, ed. Giles, pp. 18–190.
25 Furnivall, *Education in Early England*, includes John Russell's *Boke of Nurture* and Hugh Rhodes' *Boke of Nurture*.
26 Furnivall, *Political, Religious and Love Poems*, pp. 6–7.
27 Richard Rolle, *Ego dormio*, *Prose and Verse*, ed. S. J. Ogilvie-Thomson, EETS 293 (1988), p. 26.
28 Ibid., 'The form of living', *Prose and Verse*, ed. S. J. Ogilvie-Thomson, EETS 293 (1988), p. 1.
29 Bernard Hamilton, 'Perfectionism and pragmatism: Cathar attitudes to the household', in John Doran, Charlotte Methuen and Alexandra Walsham (eds), *Religion and the Household*, Studies in Church History 50 (2014), pp. 86–96.
30 Caesarius of Heisterbach, *Dialogue on Miracles*, Book V, xxii, https://legacy.fordham.edu/halsall/source/caesarius-heresies.html (accessed 17 March 2017).
31 Praepositinus of Cremona, *Summa contra haereticos*, ed. Joseph N. Garvin and James A. Corbett (South Bend, IN, 1958).
32 Ibid.
33 Marjorie Reeves, *The Influence of Prophecy in the Later Middle Ages* (Oxford, 1969), pp. 248–9.
34 PG 140.
35 *Confession of Faith against the Saracens*, PG 140.123–6.
36 PG 140.133.
37 PG 140.123–48.

38 Olivia Remie Constable, *Medieval Iberia* (Philadelphia, 1997), pp. 81–3.
39 Council of Constance, Session 2, 2 March 1415.
40 Matthew Spinka, *John Hus' Concept of the Church* (Princeton, NJ, 1966).
41 A reference to Constantine as the first Christian emperor and Sylvester I, pope from 314 to 335.
42 *Anonymi Versus de Querimonia Cleri*, *Anglo-Latin Satirical Poets*, ed. T. Wright, Rolls Series (Cambridge, 2012, reprint), II, pp. 213–18.
43 J-P. Genet (ed.), *Four English Political Tracts of the Later Middle Ages*, Camden 4th series, 18 (London, 1977), p. xiii.
44 G. R. Owst, *Literature and Pulpit in Medieval England* (Oxford, 1961), pp. 210ff.
45 Genet, *Four English Political Tracts of the Later Middle Ages*.
46 Thomas Wright (ed.), *Anglo-Latin Satirical Poets and Epigrammatists of the Twelfth Century*, 2 vols, Rolls Series 57 (London, 1872), Vol. I, p. 146, p. 153, prose to Bishop of Ely.
47 Genet, *Four English Political Tracts of the Later Middle Ages*, Ch. 4, p. 8.
48 Ibid., Ch. 5, p. 9.
49 *How Satan and his Children ...*, *The English Works of Wyclif*, ed. F. D. Matthew, EETS 74 (1880), pp. 209ff.
50 *Tam in ecclesiis quam in plateis et aliis locis profanis*, Anne Hudson, *The Premature Reformation* (Oxford, 1988), p. 69.
51 For example, Wyclif's 'Forty sermons', *Sermones Quadraginta*, and see Hudson, *The Premature Reformation*, p. 65.
52 Hudson, *The Premature Reformation*, p. 73.
53 Ibid., p. 76.
54 Ibid., p. 63.
55 Ibid., pp. 104–5.
56 Ibid., p. 155.
57 Ibid., p. 103.
58 Ibid., pp. 78–9.
59 Ibid., pp. 78–9.
60 With 13 parishes of the deanery of Bow directly under Canterbury, see A. K. McHardy, *The Church in London 1375–1392*, London Record Society 13 (London, 1977).
61 Hudson, *The Premature Reformation*, p. 135.
62 Alison Hanham (ed.), *The Cely letters (1472–1488)*, EETS 273 (1975).
63 *How Religious Men Should Keep Certain Articles*, *The English Works of Wyclif*, ed. F. D. Matthew, EETS 74 (1880), pp. 219ff.
64 Genet, *Four English Political Tracts of the Later Middle Ages*, pp. 1–21.
65 Ibid., p. 5.
66 Ibid., p. 5 (my translation).
67 *Omnes honorate fraternitatem diligite Deum timete regem honorificate.*
68 Genet, *Four English Political Tracts of the Later Middle Ages*, p. 7.
69 Ibid., p. 12. 'Honour' and 'worship' both appear in early Wycliffite translations of this passage. See table on pp. 21–2.
70 *John Benet's Chronicle*, ed. G. L. Harriss, RHS, Camden 4th Series, 9 (London, 1972), p. 194.

71 *Combustus fuit unus hereticus* at Tower Hill *qui vocatur Johannes Cardemaker de Coventria, qui tenuit multas falsas opiniones et specialiter duas.*
72 *Quod infans procreatus inter Christianos conjugatos non indegebat baptismo.*
73 Norman Tanner (ed.), *Heresy Trials in the Diocese of Norwich 1428–1431*, Camden 4th Series, 20 (London, 1977), pp. 41–3.
74 Norman Tanner, *Kent Heresy Proceedings 1511–12*, Kent Records 26 (1997), p. xii.
75 Ibid., p. 1.
76 Ibid., p. 3.
77 Ibid., pp. 3ff.
78 Ibid., pp. 4–5ff.
79 Ibid., pp. 8–15.
80 Ibid., pp. 16–24.
81 Ibid., p. 25.
82 Ibid., p. 48.
83 Ibid., pp. 43ff.
84 Ibid.
85 Ibid., p. 46.
86 Ibid., p. 50.
87 Ibid., pp. xii–xv.

CONCLUSION: RENAISSANCE AND EXPANSION

1 *Pierce the Ploughmans Crede*, ed. W. Skeat, EETS 31 (1877).
2 Olivia Remie Constable, *Medieval Iberia* (Philadelphia, 1997), pp. 364ff.
3 Samuel Hugh Moffett, *A History of Christianity in Asia*, 2 vols (New York, 2005), Vol. 2, pp. 3–4.
4 Ibid., p. 8.
5 Ibid., pp. 10–11.
6 Ibid., p. 12.

Index

References to images are in *italics*.